EISA System Architecture

by

Tom Shanley

Edited by

Don Anderson

MindShare Press

This publication contains information protected by copyright. No part of this book may be copied or reproduced in any form without prior written consent from MindShare, Inc.

©1991 and 1993 MindShare, Inc.
2202 Buttercup Dr.
Richardson, TX 75082
(214) 231-2216
fax (214) 783-4715

All rights reserved. Printed in U.S.A.
EISA System Architecture
Second Edition

ISBN 1-881609-03-0

TK
7895
.B87
S525
1993

Product names mentioned in this manual may be trademarks and/or registered trademarks of their respective companies.

Every effort has been made to supply complete and accurate information. However, MindShare, Inc. shall not be liable for any technical or editorial errors or omissions; nor for incidental or consequential damages resulting from the use of this publication.

Distributed by
Computer Literacy Bookshops Inc.
P.O. Box 641897
San Jose, CA 95164 USA

Phone (408) 435-0744
Fax (408) 435-1823
E-mail info@clbooks.com

"Any engineer... needs these books within quick reach."

"Any engineer who has to spend time on systems using an ISA or EISA bus needs these books within quick reach. In every measure, they are **elegant tools**."
–*Charles McLean, Program Manager, Amtech Systems Corporation*

"I would especially like to commend them on their outstanding publications. The books have become **some of the most useful in my library**. The co-ops in the group have found them to be especially useful."
–*Mike Demas, Applications Support Engineer, Intel Corporation*

"It's clear that MindShare really understands both the technical subject matter and the reader's learning process. The bits of historical and narrative material (the authors) inject make the contents more interesting and they help the reader get a sense of why things evolved the way that they did... The manuals continue to be useful for subsystem-level refreshers and for their reference tables."
–*Paul Alito, Vice President of R&D, Vision Integration*

"I learned more about PC interrupts in two pages of *EISA System Architecture* than in two months of digging through the so-called 'Inside' books. I'm looking forward to your PCI book. Thanks."
—*Will Gillick, Project Engineer, Mouse Corporation*

EISA System Architecture explains in depth the hardware architecture of EISA (Extension to the Industry Standard Architecture) products.

This includes IBM-compatible PCs; many of the concepts apply to other products as well.

The author tells how the EISA specifications differ from ISA. He describes the EISA bus structure, bus masters and slaves, bus arbitration, EISA interrupt handling (and how it differs from ISA), EISA CPU and bus master bus cycles, DMA and system configuration.

A separate multi-chapter section covers the EISA chip set, including major buses, functions typically provided, and a detailed introduction to the Intel 82350DT EISA chip set, focusing on the 82358 EISA Bus Controller (EBC), the 82357 Integrated Systems Peripheral (ISP) and the 82352 EISA Bus Buffers (EBBs).

For this expanded second edition, new material has been added.

The chapter on EISA configuration is updated and improved. Many subjects have enhanced treatment, with more illustrations. A helpful glossary has been added, as well as other updates to catch up with the newest evolutions in EISA.

This book presents EISA using the "building block" approach. The author defines all concepts and terms as they are introduced. Each new concept builds upon those already described. This book provides a clear, concise explanation of the EISA environment. If you design or test hardware or software that involves EISA, *EISA System Architecture* will be a valuable, time-saving tool for you.

EISA System Architecture is the second volume in the PC SYSTEM ARCHITECTURE SERIES from MindShare Press. It builds on the information in Volume 1. Look for:

Volume 1: *ISA System Architecture*
Volume 3: *80486 System Architecture*
Volume 4: *PCI System Architecture*
Volume 5: *Pentium™ Processor System Architecture*

Forthcoming volumes: *PCMCIA System Architecture* • *PowerPC System Architecture*

Dedication

This book is dedicated to my son, Ryan...a ray of sunshine; and my daughter, Jen...the teenager I would have been if I had been more sure of myself.

Acknowledgements

This book would not have been possible without the input of thousands of hardware and software people at Intel, Compaq, IBM and Dell over the past four years. They constantly sanity-check me and make me tell the truth.

Special Thanks

Special thanks to Don Anderson for his constant help, advice and friendship

Table of Contents

About This Book _____ i

Part I: The EISA Specification

Ch. 1: EISA Overview

Introduction _____ 3
Compatibility With ISA _____ 4
Memory Capacity _____ 4
Synchronous Data Transfer Protocol _____ 4
Enhanced DMA Functions _____ 5
Bus Master Capabilities _____ 6
Data Bus Steering _____ 6
Bus Arbitration _____ 6
Edge and Level-Sensitive Interrupt Requests _____ 7
Automatic System Configuration _____ 7
EISA Feature/Benefit Summary _____ 8

Ch. 2: EISA Bus Structure Overview

A Community of Processors _____ 9
    Limitations of ISA Bus Master Support _____ 10
    EISA Bus Master Support _____ 11
Types of EISA Bus masters _____ 14
EISA Slave Types _____ 15

Ch. 3: EISA Bus Arbitration

EISA Bus Arbitration _____ 17
Preemption _____ 22
Example Arbitration Between Two Bus Master Cards _____ 23
Memory Refresh _____ 25

Ch. 4: Interrupt Handling

Review of Interrupt Handling In the ISA Environment _____ 27
Shortcomings of ISA Interrupt Handling _____ 28
    Phantom Interrupts 28
    Limited Number of IRQ Lines 29
Interrupt Handling In the EISA Environment _____ 29
    Shareable IRQ Lines 29
    Elimination Of Phantom Interrupts 34

Ch. 5: Detailed Description of the EISA Bus

Introduction _____ 35
The Address Bus Extension _____ 37
The Data Bus Extension _____ 39
The Bus Arbitration Signal Group _____ 39
The Burst Handshake Signal Group _____ 41
The Bus Cycle Definition Signal Group _____ 41
The Bus Cycle Timing Signal Group _____ 42
The Lock Signal _____ 42
The Slave Size Signal Group _____ 43
The AEN Signal _____ 43
The EISA Connector Pinouts _____ 43

Ch. 6: ISA Bus Cycles

Introduction _____ 45
8-bit ISA Slave Device _____ 45
16-bit ISA Slave Device _____ 46
Transfers With 8-bit Devices _____ 46
Transfers With 16-bit Devices _____ 49
    Standard 16-bit Memory Device ISA Bus Cycle 50
    Standard 16-bit I/O Device ISA Bus Cycle 53
    Zero Wait State ISA Bus Cycle Accessing a 16-bit Device 55
ISA DMA Bus Cycles _____ 58
    ISA DMA Introduction 58
    The 8237 DMAC Bus Cycle 60

Ch. 7: EISA CPU and Bus Master Bus Cycles

Introduction To The EISA CPU and Bus Master Bus Cycle Types _____ 63
The Standard EISA Bus Cycle _____ 64

 General...64
 Analysis of the EISA Standard Bus Cycle...65
 Performance Using the EISA Standard Bus Cycle 67
The Compressed Bus Cycle **68**
 General...68
 Performance When Using Compressed Bus Cycles..69
The Burst Bus Cycle **69**
 General...69
 Analysis of the EISA Burst Transfer..70
 Performance Using Burst Transfers 74
 DRAM Memory Burst Transfers..74
 Downshift Burst Bus Master...74

Ch. 8: EISA DMA

DMA Bus Cycle Types **75**
 Introduction..75
 The Compatible DMA Bus Cycle 76
  Description...76
  Performance and Compatibility 77
 The Type "A" DMA Bus Cycle 77
  Description...77
  Performance and Compatibility 78
 The Type "B" DMA Bus Cycle...78
  Description...78
  Performance and Compatibility 79
 The Type "C" DMA Bus Cycle 79
  Description...79
  Performance and Compatibility 80
 Summary of EISA DMA Transfer Rates..80
Other DMA Enhancements **81**
 Addressing Capability 81
 Preemption 81
 Buffer Chaining..81
 Ring Buffers..82
 Transfer Size 82

Ch. 9: EISA System Configuration

The ISA I/O Address Space Problem **83**
EISA Slot-Specific I/O Address Space **86**
The EISA Product Identifier **90**

3

Expansion Card Control Bits 92
The Expansion Card Control Bits Defined by the EISA Specification 93
EISA Configuration Process 93
    General 93
    Configuration File Naming Convention 94
    The Configuration Procedure 95
    The Configuration File Macro Language 96
    An Example Configuration File 96
    Explanation of the Example Configuration File 102

Part II: The Intel 82350DT Chip Set

Ch. 10: The EISA System Buses

The Host Bus 112
The EISA/ISA Bus 113
The X Bus 113

Ch. 11: The Bridge, Translator, Pathfinder and Toolbox

The Players 117
The Bridge 117
The Translator 121
    Address Translation 121
    Command Line Translation 121
The Pathfinder 122
The Toolbox 124

Ch. 12: The Intel i82350DT EISA Chip Set

Introduction 127
The 82358DT EISA Bus Controller (EBC) and the 82352 EISA Bus Buffers 128
    General 128
    CPU Selection 129
    Data Buffer Control and the 82352 EISA Bus Buffer (EBB) 131
        General 131
        Transfer Between a 32-bit EISA Bus Master and an 8-bit ISA Slave 133
        Transfer Between a 32-bit EISA Bus Master and a 16-bit ISA Slave 140
        Transfer Between a 32-bit EISA Bus Master and a 16-bit EISA Slave 144
        Transfer Between a 32-bit EISA Bus Master and a 32-bit EISA Slave 147
        Transfer Between a 32-bit EISA Bus Master and an 32-bit Host Slave 149
        Transfer Between a 16-bit EISA Bus Master and an 8-bit ISA Slave 150

    Transfer Between a 16-bit EISA Bus Master and a 16-bit ISA Slave 152
    Transfer Between a 16-bit EISA Bus Master and a 16-bit EISA Slave 154
    Transfer Between a 16-bit EISA Bus Master and a 32-bit EISA Slave 155
    Transfer Between a 16-bit ISA Bus Master and an 8-bit ISA Slave 156
    Transfer Between a 16-bit ISA Bus Master and a 16-bit ISA Slave 157
    Transfer Between a 16-bit ISA Bus Master and a 16-bit EISA Slave 157
    Transfer Between a 16-bit ISA Bus Master and a 32-bit EISA Slave 158
    Transfer Between a 32-bit Host CPU and a 32-bit Host Slave 159
    Transfer Between a 32-bit Host CPU and an 8-bit ISA Slave 159
    Transfer Between a 32-bit Host CPU and a 16-bit ISA Slave 160
    Transfer Between a 32-bit Host CPU and a 16-bit EISA Slave 161
    Transfer Between a 32-bit Host CPU and a 32-bit EISA Slave 162
  Address Buffer Control and the 82352 EISA Bus Buffer (EBB) 162
    Host CPU Bus Master 164
    EISA Bus Master 164
    ISA Bus Master 164
    Refresh Bus Master 165
    DMA Bus Master 165
  The Host Bus Interface Unit 166
  The ISA Bus Interface Unit 169
  The EISA Bus Interface Unit 172
  Cache Support 173
  Reset Control 174
  Slot-Specific I/O Support 174
  The Clock Generator Unit 174
  I/O Recovery 175
  Testing 175
  The ISP Interface Unit 175

The 82357 Integrated System Peripheral (ISP) _____ 176
  Introduction 176
  NMI Logic 178
  Interrupt Controllers 178
  DMA Controllers 179
  System Timers 180
  Central Arbitration Control 180
  Refresh Logic 181
  Miscellaneous Interface Signals 181

Appendix

Glossary

Index

ARCHITECTURE TRAINING

Q. Who developed and teaches **IBM**'s PS/2 architecture training?

Q. Who developed and teaches **Compaq**'s EISA architecture training?

Q. Who teaches 80486 architecture at **Intel** on an ongoing basis?

Q. Who teaches PC architecture at **Dell** on an ongoing basis?

Our currently available classes include:

- ISA System Architecture
- EISA System Architecture
- PS/2 System Architecture
- 80486 System Architecture
- PCI System Architecture
- SCSI Subsystem Architecture
- PCMCIA System Architecture
- Pentium System Architecture

We also put together custom classes and enter into non-disclosure agreements with our customers, giving their people the freedom to discuss the problems that they are currently working on.

Flexible, reasonably priced, energetic...the best. **MindShare technical training**.

About This Book

The MindShare Architecture Series

The MindShare Press series of books on system architecture includes *ISA System Architecture, EISA System Architecture, 80486 System Architecture* and *PCI System Architecture*. Additionally, for information on MicroChannel architecture, see *The IBM PS/2 From the Inside Out*, published by Addison-Wesley.

Rather than duplicating common information in each book, the series uses the building-block approach. *ISA System Architecture* is the core book upon which the others build. Figure 1 illustrates the relationship of the books to each other.

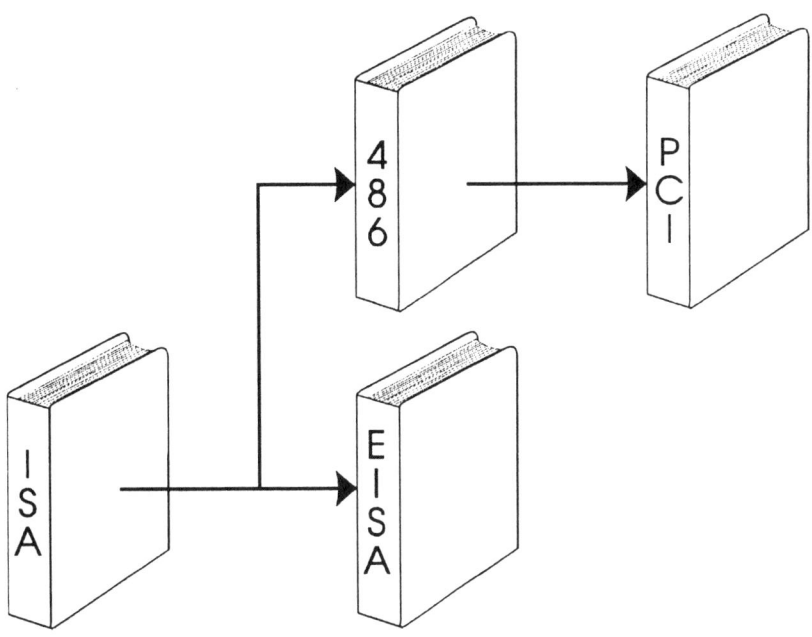

Figure 1. Series Organization

EISA System Architecture

Organization of This Book

EISA System Architecture is divided into two major parts:

- Part I: The EISA Specification
- Part II: The Intel 82350DT EISA Chip Set

Part I provides a detailed explanation of the ISA enhancements as set forth in the EISA specification, while Part II provides a detailed description of the features implemented by the Intel 82350DT chip set. The following paragraphs provide a summary of each section.

Part I: The EISA Specification

EISA Overview

This chapter provides an overview of the benefits provided by the extension to ISA, EISA.

EISA Bus Structure Overview

This chapter introduces the EISA bus structure and its relationship to the system board and expansion cards. The concepts of master and slave are introduced and defined. The types of bus masters and slaves are identified.

EISA Bus Arbitration

The bus arbitration scheme used by the EISA Central Arbitration Control is described in detail.

Interrupt Handling

An in-depth discussion of interrupt request handling in the ISA environment can be found in the chapter entitled, "Interrupt Handling," in the MindShare publication entitled *ISA System Architecture*. This chapter provides a brief review of the ISA interrupt request handling method and a detailed description of the EISA method.

Detailed Description of the EISA Bus

This chapter provides a description of all the signals on the EISA bus.

About This Book

The ISA Bus Cycle

This chapter provides a review of the ISA bus master and DMA bus cycles.

EISA CPU and Bus Master Bus Cycles

This chapter provides a detailed description of the EISA CPU and bus master bus cycle types.

EISA DMA

This chapter describes the EISA DMA capability. This includes a description of the EISA DMA bus cycle types and the other improved capabilities of the EISA DMA controller.

EISA System Configuration

In this chapter, EISA automatic system configuration is discussed. This includes a description of the slot-specific I/O address space, the EISA product identifier, and the EISA card control ports. The EISA configuration process and board description files are also covered.

Part II: The EISA Chip Set

The EISA System Buses

This chapter describes the major buses found in virtually all EISA systems. This includes the host, EISA, ISA and X buses.

The Bridge, Translator, Pathfinder and Toolbox

This chapter provides a description of the major functions performed by the typical EISA chip set. It acts as the bridge between the host and EISA buses. It translates addresses and other bus cycle information into a form understood by all of the host, EISA and ISA devices in a system. When necessary, it performs data bus steering to ensure data travels over the correct paths between the current bus master and the currently addressed device. It incorporates a toolbox including all of the standard support logic necessary in any EISA machine. It should be noted that the ISA bus is a subset of the EISA bus.

EISA System Architecture

The Intel 82350DT EISA Chip Set

This chapter provides an introduction to the Intel 82350DT EISA chip set. The focus is on the 82358DT EISA Bus Controller, or EBC, the 82357 Integrated Systems Peripheral, or ISP, and the 82352 EISA Bus Buffers, or EBBs.

Who This Book Is For

This book is intended for use by hardware and software design and support personnel. Due to the clear, concise explanatory methods used to describe each subject, personnel outside of the design field may also find the text useful.

Those interested only in the compatibility and performance-related issues can skip over the detailed discussions and home in on the issues that interest them. Those interested in a more detailed explanation of the logic behind the enhancements can read the detailed explanations of bus cycle types and the EISA chip set.

Prerequisite Knowledge

EISA stands for the (E)xtension to the (I)ndustry (S)tandard (A)rchitecture. In order to fully grasp the EISA extensions, it is necessary to first understand the ISA system architecture. The detailed description of EISA presented in this book builds upon the concepts introduced in MindShare's book entitled *ISA System Architecture* to provide a clear, concise explanation of the EISA environment.

Documentation Conventions

This section defines the typographical convention used throughout this book.

Hex Notation

All hex numbers are followed by an "h". Examples:

9A4Eh
0100h

About This Book

Binary Notation

All binary numbers are followed by an "b". Examples:

    0001 0101b
    01b

Decimal Notation

When required for clarity, all decimal numbers are followed by an "d". Examples:

    256d
    128d

Signal Name Representation

Each signal that assumes the logic low state when asserted is followed by a pound sign (#). As an example, the REFRESH# signal is asserted low when the refresh logic runs a refresh bus cycle.

Signals that are not followed by a pound sign are asserted when they assume the logic high state. As an example, DREQ3 is asserted high to indicate that a device using DMA Channel three is ready for data to be transfered.

Identification of Bit Fields (logical groups of bits or signals)

All bit fields are designated as follows:

    [X:Y],

where "X" is the most-significant bit and "Y" is the least-significant bit of the field. As an example, the ISA data bus consists of [D0:D15], where D0 is the least-significant and D15 the most-significant bit of the field.

EISA System Architecture

We Want Your Feedback

MindShare values your comments and suggestions. You can contact us via mail, phone, fax or internet email.

Phone: (214) 231-2216
Fax: (214) 783-4715
Email: shanley@mindshare.com

Mailing Address:

MindShare, Inc.
2202 Buttercup Drive
Richardson, Texas 75082

PART I:

THE EISA SPECIFICATION

EISA System Architecture

EISA Overview

Chapter 1

In This Chapter

This chapter provides an overview of the benefits provided by the extension to ISA, EISA.

The Next Chapter

The next chapter, "EISA Bus Structure Overview," provides an overview of the "equal-opportunity" environment existent within all EISA-based systems. The different types of bus masters and slaves are identified.

Introduction

EISA is a superset of the ISA 8 and 16-bit architecture, extending the capabilities of ISA while still maintaining compatibility with ISA expansion boards.

EISA introduces the following major advances:
- Supports intelligent bus master expansion cards.
- Improved bus arbitration and transfer rates.
- Facilitates 8, 16 or 32-bit data transfers by the main CPU, DMA and bus master devices.
- An efficient synchronous data transfer mechanism, permitting single transfers as well as high speed burst transfers.
- Allows 32-bit memory addressing for the main CPU, Direct Memory Access (DMA) devices and bus master cards.
- Shareable and/or ISA compatible handling of interrupt requests.
- Automatic steering of data during bus cycles between EISA and ISA masters and slaves.
- 33MB/second data transfer rate for bus masters and DMA devices.
- Automatic configuration of the system board and expansion cards.

EISA System Architecture

Compatibility With ISA

EISA systems maintain full backward compatibility with the existing ISA standard. EISA connectors are a superset of the 16-bit connectors on ISA system boards, permitting 8 and 16-bit ISA expansion cards to be installed in EISA slots. While maintaining full compatibility with ISA expansion boards and software, EISA also offers enhancements in performance and functionality for new EISA-specific boards as well as some ISA boards.

Memory Capacity

EISA systems support a 32-bit address bus. The main CPU, bus master expansion cards and DMA devices may access the entire 4GB memory space. ISA memory expansion cards can be used without modification to populate the lower sixteen megabytes. EISA memory expansion cards can add as much memory as needed for the application, up to the theoretical maximum of 4GB.

Synchronous Data Transfer Protocol

The EISA bus uses a synchronous transfer protocol. Bus master cards, DMA and the main processor synchronize their bus cycles to the bus clock. The synchronous transfer protocol also provides the cycle control necessary to execute burst cycles with a transfer rate of up to 33 MB/second.

EISA provides a number of bus cycle types covering a range of transfer speeds for different applications. The standard bus cycle requires two bus clock cycles, while the main CPU, DMA and bus masters are permitted to generate burst cycles requiring one clock cycle per transfer.

EISA Overview

Enhanced DMA Functions

EISA systems provide a number of DMA enhancements, including the ability to generate 32-bit addresses, 8, 16, and 32-bit data transfers and more efficient arbitration and data transfer types. In addition to newer, more efficient transfer types, EISA DMA also provides ISA compatible modes with ISA timing and function as the default.

DMA offers a low-cost alternative to intelligent bus master cards. The EISA DMA functions are intended for I/O devices that do not require local intelligence on the I/O expansion card.

EISA 32-bit address support enables ISA, as well as EISA DMA devices to transfer data to or from any 32-bit memory address. The default ISA DMA mode supports ISA-compatible 24-bit address generation with no software or hardware modifications. DMA software can be modified to support the 32-bit memory space, without modifications to the DMA hardware.

Any DMA channel may be programmed to perform 8, 16 or 32-bit data transfers. An 8-bit DMA device uses the lower data bus path, SD0:SD7, while a 16-bit device uses the lower two paths, SD0:SD7 and SD8:SD15. 32-bit DMA devices use all four data paths.

Using burst bus cycles, a 32-bit DMA device can transfer data at speeds up to 33 MB/second.

EISA DMA channels may be programmed to use one of four DMA bus cycle types when transferring data between the I/O device and memory. The default DMA bus cycle type, ISA-compatible, delivers a higher data transfer rate than ISA compatible computers. The improvement is the result of EISA's faster bus arbitration and requires no hardware or software modifications to ISA-compatible DMA devices. Type A and Type B cycles are EISA modes that, permit some ISA-compatible DMA devices to achieve higher performance. The burst DMA (Type "C") bus cycle type is the highest-performance DMA bus cycle and is only available to DMA devices designed specifically for burst.

EISA System Architecture

Bus Master Capabilities

EISA-based systems support intelligent EISA bus master cards, providing data rates up to 33 megabytes/second using EISA burst bus cycles. A bus master card typically includes an on-board processor and local memory. It can relieve the burden on the main processor by performing sophisticated memory access functions, such as scatter/gather block data transfers. Examples of applications that might benefit from a bus master implementation include communications gateways, disk controllers, LAN interfaces, data acquisition systems, and certain classes of graphics controllers.

Data Bus Steering

The EISA bus system permits EISA and ISA expansion cards to communicate with each other. Special system board logic ensures that data travels over the appropriate data paths and translate the control signals as necessary.

The system board data bus steering logic provides the automatic steering and control signal translation for ISA-to-ISA, EISA-to-EISA, ISA-to-EISA and EISA-to-ISA transfers.

Bus Arbitration

The EISA system board logic also provides a centralized arbitration scheme, allowing efficient bus sharing among the main CPU, multiple EISA bus master cards and DMA channels. The centralized arbitration supports preemption of an active bus master or DMA device and can reset a device that does not release the bus after preemption.

The EISA arbitration method grants the bus to DMA devices, DRAM refresh, bus masters and the main CPU on a fair, rotational basis. The rotational scheme provides a short latency for DMA devices to assure compatibility with ISA DMA devices. Bus masters and the CPU, which typically have buffering available, have longer, but predictable latencies.

EISA Overview

Edge and Level-Sensitive Interrupt Requests

In order to provide backward-compatibility with ISA systems, EISA systems support positive edge-triggered interrupts. Unlike ISA systems, however, any EISA interrupt channel can be individually programmed to recognize either shareable, level-triggered or non-shareable, positive edge-triggered interrupt requests. Level-triggered operation facilitates the sharing of a single system interrupt request line by a number of I/O devices. Level-triggered interrupts might be used, for example, to share a single interrupt request line between a number of serial ports.

Automatic System Configuration

EISA systems implement the capability to perform automatic configuration of system resources and expansion boards each time the system is powered up. System resources such as serial ports, parallel ports, VGA and other manufacturer-specific functions can be fully configured programmatically. In addition, programmable EISA expansion boards can be designed to simplify installation.

The EISA expansion card manufacturer includes a configuration file with each expansion card shipped. The configuration files can be included with either new, fully programmable EISA boards or switch-configured ISA or EISA products. The configuration files are used at system configuration time to automatically assign global system resources (such as DMA channels and interrupt levels), thus preventing resource conflicts between the installed expansion cards. For switch-configurable boards, the configuration files can be used to determine the proper assignment of resources and instruct the user about the proper selection of switch settings.

To accomplish the automatic configuration of the system board and expansion cards, EISA uses slot-specific I/O port ranges. An EISA card using these ranges can be installed into any slot in the system without the risk of I/O range conflicts. These I/O ranges can be used for expansion card initialization or for normal I/O port assignments that are guaranteed not to conflict with any other expansion board installed in the system.

EISA also includes a product identification mechanism for system boards and expansion cards. The product identifier allows products to be identified during the configuration and initialization sequences for the system and expansion

EISA System Architecture

boards. EISA includes guidelines for selection of a product identifier. The identifier of each product is selected by the product manufacturer and does not need the approval of any other party in the industry. However, a manufacturer-specific ID is assigned to each vendor by BCPR Services, the legal firm that manages the EISA specification.

EISA Feature/Benefit Summary

Table 1 - 1 provides a summary of the key features and benefits of the Extended Industry Standard Architecture.

Table 1-1. EISA Feature/Benefit Summary

Feature	Benefit
Backward compatible with all ISA expansion boards	Customer base retains value of installed ISA cards.
Board size	63 square inches of board space permits implementation of very powerful, highly-integrated expansion cards.
+5Vdc at approximately 4.5A available at each expansion slot	Ample power for expansion cards employing a large amount of highly-integrated logic.
32-bit address and data buses	Support for 4GB of memory and 32-bit transfers.
Programmable level- or edge-triggered interrupt recognition	Interrupt request lines may be shared by multiple devices.
Enhanced DMA capabilities	Both ISA and EISA DMA devices have access to memory above 16MB. New bus cycle types and 32-bit data bus allow faster transfer speeds (rates of up to 33 MB/second).
Bus Master Support	Support for up to fifteen bus master expansion cards, fast burst bus transfers, automatic data bus steering and control line translation.
Automatic system configuration	Supports automatic configuration of the EISA system board and new EISA expansion cards each time the system is powered up. Also provides help to the end user in configuring older ISA expansion cards.

EISA Bus Structure Overview

Chapter 2

The Previous Chapter

The previous chapter provided an overview of the features and benefits realized in the EISA environment.

In This Chapter

This chapter introduces the EISA bus structure and its relationship to the system board and expansion cards. The concepts of master and slave are introduced and defined. The types of bus masters and slaves are identified.

The Next Chapter

The next chapter, "EISA Bus Arbitration," describes the bus abitration mechanism implemented in all EISA systems.

A Community of Processors

The signals provided on each of EISA expansion slot can be divided into four basic categories:

- The Address Bus group
- The Control Bus group
- The Data Bus group
- The Bus Arbitration group

Three of these four signal groups are present on the expansion slots found in IBM PC/XT/AT products and compatible computers. In EISA, the Bus Arbitration group has been added.

The EISA bus not only defines the signals found on the expansion card connectors, but the permissable bus cycle types that can be run by bus masters and the software protocol that bus masters must use when communicating with each other. It also defines the support logic residing on the system board and expansion cards that is necessary to support all of the EISA capabilities.

EISA System Architecture

Examples would be the system board's Central Arbitration Control (CAC) and the data bus steering logic, which are discussed in subsequent sections.

Limitations of ISA Bus Master Support

The IBM PC XT/AT and compatible products are essentially single-processor systems. They have one microprocessor located on the system board that uses the address, control and data buses to communicate with the various memory and I/O devices found in a system.

The microprocessor on the system board is the bus master most of the time in a PC/XT/AT. It uses the buses to fetch instructions and to communicate with memory and I/O devices when instructed to do so by the currently executing instruction.

Upon occasion, however, devices other than the microprocessor require the use of the buses in order to communicate with other devices in the system. These devices are the DMA controller and the RAM Refresh logic. The DMA controller must use the buses to transfer data between I/O devices and memory. The Refresh logic must use the buses periodically to refresh the information stored in DRAM memory.

When a device other than the microprocessor (such as the DMA Controller or the Refresh logic) requires the use of the buses, it must force the microprocessor to give up control of the buses. This is accomplished by turning on the Intel microprocessor's HOLD (Hold Request) input. Upon detecting HOLD active, the microprocessor electrically disconnects itself from the address, control and data buses so the requesting device can use them to communicate with other devices. This is called "floating" the buses. The microprocessor then turns on its HLDA (Hold Acknowledge) output, informing the requesting device that it has yielded the buses to it, making it the new bus master. The device remains bus master as long as it keeps the microprocessor's HOLD input active.

When a bus master other than the microprocessor on the system board has completed using the buses, it turns off the microprocessor's HOLD input, allowing the microprocessor to re-connect itself to the buses and become bus master again.

Although It is possible for an expansion card inserted into an IBM PC/XT/AT expansion slot to become bus master, there is a major drawback. When an expansion card becomes bus master in a PC/XT/AT, it can remain bus master

EISA Bus Structure Overview

as long as it keeps the microprocessor's HOLD line active. There are no safety mechanisms built into a PC/XT/AT to prevent a bus master card from monopolizing the use of the buses to the exclusion of the microprocessor and the RAM Refresh logic on the system board and potential bus master cards inserted into other expansion slots.

If, due to poor design or a failure, a bus master expansion card should monopolize the buses for an inordinate amount of time, the main microprocessor cannot continue to fetch and execute instructions. This could have serious consequences. In addition, the Refresh logic would be unable to become bus master on a timely basis and data in DRAM memory could be lost. Finally, other bus master cards inserted in expansion slots would not be able to become bus master and transfer data. To summarize, severe problems can be incurred when bus master expansion cards are used in a PC/XT/AT.

EISA Bus Master Support

The ISA bus mastering problem is fixed in the EISA environment by the addition of the EISA bus arbitration signals and a Central Arbitration Control (CAC) on the EISA system board. The CAC provides a method for resolving situations where multiple bus masters are competing for the use of the buses. As explained in the chpater entitled, "Bus Arbitration," a bus master is not permitted to monopolize the bus in an EISA machine.

By establishing a method for resolving bus conflicts, EISA creates a system that can safely support multiple bus masters. This means that EISA products support use of the buses by:

- The main microprocessor
- The DMA Controller on the system board
- The Refresh logic on the system board
- Bus master cards inserted into expansion slots

Typically, a bus master card is quite intelligent, incorporating a microprocessor and its own local ROM, RAM and I/O devices. An example would be a disk controller card built around an 80386 microprocessor, running its own software from its local (on-board) ROM memory. It stores data received from other bus masters in its local RAM memory prior to writing it to disk. It can read large amounts of data from disk, store it in its local RAM memory and forward it to another device, such as memory on the system board, when necessary. It controls an array (group) of eight disk drives.

EISA System Architecture

Other bus masters could issue high-level commands or requests to the example disk controller. An example would be a request sent to the disk controller card to search for a database file called "TOM.DBF" on the eight disk drives it controls and, if found, read a particular record and send it back to the requesting bus master. After issuing the request to the disk controller card, the requesting bus master could surrender the EISA bus and continue other local processing until the disk controller card responds. Upon completing the search, the disk controller card would become bus master and transfer the requested data into system memory for the other bus master to use.

An EISA system can safely incorporate a number of intelligent bus master cards, each essentially running on its own. When required, they can communicate with each other and transfer data between themselves either directly or through system memory. The EISA system is designed to support multi-processing: multiple processors, each handling a portion of the overall task. Properly implemented, the parallel processing accomplished in this type of system is extremely efficient.

Figure 2 - 1 illustrates the EISA system bus structure. The basic system components are:

- The system board
- The ISA/EISA Expansion Slots

EISA Bus Structure Overview

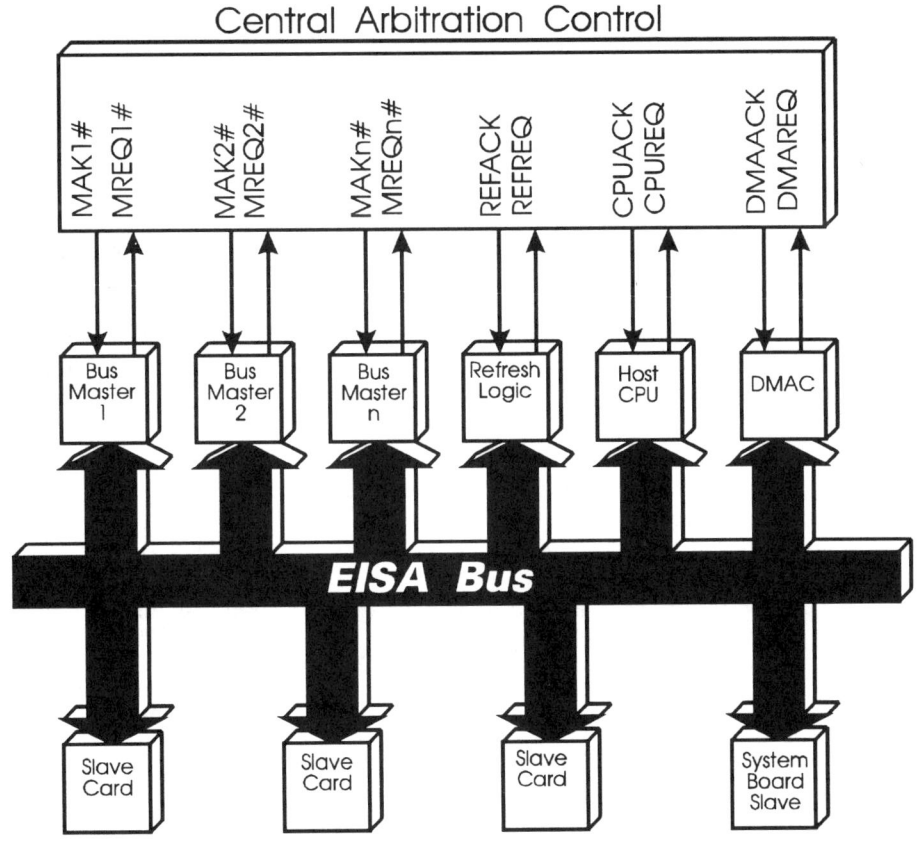

Figure 2-1. The EISA Bus: A Shared Resource

EISA System Architecture

The user may install two basic classes of devices into the expansion bus:

- ISA-compatible expansion cards
- EISA-compatible expansion cards

All EISA and ISA expansion devices fall into one of two categories:

- A **master** is a device that executes bus cycles to communicate with other devices. Any type of master can communicate with any type of slave in the system. The system board provides data bus steering logic that copies the data between data paths and translates EISA/ISA control signals when necessary.

- A **slave** is a device that a master reads from or writes to. A slave may be either a memory or an I/O slave.

There is only one type of ISA master: the ISA 16-bit bus master. This is a device that attaches to the ISA Bus and is capable of executing bus cycles to communicate with memory or I/O slaves. This is accomplished by interfacing the bus master card to DMA channel 5, 6 or 7 with the channel programmed to operate in Cascade Mode. A more detailed description of bus mastering in the ISA environment can be found in the chapter entitled, "DMA and Bus Mastering," in the MindShare publication entitled "ISA System Architecture."

Types of Bus Masters in an EISA System

In an EISA system, there are six basic types of bus masters:

- **16-bit ISA or EISA bus master**. This is a 16-bit ISA or EISA device that attaches to the EISA bus and is capable of executing bus cycles to communicate with any slave. When communicating with a 32-bit EISA slave or an 8-bit ISA slave, the data bus steering logic on the system board must sometimes aid in the transfer.

- **32-bit EISA bus master**. This is a 32-bit device that attaches to the EISA bus and is capable of executing bus cycles to communicate with any slave. When communicating with 8 or 16-bit slaves, the data bus steering logic on the system board must sometimes aid in the transfer.

- **The Main CPU**. The CPU may communicate with any ISA or EISA Slave or with devices resident on the CPU's local bus structure. When

EISA Bus Structure Overview

the microprocessor attempts to perform a transfer utilizing one or more data paths not connected to the target slave, the data bus steering logic on the system board must aid in the transfer.

- **The Refresh Logic.** Used to Refresh DRAM memory throughout the system.

- **DMA Controllers.** Used to transfer information between an I/O device and system memory.

Types of Slaves in an EISA System

Slaves fall into the following categories:

- 8-bit ISA I/O and memory slaves
- 16-bit ISA I/O and memory slaves
- 16-bit EISA I/O and memory slaves
- 32-bit EISA I/O and memory slaves
- 8, 16 or 32-bit slaves on the CPU's local bus

EISA System Architecture

EISA Bus Arbitration

Chapter 3

The Previous Chapter

The previous chapter provided background on the ISA bus' inability to support multiple processors in a fair fashion and introduced the EISA bus and the role of the Central Arbitration Control logic on the EISA system board. The types of bus masters and slaves were identified.

In This Chapter

The bus arbitration scheme used by the EISA Central Arbitration Control is described in detail.

The Next Chapter

The next chapter, "Interrupt Handling," describes the methods used to detect and service interrupt request in both the ISA and EISA environments.

The EISA Bus Arbitration Scheme

All EISA systems have a device known as the Central Arbitration Control (CAC) on the system board. The CAC's task is to arbitrate among the outstanding requests for the use of the buses and grant the buses to a single device.

There are four classifications of devices that can issue requests to the Central Arbitration Control:

- the main CPU
- Expansion bus masters
- the Refresh Controller on the system board
- the DMA Controller (DMAC) on the system board

Figure 3 - 1 illustrates the CAC's relationship to potential bus masters.

EISA System Architecture

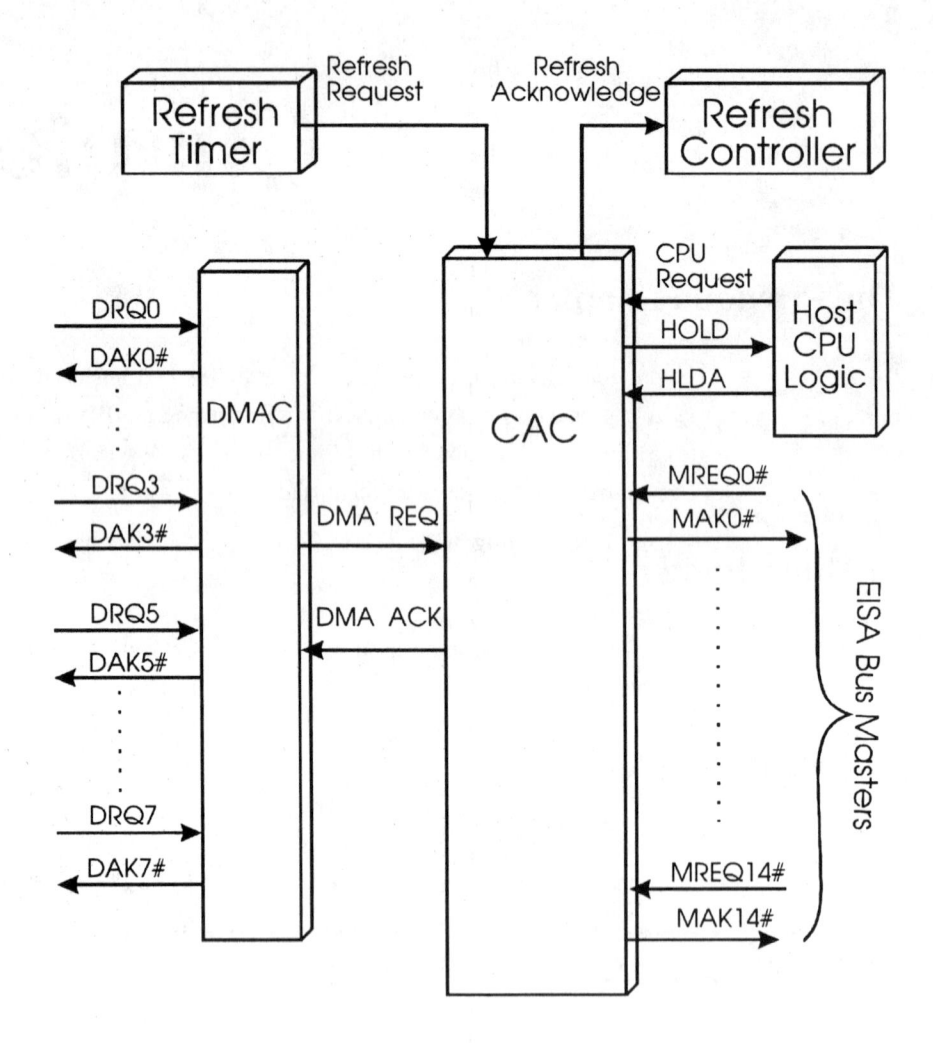

Figure 3-1. Block Diagram of the Central Arbitration Control (CAC)

The CAC uses a multi-level, rotating priority arbitration method. Figure 3 - 2 depicts this rotational priority scheme. On a fully loaded bus, the order in which devices are granted bus access is independent of the order in which they generate bus requests, since devices are serviced based on their position in the rotational order. The DMAC is given a high order of priority to assure compatibility with ISA expansion boards that require short bus latency. The EISA bus masters have a low priority and designers of EISA bus master cards must therefore provide for longer bus latency.

The top priority level uses a 3-way rotation to grant bus access sequentially to a DMA channel, the Refresh Controller, and a device from the 2-way rotation (either the main CPU or a bus master card). A DMA Channel, the Refresh Controller and a device from the 2-way rotation each gain access to the bus at least one of every three arbitration cycles (depending on what devices are requesting service). A device that does not request the bus is skipped in the

EISA Bus Arbitration

rotation. The main CPU is allowed to retain control of the buses when no other devices are requesting bus mastership. In systems that couple the main CPU with a cache controller, the host system will only require the use of the buses under the following conditions:

- a cache read miss
- an I/O read or write

In a system wherein the main CPU doesn't have a cache, the main CPU is always requesting the use of the buses.

The DMA controller is programmed during the POST to use a fixed priority scheme in evaluating which DMA channel to service next. As pictured in figure 3 - 2, this means that DMA channel zero has the highest priority, followed by two - through - seven. It should be noted that DMA channel four is unavailable because it is used to cascade the slave DMA controller through the master (see the chapter entitled, "DMA and Bus Mastering," in the MindShare publication entitled "ISA System Architecture").

NMI interrupts are given special priority. If an NMI interrupt occurs, the arbitration mechanism is modified so that the bus master cards and the DMACs are bypassed each time they come up for rotation. This gives the CPU complete control of the bus for NMI servicing.

DMA priorities can be modified by programming the DMAC Control Register to rotating priority. This scenario is pictured in figure 3 - 3. Each DMA channel then has essentially the same as all of the others.

EISA System Architecture

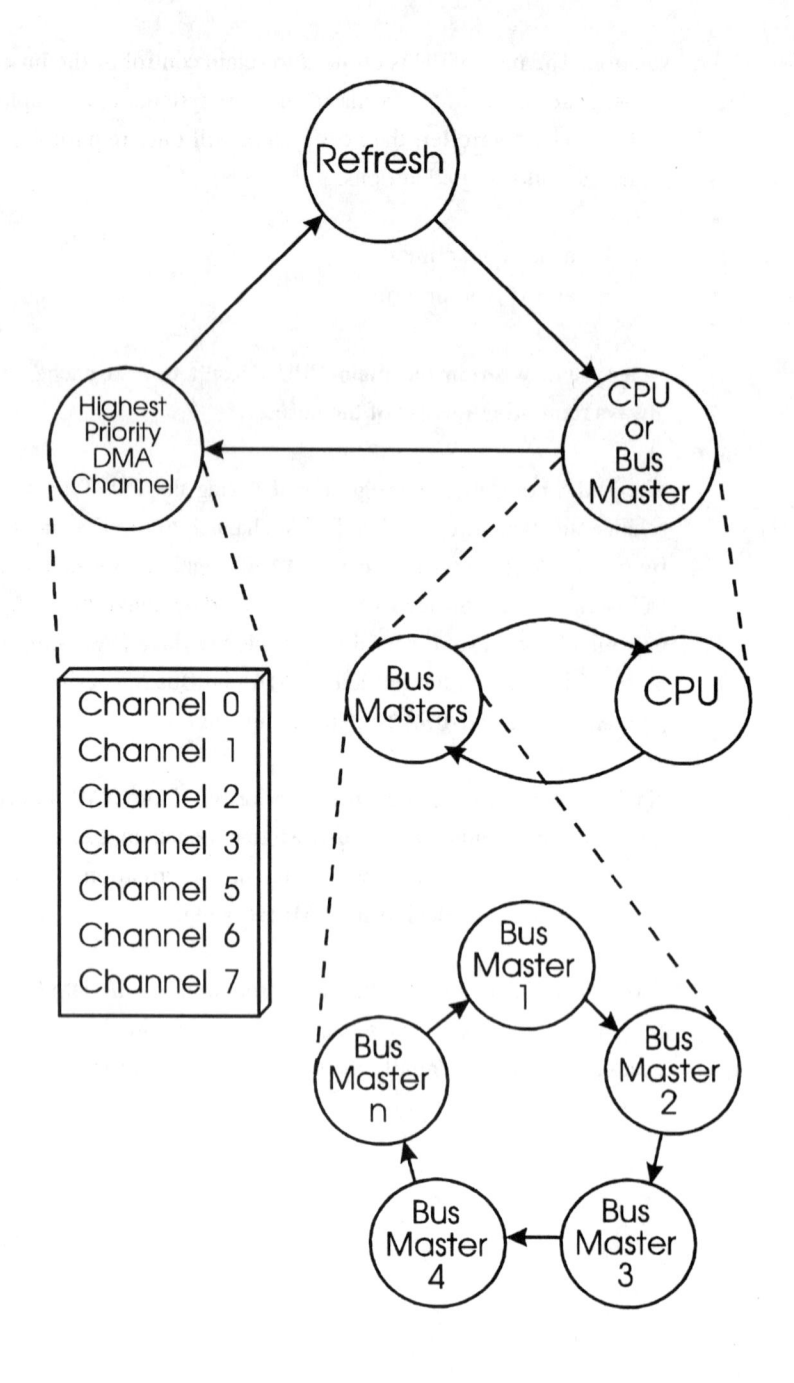

Figure 3-2. CAC With the DMACs Programmed For Fixed Priority

EISA Bus Arbitration

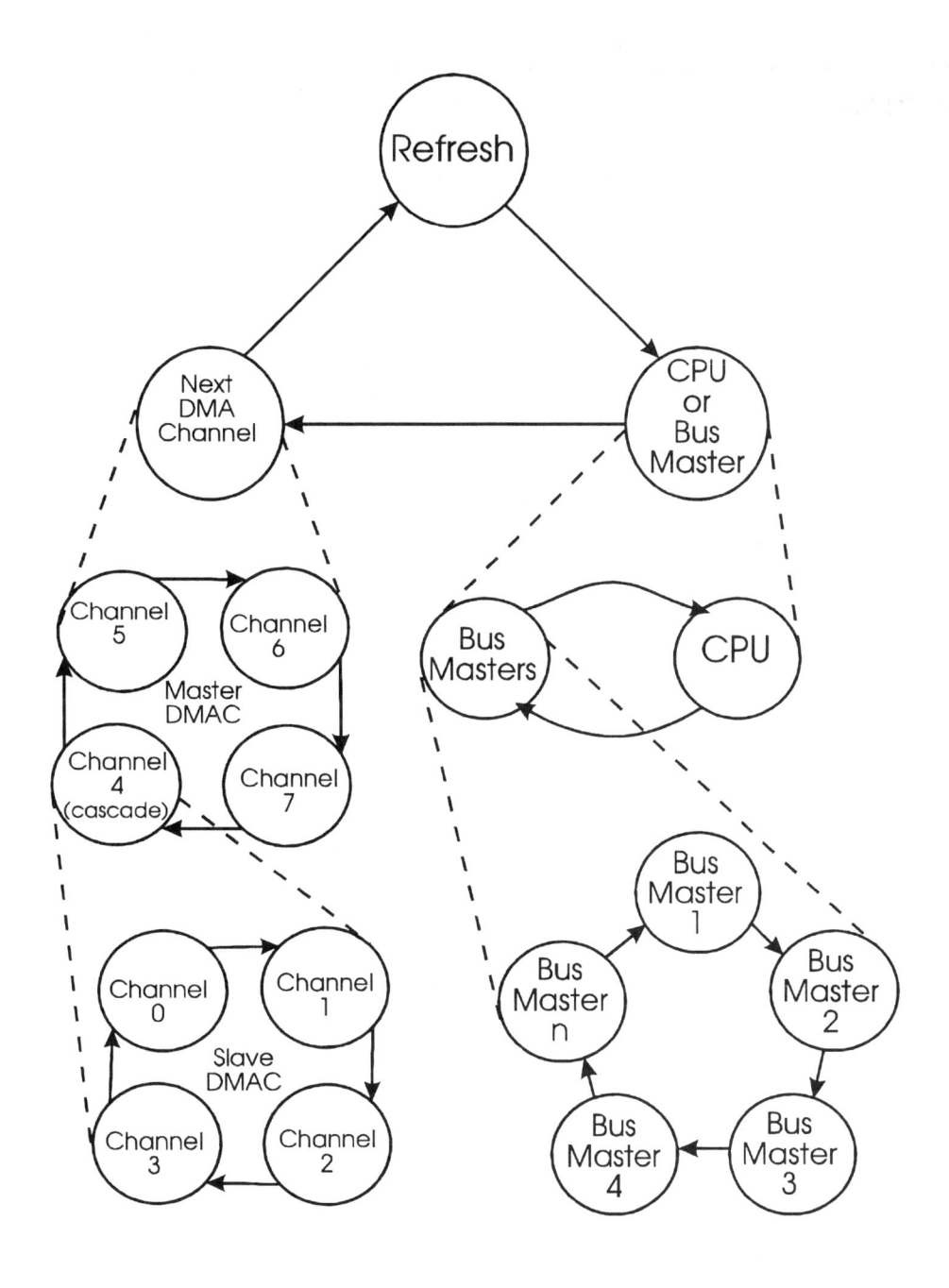

Figure 3-3. CAC With DMACs Programmed For Rotational Priority

EISA System Architecture

Preemption

When one of the potential bus masters requires the use of the buses to communicate with another device, it must turn on its request line (MREQn#) to the CAC (refer to figure 3 - 1). After deciding which device currently requesting the buses is next in the rotation, the (CAC) turns off the Acknowledge line associated with the bus master that currently owns the buses. In this way, the CAC preempts the current bus master, commanding it to relinquish control of the buses. Upon being preempted by removal of its Acknowledge, the current bus master must relinquish control of the buses within a prescribed period of time. If the current bus master is an EISA bus master card, it must release the buses within 64 cycles of the bus clock signal, BCLK. Since BCLK has a nominal frequency of 8MHz, or 125ns per cycle, 64 BCLK cycles equates to eight microseconds. If the current bus master is a DMA channel programmed for one of the new EISA bus cycle types (rather than the ISA-compatible bus cycle), the DMA channel has 32 BCLKs, or 4 microseconds, to release the buses. DMA channels programmed to run ISA-compatible DMA bus cycles cannot be preempted. Care should therefore be taken when utilizing an ISA DMA channel to perform a block data transfer using either block or demand transfer modes. If the transfer is too long, other devices requiring the use of the bus, such as the Refresh controller, may be forced to wait too long.

The current bus master indicates that it is relinquishing control of the buses by de-activating its CAC Request line. If it doesn't relinquish control with eight microseconds, the CAC takes the following actions:

- turns on the reset signal on the EISA bus to force the current bus master off the bus.
- turns on NMI, Non-Maskable Interrupt request, to alert the main microprocessor that a bus timeout has occurred.
- grants the buses to the main CPU so it can respond to the NMI.

If, on the other hand, the current bus master honors the preemption, relinquishing the buses and turning off its Request to the CAC, the CAC then grants the buses to the next bus master in the rotation that is requesting the use of the buses.

As illustrated in figure 3 - 1, the main CPU, Refresh logic and the DMA controller each have a pair of request/acknowledge lines connecting it to the

EISA Bus Arbitration

CAC. In addition, there is also a pair of request/acknowledge lines connected to each EISA slot in the system. The EISA specification provides support for up to fifteen EISA bus masters, numbered from zero to fourteen. MREQ0# and MAK0# are typically used to implement an EISA-style bus master that is embedded on the system board. MREQ1# and MAK1# are connected to EISA expansion slot one, MREQ2# and MAK2# to EISA slot two, etc. It should be noted, however, that the CAC encapsulated in the Intel 82350DT EISA chip set only has six pairs of EISA request/acknowledge lines and can therefore only support EISA bus master cards in a maximum of six EISA card slots. This explains why some EISA machines with more than six EISA slots only support bus master cards in six of them.

If the current bus master is preempted during a multiple bus cycle transfer, it will give up the buses as described above, and, after waiting two BCLKs, it will re-assert its request line to request the use of the buses again.

Example Arbitration Between Two Bus Master Cards

The timing diagram in the figure 3 - 4 illustrates bus arbitration between two Bus masters.

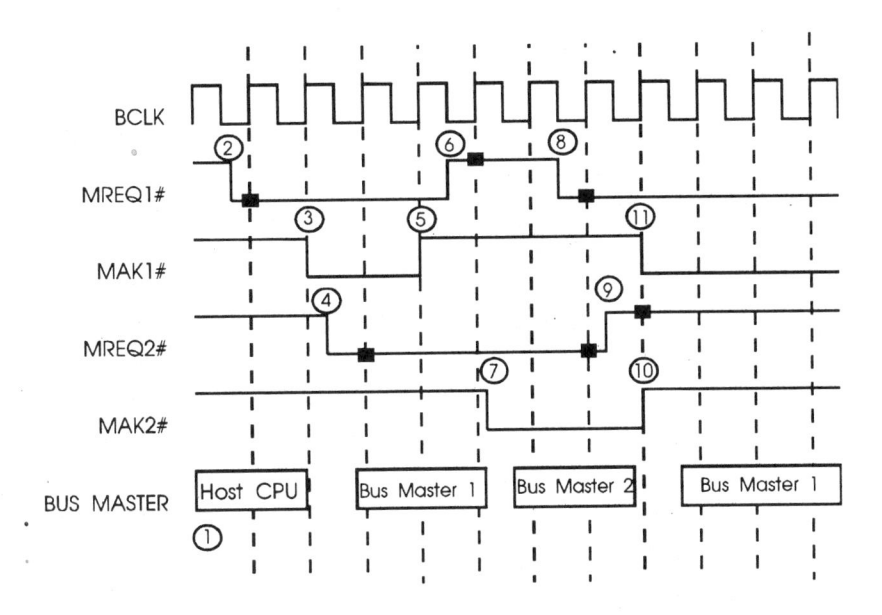

Figure 3-4. Arbitration Between Two Bus Masters

EISA System Architecture

The following steps define the sequence of events illustrated in figure 3 - 4. The step numbers correspond to the reference numbers in the illustration.

1. Initially, the Main Processor owns the buses.

2. The bus master in slot 1 requests the use of the buses by asserting MREQ1# (Master Request, Slot 1) to the Central Arbitration Control.

3. After the Central Arbitration Control has removed ownership of the buses from the Main Processor and the Main Processor signals its willingness to give up ownership, the Central Arbitration Control grants ownership to bus master 1 by asserting MACK1# (Master Acknowledge, Slot 1). Bus master 1 now owns the buses and can initiate one or more bus cycles.

4. The bus master in slot 2 signals its request for bus mastership by asserting MREQ2# to the Central Arbitration Control.

5. The Central Arbitration Control signals bus master 1 that it must give up bus mastership by removing MACK1#.

6. After having its MACK1# removed, bus master 1 has up to 8 microseconds to release the buses. This gives it time to complete one or more bus cycles prior to release. bus master 1 will signal its release of the buses by removing MREQ1#.

7. The buses are granted to bus master 2 by the Central Arbitration Control when it asserts MACK2#.

8. Bus master 1 requires the use of the buses again to either complete its previously interrupted series of transfers or to initiate a new transfer. It signals its request to the Central Arbitration Control by asserting MREQ1#.

9. Bus master 2 has finished using the buses, so it voluntarily gives up ownership by turning off MREQ2#.

10. The Central Arbitration Control removes ownership from Bus Master 2 by turning off MACK2#.

11. The Central Arbitration Control grants the buses to bus master 1 again by turning on MACK1#.

EISA Bus Arbitration

Memory Refresh

The EISA system board incorporates a Refresh controller that requests the use of the buses once every fifteen microseconds to refresh a row of DRAM memory. 16-bit ISA bus masters that hold the bus longer than fifteen microseconds must perform memory refresh bus cycles at the fifteen microsecond interval.

The EISA Refresh controller includes a 14-bit row counter that drives its contents onto address lines 2:15 when the Refresh controller becomes bus master. The Refresh controller also activates BE0#:BE3# so they can be converted to address bits zero and one.

Each time that the Refresh controller requests the use of the buses and the request is not granted within fifteen microseconds, the Refresh controller increments its uncomplete refresh count. This counter can count up to four uncompleted refresh bus cycles. When the Refresh controller succeeds in gaining control of the buses, it runs a refresh bus cycle and decrements the uncompleted refresh count by one. If more refreshes are queued up (the count isn't exhausted), the Refresh controller immediately requests the use of the buses again without waiting the normal period of fifteen microseconds.

Interrupt Handling

Chapter 4

The Previous Chapter

The previous chapter described the bus arbitration scheme utilized in EISA machines.

In This Chapter

An in-depth discussion of interrupt request handling in the ISA environment can be found in the chapter entitled, "Interrupt Handling," in the MindShare publication entitled, "ISA System Architecture." This chapter provides a brief review of the ISA interrupt request handling method and a detailed description of the EISA method.

The Next Chapter

The signals and support logic that comprise the ISA bus impose certain limitations on performance and capabilities. The EISA specification builds upon the ISA bus, adding new bus signals and system board support logic. The end result is backward-compatibility with all ISA cards and improved performance and capabilities for new EISA-style cards. The next chapter provides a detailed description of the extensions to the ISA bus and support logic.

Review of Interrupt Handling In the ISA Environment

The Intel 8259 interrupt controller's interrupt request inputs can be programmed to recognize either a positive-going pulse or a static high level as a valid interrupt request. The programmer may select either of these recognition modes for all eight inputs at once. There is no provision for the selection of either type on an input-by-input basis. On an ISA machine, the 8259 Interrupt Controllers are programmed to recognize a positive-going pulse as valid interrupt requests on its eight inputs. The following section describes the two shortcomings inherent in ISA interrupt handling.

EISA System Architecture

Shortcomings of ISA Interrupt Handling

Phantom Interrupts

Internally, the 8259 has a pull-up resistor on each of its IRQ inputs. When an ISA expansion card must generate an interrupt request, the line is driven low by the card and is then allowed to go high again. The low-to-high transition is registered as an interrupt request by the 8259 interrupt controller on the system board. The 8259 specification also demands that the IRQ line must remain high until after the leading-edge of the first interrupt acknowledge bus cycle. The pull-up resistor ensures this will be the case.

Consider the case where an ISA card is designed to keep its IRQ line low until a request must be generated. At that time, the card would allow the IRQ line to go high and would maintain the high until the request has been serviced. The transition from low-to-high would be registered as a request by the 8259. When the request has been serviced, the card would drive the line low again and keep it low until the next request is to be generated. Although this design would work, a problem may arise.

Due to the low-to-high transition, a transitory noise spike on this interrupt request line could register as a valid interrupt request. When the microprocessor issues the first of the two interrupt acknowledge bus cycles, however, the IRQ line will already be low again. This means that the IRQ line's respective IRR (Interrupt Request Register) bit will not be active. The first interrupt acknowledge is supposed to reset the highest-priority IRR bit and set its respective bit in the ISR (In-Service Register). In this case, since the IRR bit is no longer set because the request was of too short a duration (a ghost, or phantom, interrupt), the 8259 must take special action. The 8259 is designed to automatically return the interrupt vector for its number seven input in this case. When the microprocessor then generates the second interrupt acknowledge and the 8259 must respond with an interrupt vector, it will send back the vector of its number seven input. On the master 8259, this will be 0Fh, the vector of IRQ7. On the slave, it will be 77h, the IRQ15 interrupt vector. The microprocessor will therefore jump to either the IRQ7 or the IRQ15 interrupt service routine.

In these two routines, therefore, the programmer must perform a check to see if the IRQ7 or the IRQ15 was real. This is accomplished by reading the contents of the respective 8259's ISR register and checking to see if bit seven is really set. If it is, then the request is real and the programmer should execute the

Interrupt Handling

remainder of the interrupt service routine to service the request. If, on the other hand, the bit is off, it was a phantom or ghost interrupt and the programmer should just perform an interrupt return (the IRET instruction) and return to the interrupted program flow.

ISA card designers can avoid this problem by designing the card's IRQ output driver to keep the IRQ line high when not requesting service, allowing the pull-up resistor inside the 8259 to keep it high. The line will not be prone to pick up noise spikes when it's high. When a request must be generated, the card drives the IRQ line low and then lets it go high again. This low-to-high transition registers as a request in the 8259. When the microprocessor generates the first interrupt acknowledge, the line is guaranteed to be high and the request is therefore valid.

Limited Number of IRQ Lines

In the ISA environment, IRQ lines are not shareable because only one transition is registered if more than one card generates a transition. The low-to-high transition generated by the first card would be recognized by the interrupt controller and any subsequent transitions would be ignored until the first request has been serviced. More than one ISA device may share an IRQ line as long as it is guaranteed that they will never generate requests simultaneously. Since only one device may use each IRQ line, a fully-loaded machine may easily use up all of the available lines. An in-depth discussion of interrupt handling in the ISA environment may be found in the MindShare publication entitled, "ISA System Architecture."

Interrupt Handling In the EISA Environment

Shareable IRQ Lines

The interrupt controllers used in the EISA environment are a superset of the Intel 8259A controller. The 8259A allows the programmer to gang-program all eight IRQ inputs as either edge or level-triggered. In the EISA environment, machines must be capable of supporting both ISA and EISA-style cards. This means that the programmer must have the ability to individually select each IRQ input as either edge or level-triggered. The EISA interrupt controller has added an additional register for this purpose.

The ELCR, or Edge/Level Control Register, provides this selectivity. The master interrupt controller's ELCR is located at I/O address 04D0h, while the slave's is at I/O address 04D1h. Each of these registers is default programmed

EISA System Architecture

to edge-triggering upon power-up. tables 4 - 1 and 4 - 2 illustrate their respective bit assignments.

Table 4-1. Master Interrupt Controller's ELCR Bit Assignment

Bit	Description
7	0 = IRQ7 is edge-sensitive and non-shareable, 1 = IRQ7 is level-sensitive and shareable.
6	0 = IRQ6 is edge-sensitive and non-shareable, 1 = IRQ6 is level-sensitive and shareable.
5	0 = IRQ5 is edge-sensitive and non-shareable, 1 = IRQ5 is level-sensitive and shareable.
4	0 = IRQ4 is edge-sensitive and non-shareable, 1 = IRQ4 is level-sensitive and shareable.
3	0 = IRQ3 is edge-sensitive and non-shareable, 1 = IRQ3 is level-sensitive and shareable.
2	always 0 because the master's IRQ2 input is used to cascade the slave interrupt controller through the master.
1	IRQ1 is dedicated to the interrupt request output of the Keyboard interface. This bit must be 0, selecting edge-sensitive and non-shareable.
0	IRQ0 is dedicated to the interrupt request output of the System Timer. This bit must be 0, selecting edge-sensitive and non-shareable.

Interrupt Handling

Table 4-2. Slave Interrupt Controller's ELCR Bit Assignment

Bit	Description
7	0 = IRQ15 is edge-sensitive and non-shareable, 1 = IRQ15 is level-sensitive and shareable.
6	0 = IRQ14 is edge-sensitive and non-shareable, 1 = IRQ14 is level-sensitive and shareable.
5	IRQ13 is dedicated to the error output of the Numeric Coprocessor. This bit must be 0, selecting edge-sensitive and non-shareable. In reality, IRQ13 is shared by the Numeric Corocessor and the Chaining interrupt outputs of the DMA controller. More information regarding chaining can be found in the EISA chapter entitled, "DMA."
4	0 = IRQ12 is edge-sensitive and non-shareable, 1 = IRQ12 is level-sensitive and shareable.
3	0 = IRQ11 is edge-sensitive and non-shareable, 1 = IRQ11 is level-sensitive and shareable.
2	0 = IRQ10 is edge-sensitive and non-shareable, 1 = IRQ10 is level-sensitive and shareable.
1	0 = IRQ9 is edge-sensitive and non-shareable, 1 = IRQ9 is level-sensitive and shareable.
0	IRQ8 is dedicated to the alarm output of the Real-Time Clock chip. This bit must be 0, selecting edge-sensitive and non-shareable.

When programmed to recognize level-sensitive interrupt requests, the interrupt controller recognizes a low on an IRQ line as a request and an Interrupt Request line may be shared by two or more devices. The following paragraphs define how this works.

During the POST, software scans the area of memory space set aside for device ROMs, C0000h - through - DFFFFh, to see if any expansion cards have device ROMs. When a device ROM is detected, the POST jumps to the initialization routine in the ROM to execute the card's POST and to install the start addresses of its interrupt service and BIOS routines into the proper entries in the interrupt table in memory. The ROM's initialization routine reads the current pointer from the interrupt table entry, saves it and writes the pointer to the device ROM's interrupt service routine in its place. After testing and initializing the card, the ROM code performs a return to the machines POST. The POST then continues to scan the device ROM memory area for other device ROMs. If any are found, the same process is repeated. When another card is using the same IRQ line, its ROM code reads the current pointer from the interrupt table entry and saves it. This pointer points to the interrupt service routine within a previously detected device ROM for another EISA I/O card that is sharing this IRQ line. The second card's ROM code then stores a pointer

# EISA System Architecture

to its own interrupt service routine into the IRQ line's assigned interrupt table entry. In this way, a linked list of interrupt service routine start addresses is created. Any loadable-device drivers or TSRs that use shareable interrupt request lines should do the same.

Each shareable interrupt request line has a pull-up resistor on it. When no request is being generated, or when no I/O devices are physically connected to the line, the line is pulled-up to a good high level. This provides a good deal of noise immunity on the line, preventing spurious requests.

Figure 4 - 1 illustrates how multiple EISA I/O cards can share the same IRQ line. An I/O device that places a low on an interrupt request line when it generates a request may share the line with other devices that use it the same way. When a board of this type must generate a request, it acts as follows:

- Through an open-collector driver, it creates a path to ground. This places an active low level on the 8259's request input. If other I/O devices are sharing the line and generate requests simultaneously, the shared IRQ line is low.

- When an I/O board generates a request, it should also set its Interrupt Pending bit in a pre-defined I/O port on the card.

Interrupt Handling

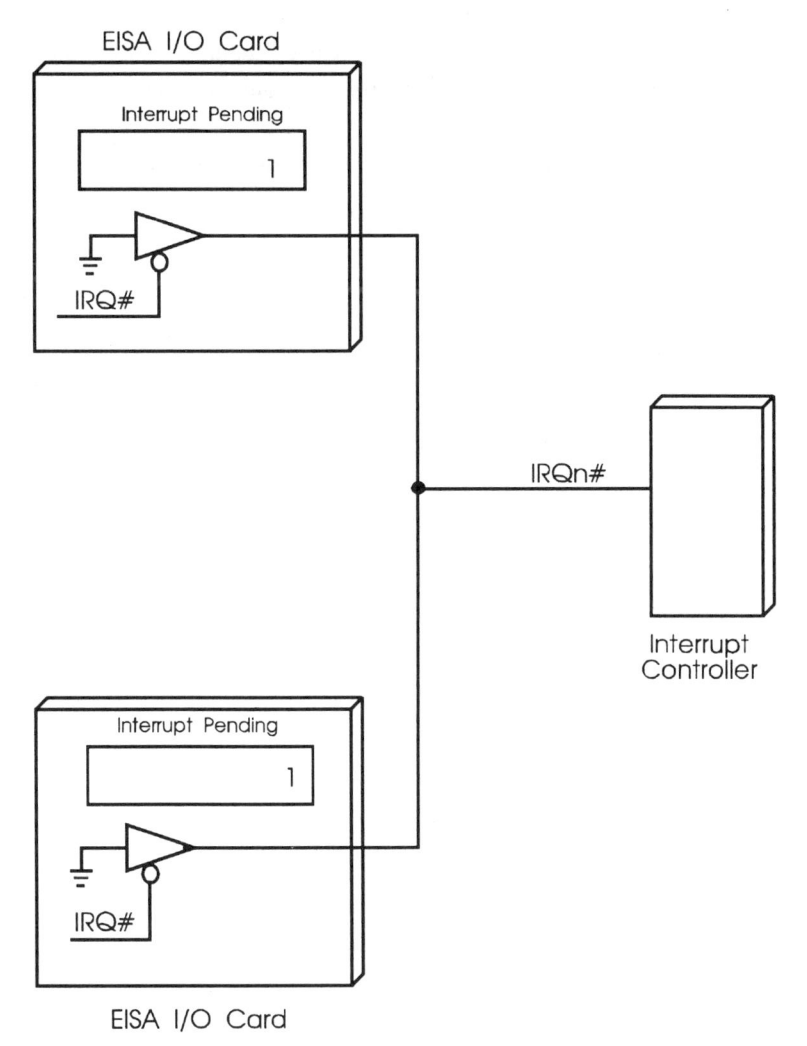

Figure 4-1. IRQ Line Sharing

When the 8259 senses a low on a shareable request input, it generates an interrupt request to the microprocessor. When the microprocessor requests the Interrupt vector, the 8259 responds with the vector for the respective line currently being serviced. The microprocessor then jumps to the interrupt service routine for the last device ROM detected during the POST. In this routine, an I/O read is performed from the card's Interrupt Pending register to determine if this card is generating a request. If the card's Interrupt Pending bit is set active, the program should continue executing the remainder of the card's interrupt service routine to service the request. If the card's Interrupt Pending bit isn't set active, however, the program should jump to the next interrupt service routine in the chain. The second service routine then polls its card's Interrupt Pending register to see if it is generating a request. The act of servicing the request (for example, sending a character to a serial port) should cause the requesting board's Interrupt Pending bit to be turned off. The board would also cease to provide a path to ground for the interrupt request line.

If more than one I/O device were generating requests simultaneously, the other board or boards would still be placing a low on the shared request line. The 8259 would therefore immediately sense another pending request and proceed as outlined above. This time, the Interrupt Pending bit for the board that was already serviced would be sensed off, and the next service routine in the chain would be jumped to see if its Interrupt Pending bit were set.

Since the program must go through a linked service routine list to determine which board is currently generating a request, it stands to reason that the lower down in the list a device is, the more time it will take to service its request (if other devices, further up the list, are also generating requests). This latency, or delay, could cause problems ranging from slow servicing of a device right up to overflow conditions and missing characters. The problem can be solved in one of two ways:

1. Move some devices to other interrupt requests lines.

2. During the configuration process, install the devices requiring the smallest latency first and the others later in the process.

Elimination Of Phantom Interrupts

All IRQ inputs that are configured as level-sensitive, shareable inputs assume the high state when no requests are pending or when the IRQ line is unused. This renders these inputs relatively noise-free, substantially decreasing the possibility of phantom interrupts.

Detailed Description of the EISA Bus

Chapter 5

The Previous Chapter

The previous chapter provided a detailed description of interrupt handling in the EISA environment.

In This Chapter

This chapter provides a description of all the signals on the EISA bus.

The Next Chapter

In the next chapter, the types of bus cycles run by the main CPU and EISA bus masters are described.

Introduction

The EISA Bus consists of two sets of signal lines:

- the ISA Bus
- the extension to the ISA Bus, the EISA bus

Figure 5 - 1 illustrates the construction of the EISA connector. When inserted, ISA boards are stopped by the EISA access key and make contact only with the ISA contacts. When an EISA board is inserted, however, an alignment notch in the board allows it to bottom out, making contact with both the ISA and the EISA contacts.

EISA System Architecture

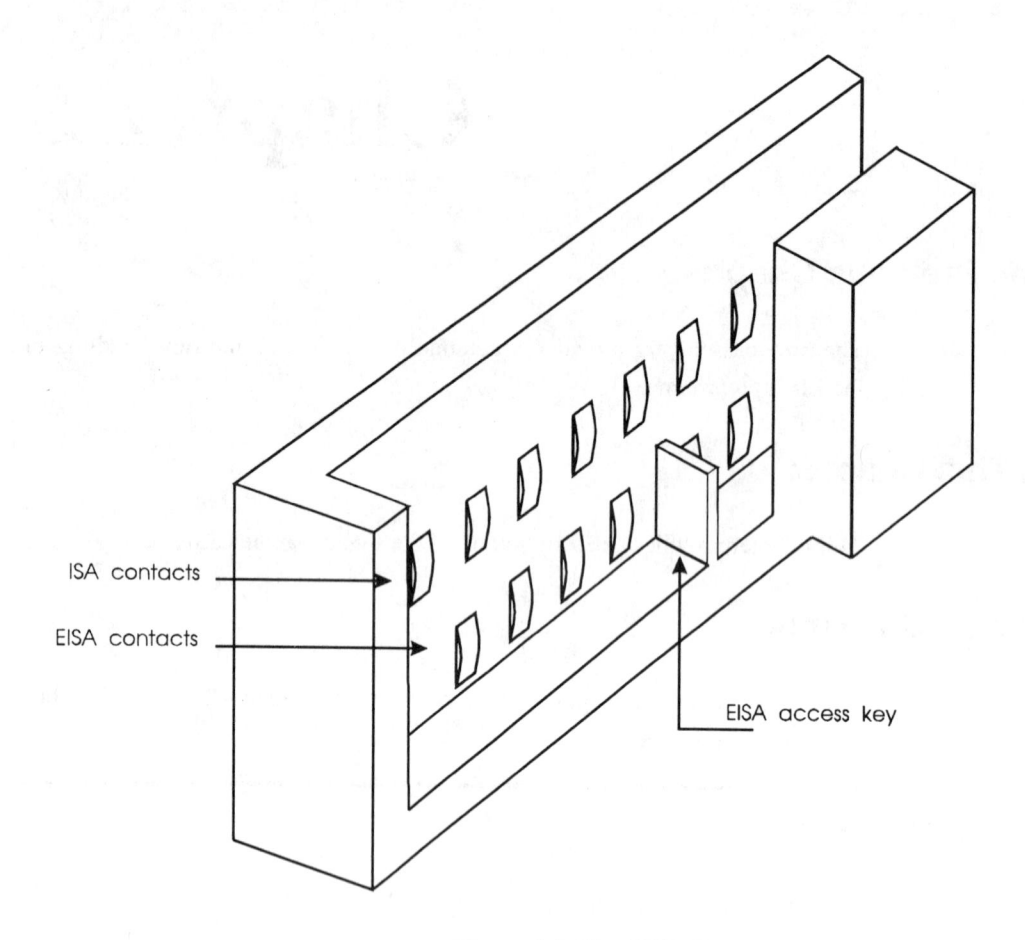

Figure 5-1. The EISA Connector

Many of the ISA signals have already been defined in preceding sections of this book and all of them are fully defined in the MindShare book entitled, *ISA System Architecture*. This section is confined to a description of the EISA signals. The following are the signal groups that comprise the EISA Bus.

- The Address Bus Extension
- The Data Bus Extension
- The Bus Arbitration signal group
- The Burst Handshake signal group
- The Bus Cycle Definition signal group
- The bus cycle timing signal group
- The Lock signal
- The Slave Size signal group
- The AEN signal

The following paragraphs provide a description of each of these signal groups.

Detailed Description of the EISA Bus

The Address Bus Extension

One of the restrictions imposed by the ISA bus structure was a function of the width of the address bus. It consisted of 24 address lines, A0 - through - A23. This allowed the microprocessor to address any memory location between address 000000h and FFFFFFh, a range of 16MB.

With the advent of multi-tasking, multi-user operating systems, access to a greater amount of memory became an imperative. The EISA specification expands the address bus to 32 bits, A0 - through - A31, and also adds the Byte Enable lines, BE0#:BE3#, to provide 32-bit bus master address support. The ISA bus includes the following address lines:

- SA0 - though SA19
- LA17 - through - LA23
- SBHE#

The EISA address bus consists of the following signals:

- SA0:SA1 (ISA bus)
- SBHE# (ISA bus)
- LA17:LA23 (ISA bus)
- LA24#:LA31# (EISA extension)
- BE0#:BE3# (EISA extension)
- LA2:LA16 (EISA extension)

The EISA specification extends the size of the LA Bus to include LA2:LA16 and LA24#:LA31#. Refer to figure 5 - 2. Combined with the previously-defined SA bus and LA signal groups on the ISA portion of the bus, this extends the address bus to a full 32-bits, allowing the current bus master to generate any memory address from 00000000h - through - FFFFFFFFh. This is a range of 4GB (giga = billion).

EISA System Architecture

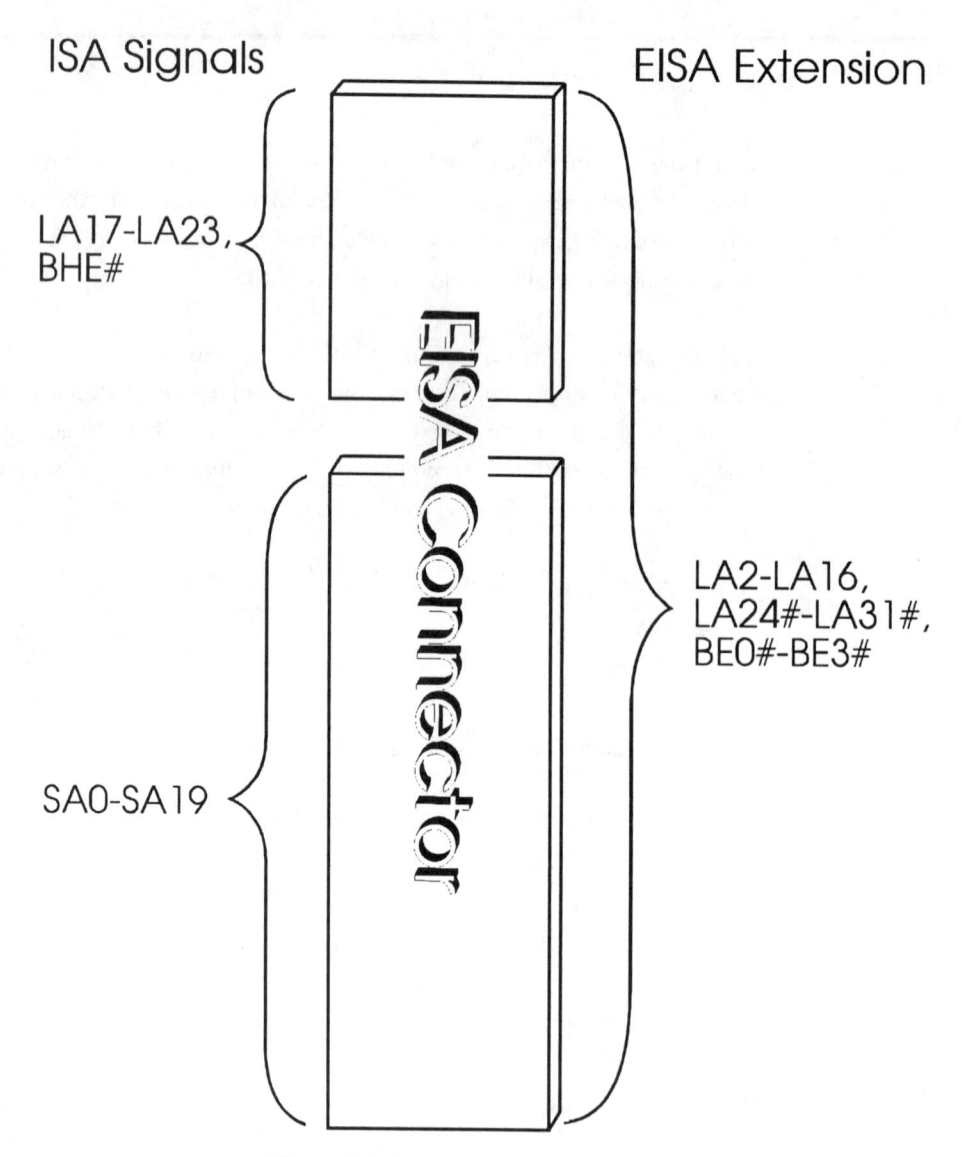

Figure 5-2. The EISA Connector -- Address Lines

The LA24# - through LA31# signals are active low to prevent 16-bit bus masters from inadvertently selecting 32-bit memory cards residing above 16 MB. When a 16-bit bus master places an address on the address bus, it is only using lines A0:A23. If address lines LA24#:LA31# were allowed to float, a 32-bit memory card that resides above the 16MB boundary might be inadvertently selected. Rather, LA24#:LA31# are pulled high with pull-up resistors on the system board, ensuring that they will be high (inactive) unless driven active (low) by a 32-bit bus master. 32-bit EISA memory cards are designed to recognize that these upper address lines carry inverted address information (0 on a line is a logical 1 and a 1 is a logical 0).

Detailed Description of the EISA Bus

Since the address information on the LA bus shows up sooner than the address on the SA bus (due to address pipelining and the fact that the LA bus bypasses the Address Latch on the system board), memory cards that use the LA lines can perform an early address decode. This allows the memory card designer to use slightly slow (cheap) memory chips and yet achieve higher throughput. In addition, the fact that the LA bus now includes the lower part of the address bus allows memory cards that use SCRAM or Page Mode RAM to determine if the next access will be in the same row of memory (because the row portion of the DRAM address is carried over the middle portion of the address bus).

The EISA specification also adds the four byte enable signal lines, BE#0:BE3#, allowing 32-bit bus masters to generate addresses in doubleword address format (A2:A31 plus the BE lines) and 32-bit slaves to see the address in 32-bit doubleword format.

The Data Bus Extension

The EISA specification extends the width of the data bus by adding two additional data paths consisting of D16:D23 and D24:D31. This allows 32-bit bus masters to transfer four bytes (a doubleword) during a single transfer when communicating with 32-bit slaves.

The Bus Arbitration Signal Group

Two signals have been added under EISA to allow implementation of bus master cards. They are described in table 5 - 1.

EISA System Architecture

Table 5-1. EISA Bus Master Handshake Lines

Signal Name	Full Name	Description
MREQx#	Master Request for Slot x	When a bus master in a slot requires the use of the buses to perform a transfer, it asserts its slot-specific MREQx# signal line. This signal is applied to the Central Arbitration Control (CAC) on the system board, which then arbitrates its priority against other pending bus requests.
MAKx#	Master Acknowledge for Slot x	When the Central Arbitration Control (CAC) is ready to grant the buses to a requesting bus master (MREQx is active), the CAC asserts the bus master's MAKx# slot-specific signal line to inform the bus master that it has been granted the buses.

Figure 5 - 3 illustrates the relationship of the master request and acknowledge lines to the CAC. The subject of bus arbitration is covered in detailed the chapter entitled, "Bus Arbitration."

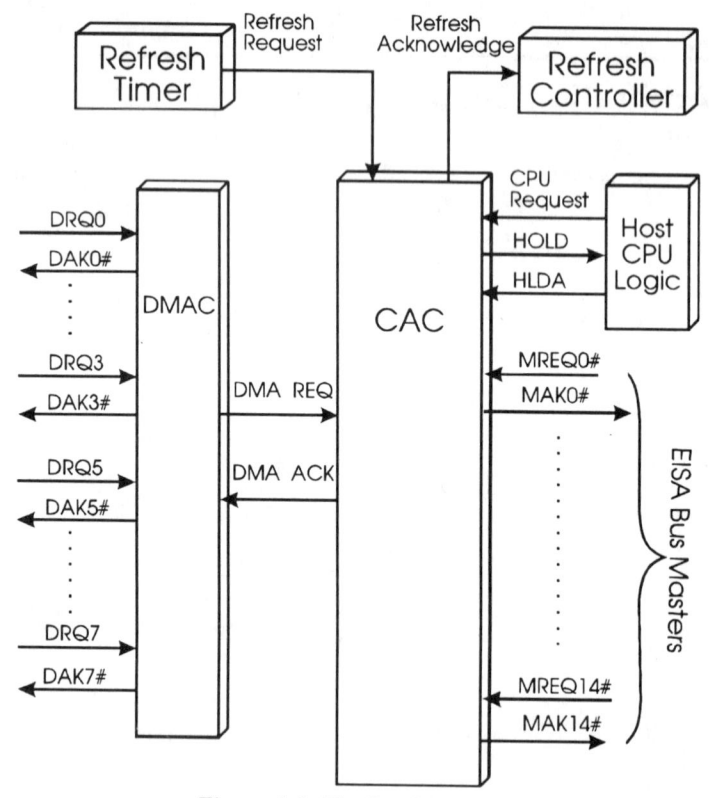

Figure 5-3. The Bus Master Handshake Lines

Detailed Description of the EISA Bus

The Burst Handshake Signal Group

The EISA specification adds two signal lines to support initiation of burst mode (Type "C") bus cycles. They are described in table 5 - 2.

Table 5-2. The Burst Handshake Lines

Signal Name	Full Name	Description
SLBURST#	Slave Burst	A slave asserts SLBURST# to indicate that it supports Burst cycles. If the slave supports Burst cycles, it will assert this signal regardless of the state of the MSBURST# signal line.
MSBURST#	Master Burst	During a bus cycle, the current bus master asserts this line as a response to an active level on the SLBURST# handshake line. It informs the addressed slave that the bus master supports Burst cycles.

The subject of burst mode (Type "C") bus cycles is covered in detail in the chapter entitled, "EISA CPU and Bus Master Bus Cycles."

The Bus Cycle Definition Signal Group

The EISA specification defines a new set of Bus Cycle Definition signal lines. The current EISA bus master uses them to inform the currently addressed slave of the type of bus cycle in progress. Table 5 - 3 defines the new signals.

Table 5-3. EISA Bus Cycle Definition Lines

Signal Name	Full Name	Description
M/IO#	Memory or I/O	During a bus cycle, M/IO# is set high if a memory address is on the address bus. It will be set low if it's an I/O address.
W/R#	Write or Read	During a bus cycle, W/R# is set high if a write bus cycle is in progress and low if a read bus cycle is in progress.

EISA System Architecture

The Bus Cycle Timing Signal Group

Under the EISA specification, the following signals were added to define the address and data portions of the bus cycle, as well as the end of the bus cycle.

Signal Name	Full Name	Description
START#	Start phase	Every EISA bus cycle consists of two phases: the Start and Command phases. The address and the M/IO# control line are output by the current bus master and decoded by the target slave during the Start phase. The Start phase corresponds to address time and is therefore one BCLK is duration.
CMD#	Command phase	Every EISA bus cycle consists of two phases: the Start and Command phases. The data is transferred during the Command phase. CMD# goes active at the trailing edge of the START# signal (trailing edge of Ts) and stays active until the end of the bus cycle. When a bus cycle has wait states inserted, the CMD# signal will be active for multiple cycles of BCLK.
EXRDY	EISA Ready	Asserted by an EISA slave to request the insertion of wait states in the current bus cycle. It is sampled on each falling edge of BCLK after the CMD# line goes active. When sensed active, the bus cycle will be terminated at the next rising edge of BCLK.

The Lock Signal

The LOCK# signal can be asserted by the current bus master to prevent other bus masters from arbitrating for the use of the bus. This allows the current bus master to complete one or more memory accesses prior to surrendering control to another bus master. The purpose of the bus lock capability is to prevent two bus masters that share a memory location as a software semaphore from becoming de-synchronized with each other.

Detailed Description of the EISA Bus

The Slave Size Signal Group

When the current bus master addresses an EISA-style slave, the slave will assert one of these two signals to indicate the data paths it can use and the fact that it is an EISA-style slave. Table 5 - 4 describes these two signals.

Table 5-4. The EISA Type/Size Lines

Signal Name	Full Name	Description
EX32#	EISA Slave Size 32	When a 32-bit EISA slave decodes its address, it asserts EX32# to inform the current bus master that it can handle 32-bit transfers.
EX16#	EISA Slave Size 16	When a 16-bit EISA slave decodes its address, it asserts EX16# to inform the current bus master that it can handle 16-bit transfers.

The AEN Signal

The following paragraph describes the manner in which the AEN signal is used under the ISA specification.

When either the master or slave DMA Controller (DMAC) on the system board becomes bus master, it sets AEN active as a substitute for BALE#, indicating that a valid memory address is present on the address bus. Memory cards should decode the address on the address bus. I/O cards should also monitor the AEN signal line and ignore the address on the bus when AEN is active. This is necessary because the DMAC will set either the IORC# or IOWC# line active and I/O devices would think there was an I/O address on the bus when there really wasn't.

It should be noted that AEN has another, special, usage in the EISA environment. This additional function is discussed in the chapter entitled, "EISA System Configuration."

The EISA Connector Pinouts

The EISA connector is an extended version of the ISA connector. The ISA connector is divided into an 8-bit connector and a 16-bit extension. In figure 5 - 4, the upper half of the EISA connector, rows A and B, comprise the 8-bit portion that is compatible with the IBM PC and XT expansion connector and

EISA System Architecture

the 8-bit portion of the connector found in the IBM PC/AT. On the lower half of the EISA connector in the figure, rows C and D comprise the 16-bit portion that is compatible with the 16-bit extension to the 8-bit connector found in the IBM PC/AT. The pins on the EISA connector are arranged in eight rows. Rows A, B, C, and D comprise the ISA group, while rows E, F, G and H comprise the EISA group.

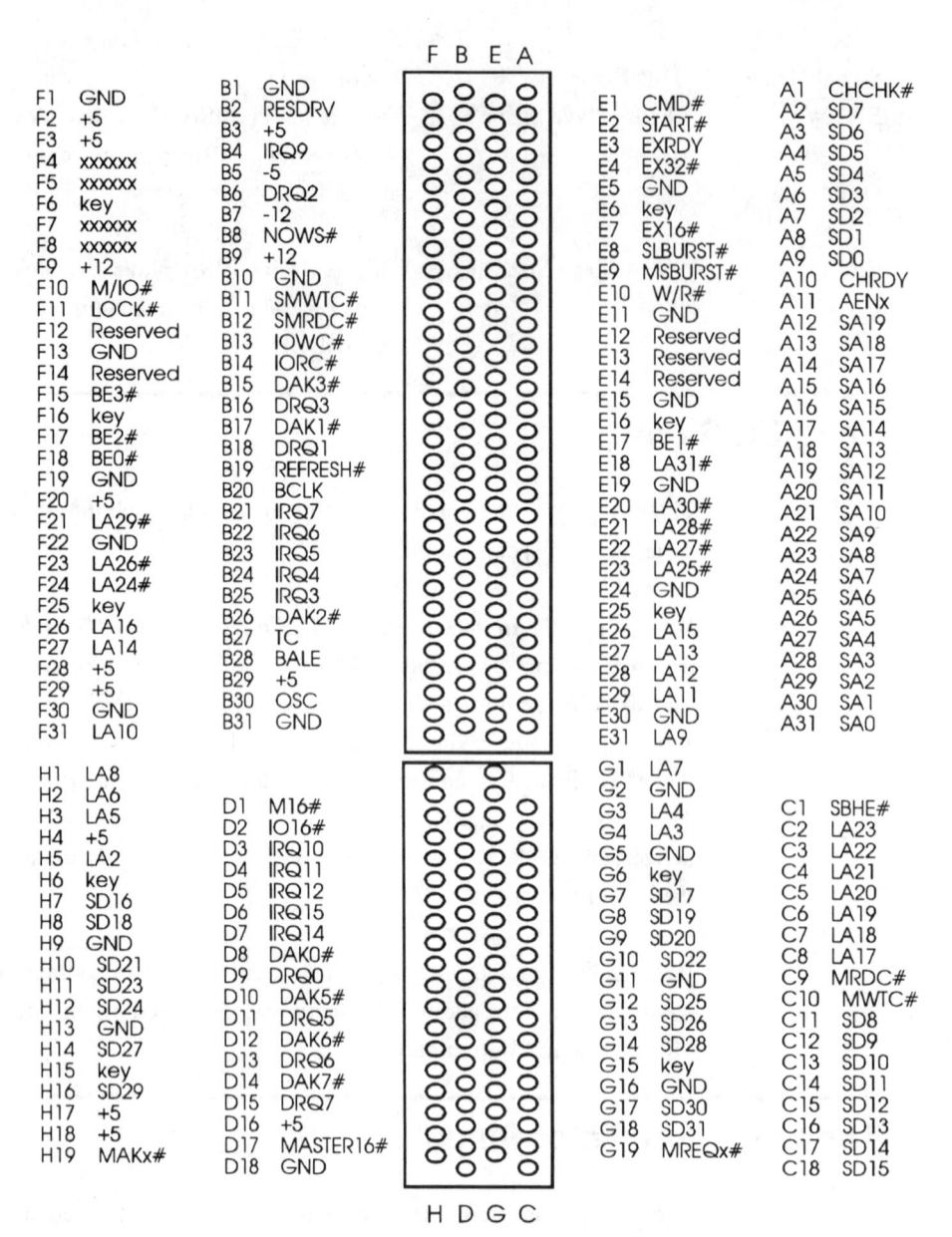

F1	GND	B1	GND	E1	CMD#	A1	CHCHK#
F2	+5	B2	RESDRV	E2	START#	A2	SD7
F3	+5	B3	+5	E3	EXRDY	A3	SD6
F4	xxxxxx	B4	IRQ9	E4	EX32#	A4	SD5
F5	xxxxxx	B5	-5	E5	GND	A5	SD4
F6	key	B6	DRQ2	E6	key	A6	SD3
F7	xxxxxx	B7	-12	E7	EX16#	A7	SD2
F8	xxxxxx	B8	NOWS#	E8	SLBURST#	A8	SD1
F9	+12	B9	+12	E9	MSBURST#	A9	SD0
F10	M/IO#	B10	GND	E10	W/R#	A10	CHRDY
F11	LOCK#	B11	SMWTC#	E11	GND	A11	AENx
F12	Reserved	B12	SMRDC#	E12	Reserved	A12	SA19
F13	GND	B13	IOWC#	E13	Reserved	A13	SA18
F14	Reserved	B14	IORC#	E14	Reserved	A14	SA17
F15	BE3#	B15	DAK3#	E15	GND	A15	SA16
F16	key	B16	DRQ3	E16	key	A16	SA15
F17	BE2#	B17	DAK1#	E17	BE1#	A17	SA14
F18	BE0#	B18	DRQ1	E18	LA31#	A18	SA13
F19	GND	B19	REFRESH#	E19	GND	A19	SA12
F20	+5	B20	BCLK	E20	LA30#	A20	SA11
F21	LA29#	B21	IRQ7	E21	LA28#	A21	SA10
F22	GND	B22	IRQ6	E22	LA27#	A22	SA9
F23	LA26#	B23	IRQ5	E23	LA25#	A23	SA8
F24	LA24#	B24	IRQ4	E24	GND	A24	SA7
F25	key	B25	IRQ3	E25	key	A25	SA6
F26	LA16	B26	DAK2#	E26	LA15	A26	SA5
F27	LA14	B27	TC	E27	LA13	A27	SA4
F28	+5	B28	BALE	E28	LA12	A28	SA3
F29	+5	B29	+5	E29	LA11	A29	SA2
F30	GND	B30	OSC	E30	GND	A30	SA1
F31	LA10	B31	GND	E31	LA9	A31	SA0
H1	LA8			G1	LA7		
H2	LA6			G2	GND		
H3	LA5	D1	M16#	G3	LA4	C1	SBHE#
H4	+5	D2	IO16#	G4	LA3	C2	LA23
H5	LA2	D3	IRQ10	G5	GND	C3	LA22
H6	key	D4	IRQ11	G6	key	C4	LA21
H7	SD16	D5	IRQ12	G7	SD17	C5	LA20
H8	SD18	D6	IRQ15	G8	SD19	C6	LA19
H9	GND	D7	IRQ14	G9	SD20	C7	LA18
H10	SD21	D8	DAK0#	G10	SD22	C8	LA17
H11	SD23	D9	DRQ0	G11	GND	C9	MRDC#
H12	SD24	D10	DAK5#	G12	SD25	C10	MWTC#
H13	GND	D11	DRQ5	G13	SD26	C11	SD8
H14	SD27	D12	DAK6#	G14	SD28	C12	SD9
H15	key	D13	DRQ6	G15	key	C13	SD10
H16	SD29	D14	DAK7#	G16	GND	C14	SD11
H17	+5	D15	DRQ7	G17	SD30	C15	SD12
H18	+5	D16	+5	G18	SD31	C16	SD13
H19	MAKx#	D17	MASTER16#	G19	MREQx#	C17	SD14
		D18	GND			C18	SD15

Figure 5-4. The EISA Connector Pin Assignments

ISA Bus Cycles

Chapter 6

The Previous Chapter

The previous chapter provided a functional description of the EISA bus signals.

This Chapter

This chapter provides a review of the ISA bus master and DMA bus cycles.

The Next Chapter

The next chapter provides a detailed description of the EISA CPU and bus master bus cycle types.

Introduction

In order to define extensions to ISA, or EISA, the writers of the EISA specification had to first document ISA. The following descriptions of ISA bus cycles are based on the descriptions found in the EISA specification.

The Bus Clock, or BCLK, is supplied to the ISA bus by the system board and defines the time slots (Tstates) that comprise a bus cycle. In order to maintain ISA compatibility, the maximum clock rate used for bus cycles on the EISA Bus is 8.33MHz.

8-bit ISA Slave Device

An 8-Bit ISA slave device interfaces only to the least-significant eight data bus bits and uses only ISA address bus bits SA0:SA19. This is the simplest and slowest of the slave devices and was first developed for use with the IBM PC. These devices didn't have to be very fast because the PC was based on an Intel 8088 microprocessor running at 4.77MHz.

At 4.77MHz, the clock period is 209.64ns and a 0-wait state bus cycle consists of four clock cycles, or 838.6ns. In other words, devices with an access time of

EISA System Architecture

up to 836ns could be interfaced to the microprocessor without incurring any wait states. Since the designer must account for the cycle time of DRAMs (typically double the access time), not the stated access time, this means that DRAMs with an access time of up to 400ns could be interfaced to the microprocessor without incurring wait states.

16-bit ISA Slave Device

A 16-bit ISA slave device interfaces to sixteen ISA data bus bits and uses ISA address bus lines SA0:SA19, LA17:LA23 and SBHE#. 16-bit devices were developed for use with the IBM PC-AT. Some of these devices were designed to operate in the original 6MHz version of the IBM PC-AT, while most were designed to work with the 8MHz version.

The 6MHz PC-AT could interface with a slave device having an access time of up to approximately 332ns and incur no wait states. This being the case, DRAMs with an access time of up to approximately 165ns could be accessed with 0-wait states.

The 8MHz PC-AT could interface with a slave device having an access time of up to approximately 250ns and incur no wait states. DRAMs with an access time of up to approximately 125ns could therefore be accessed with 0-wait states.

Transfers With 8-bit Devices

The ISA bus cycle types utilized to communicate with 8-bit devices include:

- Standard 8-bit device ISA bus cycle: 4-wait states
- Shortened 8-bit device bus cycle: 1-, 2-, or 3-wait states
- Stretched 8-bit device bus cycle: more than 4-wait states

The steps below describe the sequence of events that take place during an 8-bit bus cycle using the default READY# timing and explains how the default timing can be either shortened or stretched. Figure 6 - 1 illustrates an example bus cycle. The step numbers in the text that follows corresponds to the numbered reference points in figure 6 - 1.

1. The address being presented by the current bus master begins to appear on the LA Bus at the start of address time. This corresponds to the leading edge of Ts. If the system board is based on an 80286 or 80386

ISA Bus Cycles

microprocessor and address pipelining is active, the address may actually be present on the LA bus prior to the beginning of the bus cycle (as is the case in this example). 16-bit ISA memory expansion cards can use the portion of the address on the LA bus to perform an early address decode. 8-bit ISA expansion cards do not have access to the LA bus and therefore cannot perform an early address decode. I/O cards only use the lower 16 address bits and therefore cannot take advantage of address pipelining.

2. BALE goes active half way through address time, gating the address through the system board Address Latch onto the SA Bus.

3. If this is a write bus cycle, the microprocessor's output data is gated onto the SD bus half way through address time. It remains on the SD bus until half a BCLK cycle into the next bus cycle (half way through address time of the next transfer).

4. The trailing-edge of BALE (at the beginning of data time) causes the system board Address Latch to latch the address being output by the CPU so it will remain static on the SA Bus for the remainder of the bus cycle. Also at this time, the addressed slave device can safely complete the decoding process.

5. At the end of address time, the M16# signal is sampled inactive by the system board Bus Control logic, indicating that the command lines SMRDC and SMWTC will not be activated until half way through the first data time.

6. M16# is also sampled half way through the first data time indicating that the addressed expansion board is either an 8-bit device or a 16-bit I/O device.

   The appropriate command line (SMRDC#, SMWTC#, IORC# or IOWC#) is set active half way through data time. During a transfer with an 8-bit device, the activation of the command line is delayed until the midpoint of data time to allow more time for address decode before command line activation. The command line remains active until the end of the bus cycle (end of last Tc).

7. At the midpoint of the second data time, the IO16# signal is sampled inactive by the system board Bus Control logic, indicating that the addressed expansion board is an 8-bit device.

EISA System Architecture

Half way through the second data time and half way through each subsequent data time, the Default Ready Timer on the system board samples the NOWS# line. If sampled active, the CPU READY# line is activated and the bus cycle ends on the next rising edge of BCLK (the end of the current data time). In this way, an ISA board can terminate a bus cycle earlier than the default number of BCLK cycles (wait states) by activating NOWS#.

8. This item does not have a corresponding numbered reference point on the timing diagram. A bus cycle addressing an 8-bit ISA device defaults to six BCLK cycles (four wait states) if the following two conditions are met:

    - the bus cycle isn't terminated earlier by the assertion of NOWS#.
    - CHRDY is active when sampled during the first half of the last data time of the default cycle (first half of the 5th data time).

    This means that the duration of an ISA bus cycle accessing an 8-bit device defaults to four wait states unless shortened by NOWS# (to 3, 4, or 5 BCLK cycles) or lengthened by CHRDY. The bus cycle ends at the trailing edge of the fifth data time.

9. During a read bus cycle, the microprocessor reads the data on the data bus at the trailing edge of the last BCLK (Tc) of the bus cycle and the bus cycle is then terminated. The command line (SMRDC#, IORC#, etc.) is de-activated at that time.

When a write bus cycle terminates, the MWTC#, SMWTC# or IOWC# command line is de-activated. Write data remains on the SD bus until half way through address time of the next bus cycle. This accommodates the hold time of the device being written to and doesn't disturb the device being addressed in the next bus cycle because the command line for that bus cycle hasn't been activated yet.

ISA Bus Cycles

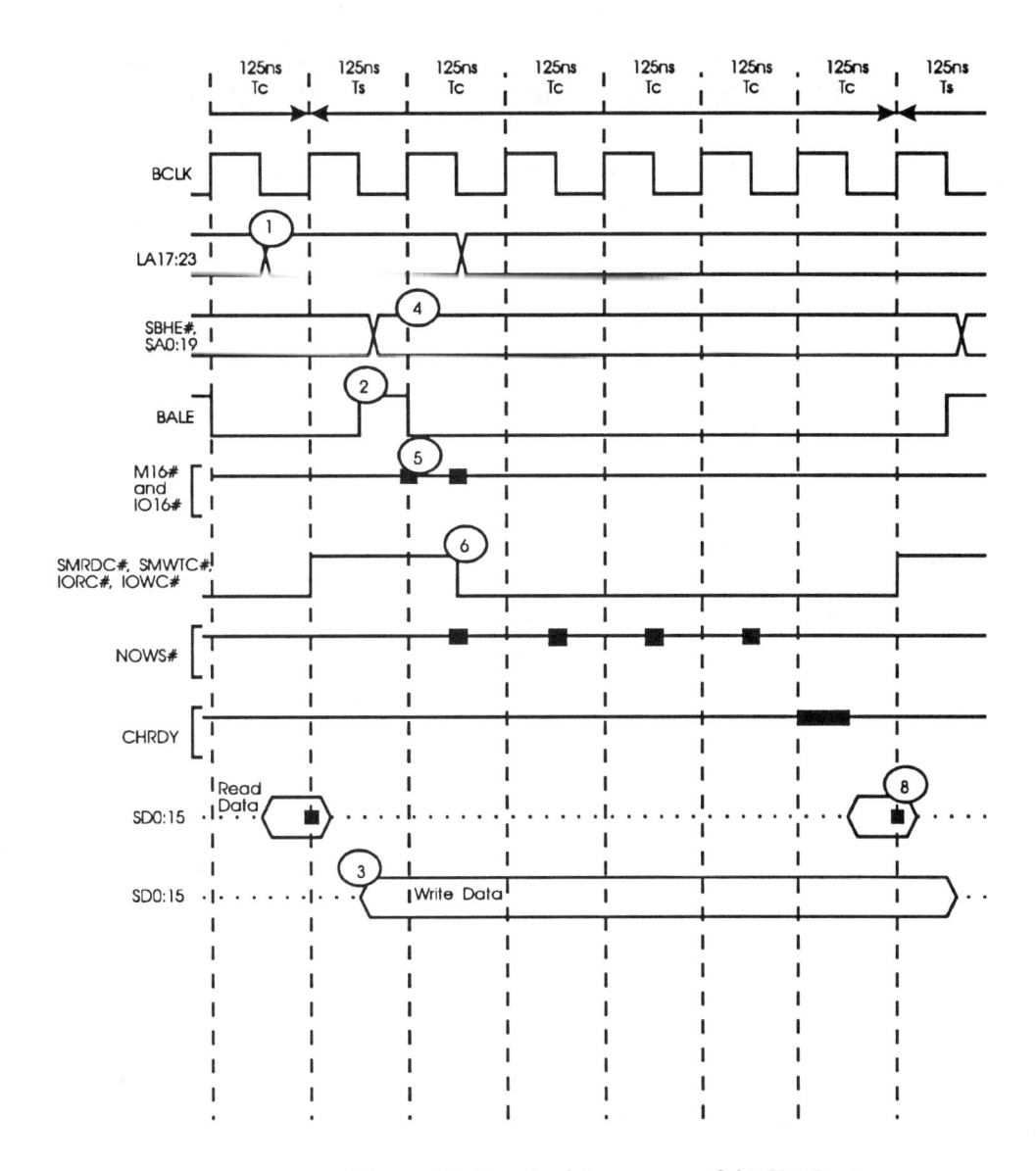

Figure 6-1. Standard Access to an 8-bit ISA Device

Transfers With 16-bit Devices

The ISA bus cycle types utilized to communicate with 16-bit devices include:

- Standard 16-bit device ISA bus cycle (Memory & I/O): 1-wait state
- Shortened 16-bit device ISA bus cycle (Memory only): 0-wait state
- Stretched 16-bit device ISA bus cycle: more than 1-wait state

EISA System Architecture

Standard 16-bit Memory Device ISA Bus Cycle

Figure 6 - 2 illustrates the timing of a bus cycle on the ISA bus when the current bus master is communicating with a one wait state 16-bit memory device. The timing diagram and the following numbered steps illustrate the sequence of events that occur during a default ISA 16-bit memory access. Each of the numbered steps corresponds to the numbered reference points in figure 6 - 2.

1. If the system board is based on an 80286 or 80386 microprocessor and address pipelining is active, the address is present on the LA Bus prior to the beginning of the bus cycle. This allows the addressed memory slave to start decoding the address early which may speed up access.

2. BALE is set active halfway through address time. On the rising edge of BALE, 16-bit ISA Memory devices can begin to decode the LA lines to determine if the address is for them. Also when BALE goes active the lower portion of the address from the processor is transferred through the system board's Address Latch onto the SA Bus.

3. The addressed memory board activates M16# as a result of decoding the LA lines, indicating to the system board's Bus Control Logic that it is capable of handling a 16-bit transfer without data bus steering being performed by the steering logic on the system board.

4. If this is a write bus cycle, the microprocessor's output data is gated onto the SD bus half way through address time and remains on the SD bus until half a BCLK cycle into the next bus cycle (half-way through address time of the next bus cycle).

5. At the end of address time, the trailing edge of BALE causes two events to take place:

ISA Bus Cycles

   a. 16-bit ISA Memory devices latch the LA lines so the addressed device will not be deselected when the LA lines are pipelined before the end of the current bus cycle.

   b. the Address Latch on the system board latches the lower twenty bits of the address, SA0:SA19, so they remain static on the SA bus for the remainder of the bus cycle. The addressed slave device can safely decode the SA address on the bus on the falling edge of BALE.

6. The system board's Bus Control Logic samples M16# at the end of address time to determine if the addressed device can take advantage of the MRDC# or MWTC# command lines being activated immediately.

   The appropriate command line (MRDC# or MWTC#) is set active at the leading edge of data time if M16# was sampled active. This command line remains active until the end of the bus cycle (end of last Tc).

   If M16# is sampled inactive the command line (MRDC# or MWTC#) is activated half way through data time.

7. The system board's Bus Control Logic samples M16# a second time at the midpoint of the first data time to determine if data bus steering is necessary. Since this is an access to a 16-bit device, no steering is necessary.

   Also at the midpoint of the first data time, the Default Ready Timer on the system board samples the NOWS# line. If sampled active, the microprocessor's READY# line is set active and the bus cycle terminates at the end of the first data time. In this way, a 16-bit ISA memory board can complete a bus cycle in two BCLK cycles. (It should be noted, however, that the Default Ready Timer ignores NOWS# during I/O bus cycles.)

8. During address pipelining, the microprocessor is free to output the address for the next bus cycle during the current bus cycle. Only the upper portion of the pipelined address appears at this time on the LA bus because these bits are buffered but not latched from the microprocessor's address bus. The remainder of the address will not appear on the SA bus until the midpoint of address time in the next bus cycle.

9. CHRDY is sampled by the Default Ready Timer at the beginning of the second data time to determine if the device will be ready to complete the bus cycle at the end of this BCLK cycle. If the device cannot complete the bus cycle by the end of this BCLK cycle, it should pull the CHRDY line

EISA System Architecture

inactive. If CHRDY were sampled inactive by the Default Ready Timer, it would respond by extending the bus cycle by adding another data time. CHRDY is then checked at the beginning of each additional data time until the device releases CHRDY to indicate that the bus cycle can be completed.

10. An ISA 16-bit memory bus cycle defaults to three BCLK cycles (one wait state) if the bus cycle isn't terminated earlier by the assertion of NOWS# and if CHRDY stays active throughout the bus cycle. This means that the length of an ISA bus cycle when accessing a 16-bit memory card defaults to one wait state unless shortened by NOWS# or lengthened by CHRDY. READY# is then set active to the microprocessor, telling it to read the data from the data bus.

When a memory write bus cycle terminates, the MWTC# command line is de-activated, but the data remains on the SD Bus for the first half of address time in the next bus cycle. This provides hold time for the device being written to and doesn't affect the device being addressed in the next bus cycle because the command line hasn't been activated yet.

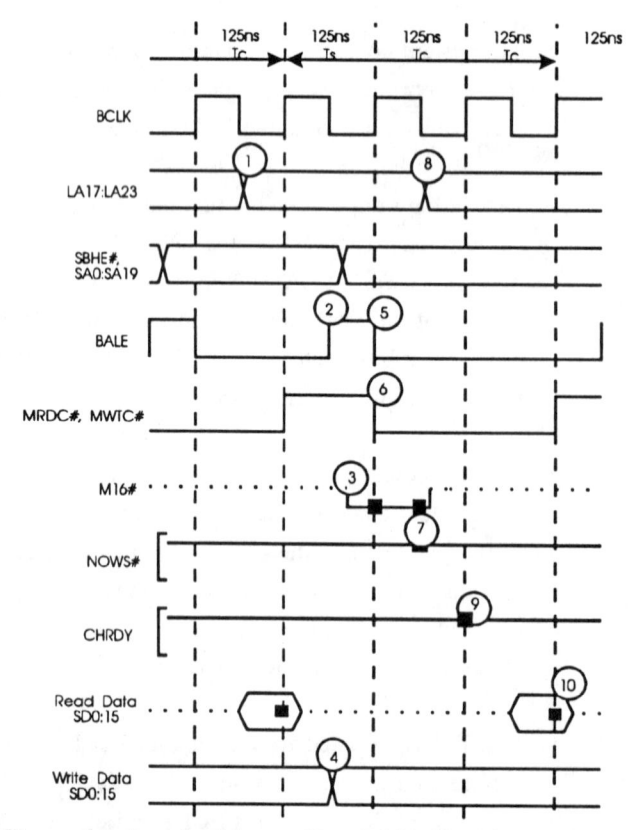

Figure 6-2. Standard Access To a 16-bit ISA Memory Device

ISA Bus Cycles

Standard 16-bit I/O Device ISA Bus Cycle

Figure 6 - 3 illustrates the timing of a bus cycle on the ISA bus when the current bus master is communicating with a 16-bit I/O device. The timing diagram and the following numbered steps illustrate the sequence of events that occur during a default ISA 16-bit memory access. Each of the numbered steps corresponds to the numbered reference points in figure 6 - 3.

1. If the system board is based on an 80286 or 80386 microprocessor and address pipelining is active, the address is present on the LA Bus prior to the beginning of the bus cycle. The LA Bus has no impact on I/O bus cycles since the LA bus will always be zeros during I/O operations.

2. BALE is set active halfway through address time, gating the address through the system board's Address Latch onto the SA Bus.

3. If this is a write bus cycle, the microprocessor's output data is gated onto the SD bus half way through address time and remains on the SD bus until half a BCLK cycle into the next bus cycle (half-way through address time of the next bus cycle).

4. At the start of data time, the trailing edge of BALE causes the Address Latch on the system board to latch the lower twenty bits of the address, SA0:SA19, so it remains static on the SA bus for the remainder of the bus cycle. The addressed slave device can safely latch the SA address on the bus on the falling edge of BALE.

5. The appropriate command line (IORC# or IOWC#) is also set active at the midpoint of data time. This command line remains active until the end of the bus cycle (end of last Tc).

6. At the midpoint of the first data time, the Default Ready Timer on the system board ignores the NOWS# line since an I/O device is being accessed. This is done to prevent two back-to-back I/O write bus cycles from accessing the I/O device too quickly. This could violate the I/O recovery time of the I/O device, causing improper operation.

7. During address pipelining, the microprocessor is free to output the address for the next bus cycle during the current bus cycle. Only the upper portion of the pipelined address appears at this time on the LA bus because these bits are buffered but not latched from the microprocessor's address bus. The

EISA System Architecture

remainder of the address will not appear on the SA bus until the midpoint of address time in the next bus cycle.

8. IO16# is sampled at the midpoint of the second data time to determine if the I/O device is an 8 or 16-bit device. If sampled active, no data bus steering will be performed and the bus cycle is terminated on the next rising edge of BCLK, which is the end of the second data time. The bus cycle will not be terminated if the CHRDY line is sampled inactive.

9. CHRDY is sampled by the Default Ready Timer at the end of the second data time to determine if the device is ready to complete the bus cycle. If the device cannot complete the bus cycle by the end of the second BCLK cycle, it should have pulled the CHRDY line inactive. If CHRDY were sampled inactive by the Default Ready Timer, it would respond by extending the bus cycle by one data time. CHRDY is then checked at the beginning of each additional data time until the device releases CHRDY to indicate that the bus cycle can be completed.

10. An ISA 16-bit I/O bus cycle defaults to three BCLK cycles (one wait state) if CHRDY stays active throughout the bus cycle. The bus cycle cannot be terminated earlier by the assertion of NOWS#. This means that the length of an ISA bus cycle when accessing a 16-bit I/O card defaults to one wait state unless lengthened by CHRDY. READY# is then set active to the microprocessor, telling it to read the data from the data bus.

When an I/O write bus cycle terminates, the IOWC# command line is de-activated, but the data remains on the SD Bus for the first half of address time in the next bus cycle. This accommodates the hold time of the device being written to and doesn't disturb the device being addressed in the next bus cycle because the command line for that bus cycle hasn't been activated yet.

ISA Bus Cycles

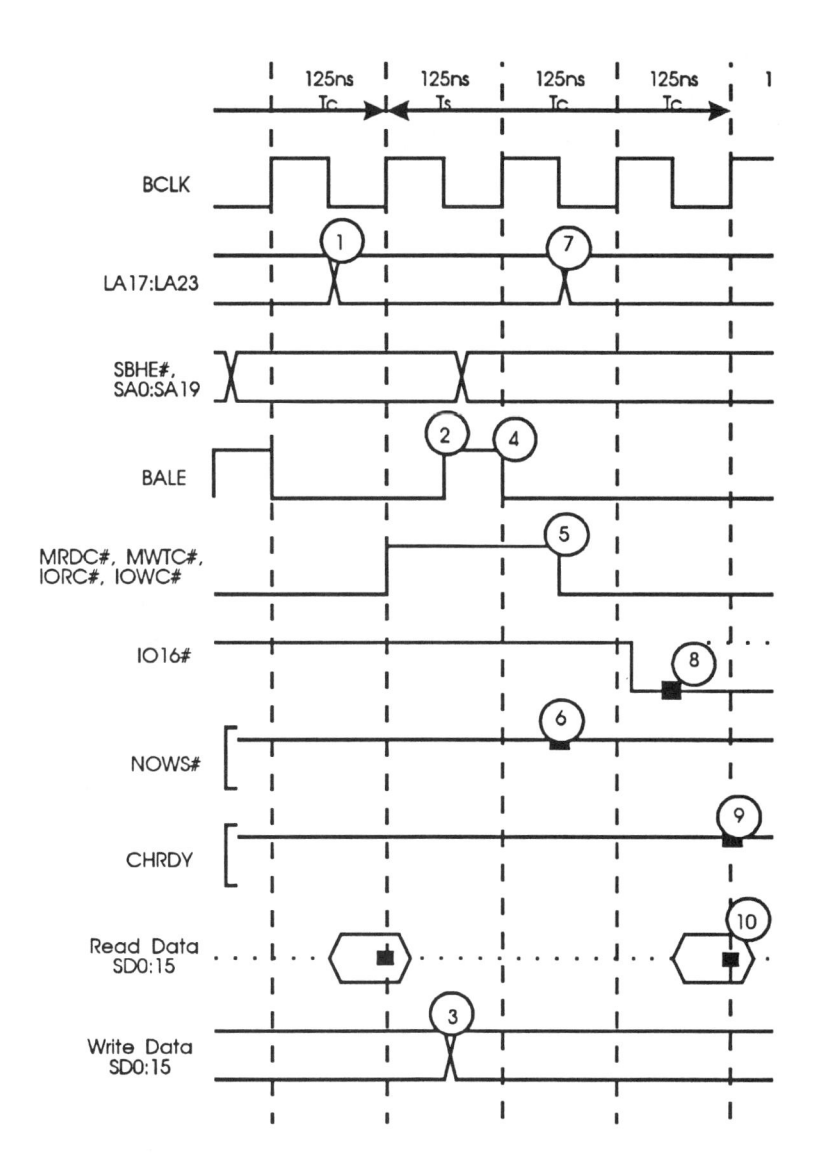

Figure 6-3. Standard Access to 16-bit I/O device

Zero Wait State ISA Bus Cycle Accessing a 16-bit Device

Figure 6 - 4 illustrates the timing of a bus cycle on the ISA bus when the current bus master is communicating with a zero wait state 16-bit device. Note that only 16-bit memory devices can complete bus cycles at zero wait states. The timing diagram and the following numbered steps illustrate the sequence of events during this bus cycle. Each of the numbered steps corresponds to the numbered reference points in figure 6 - 4.

1. In this example, Address Pipelining is active and the LA address is present on the ISA bus prior to the beginning of the bus cycle. This allows the addressed slave to start decoding the address early. In some cases, this allows a device to operate at 0-wait states.

2. BALE is set active halfway through address time. On the rising edge of BALE, 16-bit ISA Memory devices can begin to decode the LA lines to determine if the address is for them. Also when BALE goes active the lower portion of the address from the processor is transferred through the system board's Address Latch onto the SA Bus.

3. The addressed memory board activates M16# as a result of decoding the LA lines, indicating to the system board's Bus Control Logic that it is capable of handling a 16-bit transfer without data bus steering being performed by the steering logic on the system board.

4. If this is a write bus cycle, the microprocessor's output data is gated onto the SD bus half way through address time and remains on the SD bus until half a BCLK cycle into the next bus cycle (half-way through address time of the next bus cycle).

5. At the end of address time, the trailing edge of BALE causes two events to take place:

    a. 16-bit ISA Memory devices latch the LA lines so the addressed device will not be deselected when the LA lines are pipelined before the end of the current bus cycle.

    b. the Address Latch on the system board latches the lower twenty bits of the address, SA0:SA19, so they remain static on the SA bus for the remainder of the bus cycle. The addressed slave device can safely decode the SA address on the bus on the falling edge of BALE.

ISA Bus Cycles

6. The system board's Bus Control Logic samples M16# at the end of address time to determine if the addressed device can take advantage of the MRDC# or MWTC# command lines being activated immediately.

   M16# is sampled active and the appropriate command line (MRDC# or MWTC#) is set active at the leading edge of data time. This command line remains active until the end of the bus cycle (end of Tc).

7. The system board's Bus Control Logic samples M16# a second time at the midpoint of the first data time to determine if data bus steering is necessary. Since this is an access to a 16-bit device, no steering is necessary.

   Since the M16# line is active, the Default Ready Timer samples the NOWS# line to see if the bus cycle can end in zero ISA wait states. In this example M16# is sampled active, forcing the Default Ready Timer to activate the microprocessor's READY# line before the end of the current data time. In this way, faster ISA boards can complete a bus cycle in two rather than three BCLK cycles.

8. Since the LA lines have already done their job, (the addressed device has already decoded the LA lines and latched the chip select), the microprocessor is free to output the address for the next bus cycle.

9. During a read, the microprocessor latches the contents of the data bus, thereby ending the bus cycle. During a write, the microprocessor ends the bus cycle.

EISA System Architecture

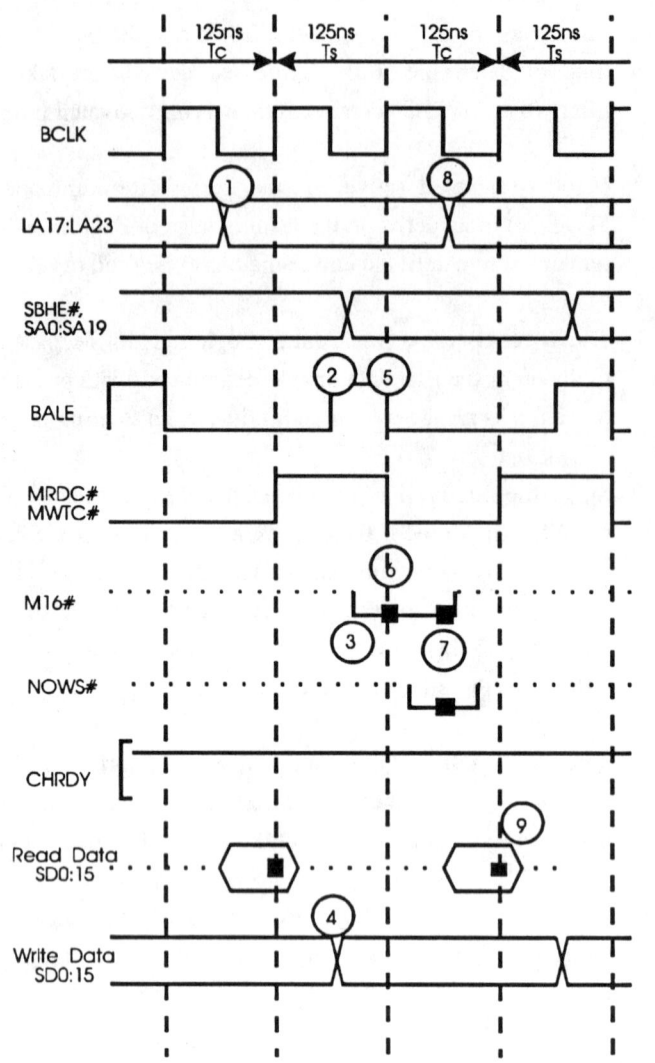

Figure 6-4. Zero Wait State Access To a 16-bit ISA Memory Device

ISA DMA Bus Cycles

ISA DMA Introduction

ISA machines use two Intel 8237 DMACs on the system board to implement the DMA logic. One of the DMACs is connected to the other in a master/slave configuration using channel 0 on the master as the cascade input from the slave. Since each 8237 DMAC provides four DMA channels and one on the master is used as the cascade input from the slave, the ISA system provides a total of seven DMA channels. The four inputs to the slave DMAC are

ISA Bus Cycles

designated as channels 0 - through - 3, while the three inputs to the master are designated as channels 5 - through - 7.

In addition, the ISA machine implements the two DMACs in such a fashion that the three channels on the master (channels 5 - through - 7) are capable of performing 16-bit transfers, while the four channels on the slave (channels 0 - through - 3) are capable of performing 8-bit transfers.

Each DMA block data transfer can consist of up to 64K individual transfers. This limitation is imposed by the 16-bit Transfer Count Register associated with each channel. This allows each of the four 8-bit channels to transfer up to 64KB of data, while the 16-bit channels can transfer up to 128KB of data.

Each DMA channel can address any memory location within the 16MB range from 000000h to FFFFFFh. This limitation is imposed by the combination of the 16-bit Memory Address Register associated with each channel in the DMAC and the 8-bit Page Register associated with each channel. This pair of registers associated with each channel provide a 24-bit memory address capability.

ISA Expansion boards can become bus masters if they are connected to one of the three 16-bit DMA channels on the master DMAC (Channels 5 - through - 7) and the channel is programmed as a cascade channel. The ISA board may then request the use of the bus through the auspices of the master DMAC on the system board.

When a DMAC is bus master, it uses its own clock when executing bus cycles. This clock is referred to as the DMA clock and is 1/2 the BCLK frequency. Depending on the unit and the selected processor speed, this will yield a DMA clock of either 3MHz (6MHz AT), 4MHz (8MHz ISA-compatible machine), or 4.165MHz (8.33MHz ISA-compatible machine).

EISA System Architecture

The 8237 DMAC Bus Cycle

The 8237 is built around a state machine with seven possible states, each one DMA clock period wide. The following table lists the clock period for the three possible processor speed settings:

Speed Setting	DMA Clock Frequency	DMA Clock Period
6MHz	3MHz	333.3ns
8MHz	4MHz	250ns
8.33MHz	4.165MHz	240ns

Prior to receiving a DMA Request, the DMAC is in the idle state, Si. When a DREQ is sensed, the DMAC enters a state where it asserts HOLD (Hold Request) to the microprocessor and awaits the HLDA (Hold Acknowledge). This state is called SO (the letter O). The DMAC remains in the SO state until HLDA is sensed active.

The DMAC can then proceed with the DMA transfer. S1, S2, S3 and S4 are the states used to execute a transfer (of a byte or word) between the requesting I/O device and system memory. In addition, when accessing a device that is slow to respond, a DMA transfer cycle can be stretched by de-asserting the DMAC's READY input until the device is ready to complete the transfer. This will cause the DMAC to insert wait states, Sw, in the bus cycle until READY goes active again.

The following actions take place during states S1 - through - S4:

ISA Bus Cycles

State	Actions Taken
S1	During Block and Demand transfers, the middle byte of the memory address, A8:A15, only changes once every 256th transfer. For this reason, the DMAC only enters the S1 state every 256th transfer to update the middle byte of the address that is contained in the external DMA address latch. Starting at the trailing edge of S1, the middle byte of the memory address is output onto data bus pins D0:D7 and is then latched into the external DMA Address Latch during S2. The DMAC also sets its AEN output active, causing the external DMA address latch to output and acting as an enable for the DMA Page Register addressing.
S2	During S2, the lower byte (A0:A7) of the memory address is output directly onto the address bus, A0:A7. If S2 was preceded by S1, the DMAC pulses its ADSTB output, causing the new middle byte of the address to be latched into the external DMA address latch. If S2 wasn't preceded by S1, ADSTB isn't pulsed, but the DMAC's AEN output is set active. This causes the external DMA address latch to output the previously latched middle byte and acting as an enable for the DMA Page Register addressing. In addition, DAKn# is asserted to tell the I/O device that the transfer is in progress.
S3	S3 will only occur in a bus cycle if Compressed Timing hasn't been selected for this DMA channel. See text below for a discussion of Compressed Timing. During S3, the MRDC# or the IORC# line is set active. If the DMA channel is programmed for extended writes, the MWTC# or IOWC# line is also set active during S3.
S4	If the DMA channel was not programmed for extended write, the MWTC# or IOWC# is set active at the start of S4. If extended write had been selected, the write command line was already set active at the start of S3. The actual read/write takes place at the trailing edge of S4 when both the Read and Write command lines are de-asserted by the DMAC. This completes the transfer of a byte or word between memory and the requesting I/O device.

EISA System Architecture

When Compressed Timing is selected, S3 is eliminated from the DMA transfer cycle. The only real purpose of S3 is to allow the Read command line to be asserted for twice the duration it is when Compressed Timing is active. Not all memory and I/O devices will tolerate this abbreviated Read command line, so it must be used cautiously.

When Extended Write is selected, it causes the Write command line to be set active during S3 rather than S4, effectively doubling the duration of the Write command line's active period.

It should be obvious that Extended Write and Compressed Timing are mutually exclusive because S3 is essential for Extended Write and is eliminated when Compressed Timing is selected.

Table 6 - 1 illustrates the transfer speeds possible at the three clock speeds under the following conditions:

- Compressed Timing turned off
- Compressed Timing turned on

The table assumes that the transfer is no more than 256 bytes in length. This was done for simplicity's sake. Every 256 transfers the DMAC must insert an S1 state in the next bus cycle to update the middle byte of the memory address (A8:A15), which must be latched into the external DMA Address Latch. This adds one DMA clock period to the length of every 257th bus cycle.

Table 6-1. ISA DMA Transfer Rates

	Compressed Off			Compressed On		
DMA Clock Frequency	3MHz	4MHz	4.165MHz	3MHz	4MHz	4.165MHz
Transfers per Second	1M/s	1.3M/s	1.39M/s	1.5M/s	2M/s	2.08M/s

When looking at table 6 - 1, keep in mind that each bus cycle consists of three DMA clock cycles with Compressed Timing turned off and two DMA clock cycles with Compressed Timing turned on.

Chapter 7

EISA CPU and Bus Master Bus Cycles

The Previous Chapter

The previous chapter provided a review of the bus master and DMA bus cycles in the ISA environment.

This Chapter

This chapter provides a detailed description of the EISA CPU and bus master bus cycle types.

The Next Chapter

The next chapter provides a detailed description of the EISA DMA bus cycle types.

Introduction To The EISA CPU and Bus Master Bus Cycle Types

In order to maintain complete ISA compatibility, ISA bus cycles are executed precisely as they are in an ISA machine. These bus cycle types have been described in the preceding chapter.

As stated earlier, an Intel processor is capable of executing seven types of bus cycles:

- Memory Data Read and Memory Instruction Read. These two types are actually identical, reducing the total to six bus cycle types.
- Memory Data Write
- I/O Data Read
- I/O Data Write
- Interrupt Acknowledge
- Halt or Shutdown

EISA System Architecture

Of these six, only four are ever seen by the expansion boards on the ISA bus:

- Memory Read
- Memory Write
- I/O Read
- I/O Write

In an EISA system, the main CPU is capable of performing three variants of each of these four bus cycle types when communicating with a device over the EISA bus:

- Standard timing
- Compressed timing (not implemented in current machines)
- Burst timing

EISA bus masters are capable of executing two of these three variants:

- Standard timing
- Burst timing

The Standard EISA Bus Cycle

General

The standard EISA bus cycle type is based upon a 0-wait state bus cycle. Unless wait states are inserted by the slave, it completes in two BCLK periods. Each wait state adds one additional BCLK period. The following formula is used to calculate the total transfer time:

Total Transfer Time = N*(2+Tw)*(1 BCLK period)

where: Tw = number of wait states per bus cycle
N = number of bus cycles for overall transfer

As an example, a transfer of 64 doublewords (256 bytes) completes in 15.36 microseconds for a 32-bit transfer with a 8.33MHz BCLK, while a 16-bit transfer completes in 30.72 microseconds. This example assumes that no preempts occur during the transfer and the addressed slave is a 0-wait state device.

EISA CPU and Bus Master Bus Cycles

Analysis of the EISA Standard Bus Cycle

The timing diagram in figure 7 - 1 illustrates the timing for three bus cycles, the first of which has 1-wait state and the last two are 0-wait state bus cycles. The following numbered steps correspond to the reference points in the illustration.

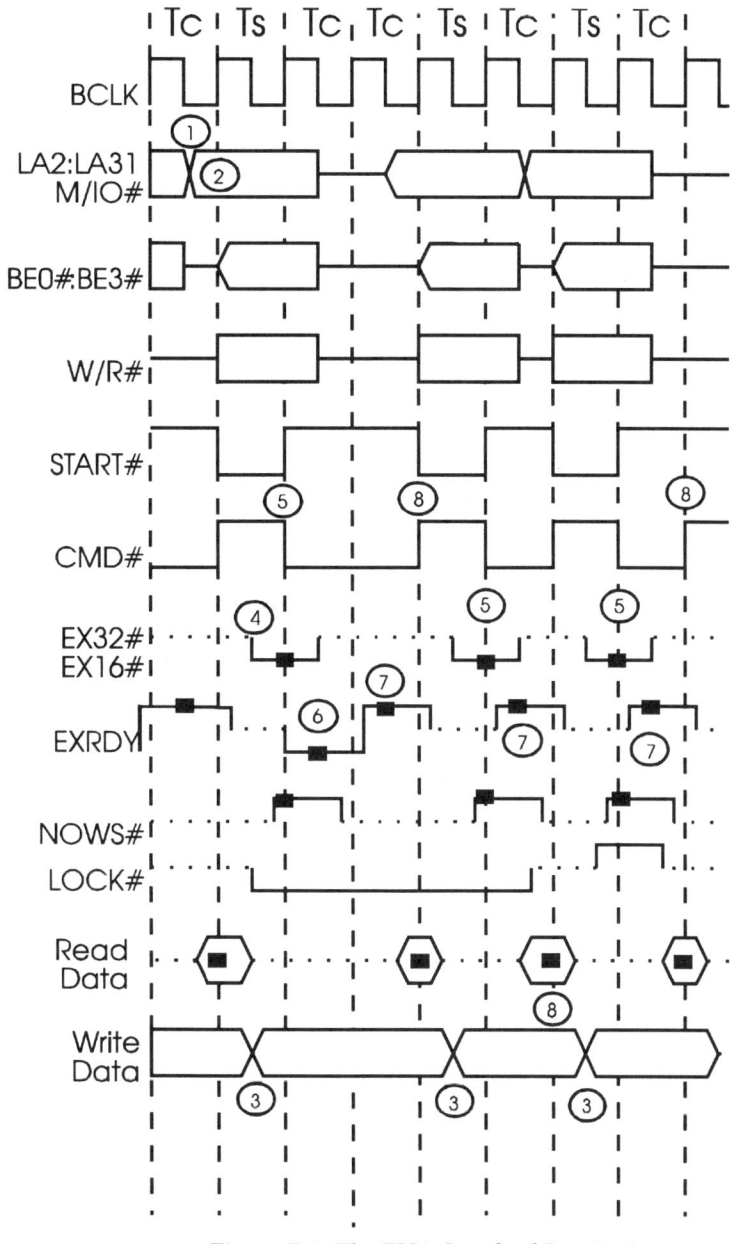

Figure 7-1. The EISA Standard Bus Cycle

EISA System Architecture

1. The first bus cycle after bus grant cannot use address pipelining. After the first bus cycle, however, the bus master can use address pipelining to output the address and M/IO# early.

2. After the bus master (or CPU) has requested and been granted the buses, the bus cycle begins on the rising edge of BCLK (the leading edge of Ts) with the assertion of the START# signal by the current bus master. START# remains active for a full BCLK cycle (all of Ts). At the leading edge of START#, the bus master or CPU places the address on the LA bus and Byte Enables and also outputs M/IO#. If address pipelining is active, the address, Byte Enables and M/IO# may be placed on the bus during the previous bus cycle. W/R# is set to the appropriate state at the beginning of the bus cycle.

3. If a write bus cycle is in progress, the bus master begins to drive the data onto the appropriate data paths at the midpoint of Ts.

4. The addressed EISA slave decodes the address and asserts either EX16# or EX32# to indicate that it is an EISA device and the data size it's prepared to handle. I/O devices should also ensure that the AEN signal is inactive before decoding an address. AEN is set active by the DMA controller when it is placing a valid memory address on the address bus. In order to maintain ISA bus master compatibility, an EISA I/O slave should assert IO16# as well as EX16# or EX32#. EISA slaves that do not need to maintain ISA bus master compatibility do not need to assert IO16#. The system board develops M16# from EX16# or EX32# to maintain ISA bus master compatibility when communicating with ISA memory slaves.

   Note: EISA compressed mode is not supported in current implementations of EISA; however, if implemented the addressed slave should assert NOWS# prior to the end of Ts.

5. If the addressed slave must latch the address information, it should be latched on the trailing edge of START#. The system board's Data Bus Steering logic samples the EX16# and EX32# lines to see if steering is necessary. CMD# will be set active by the system board coincidentally with the trailing edge of START#. Only the system board drives the CMD# line. CMD# then remains active until the end of the bus cycle.

EISA CPU and Bus Master Bus Cycles

If compressed mode were implemented, the main CPU logic would sample the NOWS# line to see if the addressed slave supports EISA compressed mode bus cycles.

6. EXRDY is sampled at the falling edge of every BCLK after CMD# goes active. If sampled inactive (low), the bus cycle will be extended by one wait state (an additional Tc). Designers of EISA expansion cards are guaranteed that the address presented on the LA bus, the Byte Enable lines and the state of M/IO# will remain on the bus until the midpoint of the first Tc period of the bus cycle.

7. If EXRDY is sampled active at the midpoint of Tc, the bus cycle will be terminated at the end of Tc. If the current bus master has another bus cycle to run and it uses address pipelining, the address for the next bus is placed on the LA bus, the Byte Enable lines and M/IO#.

8. After EXRDY is sampled active at the midpoint of Tc, the bus cycle is terminated at the end of the BCLK cycle. The system board logic removes the CMD# signal. If a read bus cycle is in progress, the bus master reads the data from the data bus. If a write bus cycle is in progress, the bus master ends the bus cycle but continues to drive the data onto the data bus until the midpoint of Ts of the next bus cycle. This is done to ensure that the hold time for the currently addressed device is satisfied.

Performance Using the EISA Standard Bus Cycle

Assuming that the current bus master and the currently addressed slave are both 32-bit devices, that the BCLK frequency is 8.33MHz, and that the bus master performs a series of 32-bit transfers, the transfer rate would be 16.66MB/second:

> 120ns per BCLK cycle x 2 BCLK cycles per transfer
> = 240ns per transfer, divided into one second
> = 4.166M transfers/second, at 4 bytes/transfer
> = 16.66MB/second

If the currently addressed slave is a 16-bit device, the transfer rate would be 8.33MB/second.

EISA System Architecture

The Compressed Bus Cycle

General

Currently available EISA chip sets do not support the EISA Compressed bus cycle. For this reason, a detailed analysis of the Compressed bus cycle is reserved for a future printing (when it is implemented).

Only the main CPU can utilize EISA Compressed bus cycles when communicating with EISA memory or I/O slaves that support Compressed mode. Using the Compressed bus cycle, the CPU can complete a transfer every 1.5 BCLK cycles. The following formula may be used to calculate the overall transfer rate when transferring a block of data between the main CPU and a slave that supports Compressed bus cycles:

Total Transfer = N * (1.5 BCLK periods)

where: N = the total number of bus cycles for the overall block transfer

As an example, a transfer of 64 doublewords (256 bytes) completes in 11.52 microseconds for a 32-bit transfer with a 8.33MHz BCLK, while a 16-bit transfer completes in 23.04 microseconds. This example assumes that no preempts occur during the transfer and the addressed slave is a 0-wait state device.

Using the Compressed bus cycle, the CPU presents a new address every 1.5 BCLK periods (instead of two) and the system board shortens the length of the CMD# active period to one-half of a BCLK period.

If a slave supports Compressed bus cycles, it must assert NOWS# prior to the end of Ts. The slave must not de-assert EXRDY after asserting NOWS#. If the system board samples NOWS# active at the leading edge of CMD# and the system board design supports Compressed mode, the CMD# pulse width is shortened to .5 BCLK periods. Since the main CPU logic might not support Compressed mode, or the current bus master might not be the main CPU, the slave must be prepared to accept CMD# with a duration of one BCLK or longer.

EISA CPU and Bus Master Bus Cycles

Performance When Using Compressed Bus Cycles

If both the main CPU and the currently addressed slave support Compressed mode, the BCLK frequency is 8.33MHz, and both the master and the salve are 32-bit devices, the transfer rate for a block data transfer would be 22.22MB/second:

120ns per BCLK cycle x 1.5 BCLK cycles per transfer
= 180ns per transfer, divided into one second
= 5.55M transfers/second, at 4 bytes/transfer
= 22,22MB/second

If the currently addressed slave is a 16-bit device, the transfer rate would be 11.11MB/second.

The Burst Bus Cycle

General

A burst transfer is used to transfer blocks of data between the current bus master and EISA memory. A burst must consist of all reads or all writes. Reads and writes may not be mixed within a burst. In other words, the state of the W/R# bus cycle definition line may not be changed during a burst. After the initial transfer in a block data transfer, each subsequent EISA Burst bus transfer can be completed in one BCLK period. The initial transfer requires the time periods consisting of Ts and Tc to transfer the first data item and for the master and slave to agree to use burst mode for the subsequent transfers. Unless wait states are inserted by the slave, each subsequent transfer can then be completed in one BCLK period. Each wait state adds one additional BCLK period. The following formula is used to calculate the total transfer time:

Total Transfer Time = (1 + Twi + N) * one BCLK period

where: Twi = wait states per transfer
N = number of bus cycles for overall transfer

As an example, a transfer of 64 doublewords (256 bytes) completes in 7.8 microseconds for a 32-bit transfer with a 8.33MHz BCLK, while a 16-bit transfer completes in 15.6 microseconds. This example assumes that no preempts occur during the transfer and the addressed slave is a 0-wait state device.

EISA System Architecture

Analysis of the EISA Burst Transfer

The timing diagram in figure 7 - 2 illustrates the timing for five transfers performed using Burst mode. The following numbered steps correspond to the reference points in the illustration.

A 16-bit Burst transfer is identical with the exception that EX16# is generated by the slave instead of EX32#.

1. The current bus master can use address pipelining to output the first address and M/IO# early.

2. At the beginning of the first bus cycle in the transfer, the current EISA bus master activates the START# signal. An active level on START# indicates that the bus master has placed a valid address and bus cycle definition on the buses. The EISA Bus Controller, or EBC, on the system board samples START# active and recognizes that an EISA bus master, rather than an ISA bus master, has initiated a bus cycle. In response, the EBC will generate BALE during Ts. This is done in case the EISA bus master is addressing an ISA device. In addition, the bus master sets the Byte Enable lines and W/R# to the appropriate state. W/R# will remain in the selected state (Write or Read) throughout the burst transfer.

3. If this is a write transfer, the bus master starts to drive the data onto the data bus at the midpoint of Ts.

4. At the end of Ts, the current bus master and the system board logic sample EX16# and EX32#. An active level on either of these lines indicates that the currently addressed device is an EISA device and what data paths it is capable of using. The bus master de-activates START# and the system board logic activates the CMD# signal to indicate data transfer time has begun. If the bus master is capable of using burst transfers, it samples SLBURST# to determine if the addressed slave also supports burst. In this example, SLBURST# is sampled active, indicating that the slave supports burst mode.

5. In response to sampling an active level on SLBURST#, the bus master activates MSBURST# at the midpoint of Tc to indicate to the slave that it also supports burst mode and will use it for the remaining transfers in the burst. Also, the bus master samples EXRDY at the midpoint of Tc to determine if the addressed slave will be ready to complete the first transfer at the end of the current Tc. In this example, EXRDY is sampled active,

EISA CPU and Bus Master Bus Cycles

indicating that the first transfer can be completed at the end of this Tc period. In response. the bus master pipelines out the second address starting at the midpoint of Tc.

6. At the end of the first Tc period, the bus master completes the first transfer in the burst. If a read burst is in progress, the bus master reads the data off the appropriate data paths. If a write burst is in progress, the bus master starts to drive the data for the second transfer onto the appropriate data paths. The slave samples MSBURST# at the end of each Tc period to determine if the bus master will use burst mode for the remaining transfers. In this example, MSBURST# is sample active, so a burst transfer will occur.

7. At the midpoint of the second Tc, the bus master samples EXRDY to determine if the slave will be ready to end the second transfer at the end of this Tc period. In this example, it is sampled active, indicating the slave will be ready. In response, the bus master begins to drive the third address out at the midpoint of Tc.

8. At the end of the second Tc, the slave samples MSBURST# again to determine if the bus master is still bursting. The active state indicates it is. The bus master ends the second transfer. If a read burst is in progress, the bus master reads the data off the appropriate data paths. If a write burst is in progress, the bus master starts to drive the data for the third transfer onto the appropriate data paths.

9. At the midpoint of the third Tc, the bus master samples EXRDY to determine if the slave will be ready to complete the third transfer at the end of this Tc period. In this example, EXRDY is sample inactive, indicating it will not be ready. This will cause the bus master to insert a wait state of one TC duration to stretch the data transfer time for the third transfer. If a read transfer is in progress, the bus master will not read the third transfer's data off the bus at the end of this Tc. If a write transfer, the bus master will continue to drive the data for the third transfer onto the data bus during the next Tc. The bus master still pipelines out the address for the fourth transfer, however, starting at the midpoint of the third Tc period.

10. At the midpoint of the fourth Tc, the bus master samples EXRDY to determine if the slave will be ready to complete the third transfer at the end of this Tc period. Since EXRDY is sampled active, it will be ready. The bus master does not pipeline out the address for the fifth transfer yet and continues to drive the data for the third transfer onto the data bus.

11. The bus master completes the third transfer. If a read burst is in progress, the bus master reads the data off the appropriate data paths. If a write burst is in progress, the bus master starts to drive the data for the third transfer onto the appropriate data paths.

12. At the midpoint of the fifth Tc period, the bus master samples EXRDY# to determine if the slave will be ready to end the fourth transfer at the end of the current Tc period. Since EXRDY is sampled active, the slave will be ready to end the transfer. The bus master also pipelines out the fifth address at the midpoint of Tc.

13. The bus master completes the fourth transfer. If a read burst is in progress, the bus master reads the data off the appropriate data paths. If a write burst is in progress, the bus master starts to drive the data for the fifth transfer onto the appropriate data paths.

14. At the midpoint of the sixth Tc, the bus master samples EXRDY# to determine if the slave will be ready to end the fifth transfer at the end of the current Tc period. Since EXRDY is sampled active, the slave will be ready to end the transfer. Since this is the end of the sample burst, the bus master de-activates MSBURST# to inform the slave that the last transfer of the burst is in progress. In this example, the bus master pipelines out the next address at the midpoint of Tc. In this example, the bus master is addressing a device other than the memory slave, causing the slave to release SLBURST#.

15. At the end of the sixth Tc period, the bus master ends the last transfer of the burst. If a read burst is in progress, the bus master reads the data off the appropriate data paths. If a write burst is in progress, the bus master ends the transfer and ceases to drive the data bus. This completes the example burst transfer.

16. The bus cycle following the burst is a standard EISA bus cycle. Since the bus master is setting W/R# low, it is a read. The bus master samples EXRDY active at the midpoint of Tc and the bus master reads the data off the data bus at the end of Tc and end the bus cycle.

17. The next bus cycle is also a standard EISA bus cycle. The high of W/R# indicates that a write is in progress. The bus master begins to drive the data onto the data bus at the midpoint of Ts, samples EXRDY active at the midpoint of Tc, and will therefore end the bus cycle at the end of Tc.

EISA CPU and Bus Master Bus Cycles

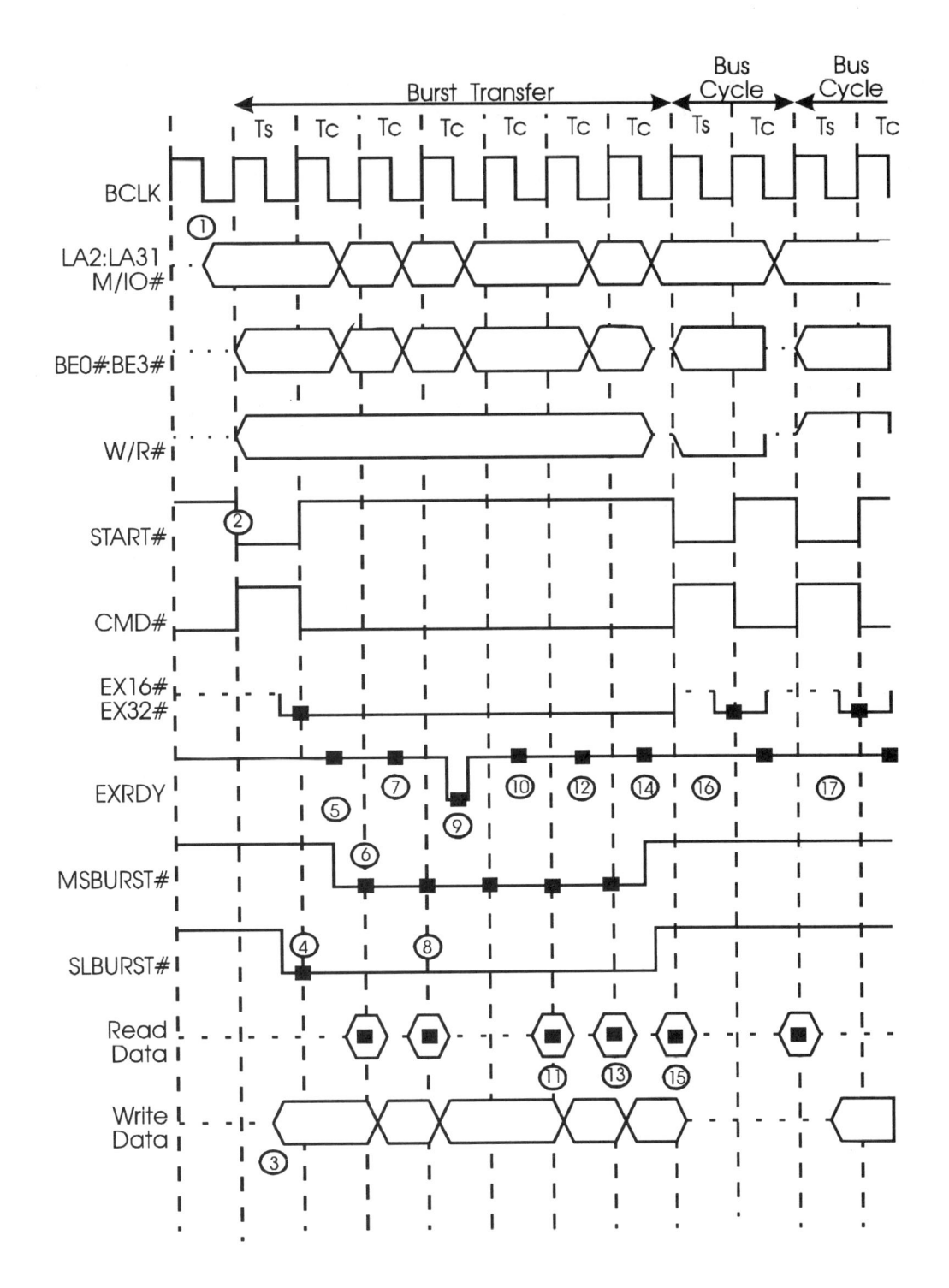

Figure 7-2. The EISA Burst Transfer

EISA System Architecture

Performance Using Burst Transfers

Once a 32-bit bus master and a 32-bit slave have switched into burst mode, the second through the nth transfers may be completed at the following rate:

    8.33MHz BCLK = 120ns per BCLK cycle
    1 second/120ns per transfer = 8.33M transfers/second
    8.33M transfers/second x 4 bytes per transfer = 33.33MB/second

If the bus master and/or the slave are 16-bit devices, the maximum transfer rate would be 16.66MB/second.

DRAM Memory Burst Transfers

The addresses output by the bus master when bursting to or from Page Mode or Static Column (SCRAM) DRAM memory must be within a 1024 byte DRAM memory row (address lines LA10:LA31 cannot change during the burst). The addresses within the burst do not have to be sequential. They only have to be within the same row. To change DRAM rows, the burst transfer must be terminated by the bus master by setting MSBURST# inactive on the last cycle in the row, and the burst sequence is then restarted within a new row.

Downshift Burst Bus Master

A downshift burst bus master is a 32-bit burst bus master that can convert to a 16-bit burst bus master on-the-fly. In other words, if the bus master samples EX16# and SLBURST# active at the end of Ts, it automatically adjusts itself to only use the lower two data paths during the burst. The bus master is responsible for copying data to the appropriate data paths during the burst. The system board Data Bus Steering logic will not take care of data copying. At the start of the first transfer in the burst, the downshift bus master must indicate its ability to downshift by setting MASTER16# active while START# is active (in other words, for the duration of Ts).

EISA DMA

Chapter 8

The Previous Chapter

The previous chapter described the bus cycle types that may be run by the main CPU or an EISA bus master.

In This Chapter

This chapter describes the EISA DMA capability. This includes a description of the EISA DMA bus cycle types and the other improved capabilities of the EISA DMA controller.

The Next Chapter

The next chapter provides an introduction to the bus structure hierarchy in a typical EISA system. It describes the distribution of functions between the host bus, EISA bus and the X-bus on the typical EISA system board and the relationship of the functional areas to each other.

DMA Bus Cycle Types

Introduction

The EISA DMA controller incorporates seven DMA channels, each capable of performing 8, 16 or 32-bit transfers. In addition, each DMA channel may be individually programmed to utilize one or four types of bus cycles when performing data transfers between an I/O device and memory. The following sections describe the bus cycle types and other improvements. Detailed timing diagrams and register-level programming information may be found in the EISA specification.

EISA System Architecture

The Compatible DMA Bus Cycle

Description

Each of the seven DMA channels is default programmed to use ISA-compatible DMA bus cycles to transfer data between an I/O device and memory. As in an ISA machine, channels 0- through - 3 are default programmed for 8-bit transfers, while channels 5 - through- 7 are default programmed for 16-bit transfers. Any DMA channel may be re-programmed to perform 8, 16, or 32-bit transfers using the ISA-compatible bus cycle.

When programmed to use ISA-compatible DMA bus cycles, a transfer is performed every eight BCLK periods. Table 8 - 1 defines the duration of key signals during an ISA-compatible DMA bus cycle.

Table 8-1. The DMA ISA-Compatible Bus Cycle

Event	Duration
Memory address present	8.0 BCLKs
Duration of data transfer period during a memory-to-IO transfer (CMD# active)	4.5 BCLKs
Duration of MRDC# during memory-to-IO transfer	4.5 BCLKs
Duration of IORC# during IO-to-memory transfer	6.5 BCLKs
Duration of IOWC# during a memory-to-IO transfer	4.0 BCLKs
Duration of MWTC# during IO-to-memory transfer	4.0 BCLKs

The duration of the key signals illustrated in table 8 - 1 give an idea as to the amount of time the memory and I/O device have to recognize that they are being addressed and to either accept or output data. Comparing this table to the tables in the following sections on the other three DMA bus cycle types, it is clear that the amount of time allotted for address decode and data movement becomes increasingly shorter for the faster bus cycle types.

EISA DMA

Performance and Compatibility

Table 8 - 2 defines the data transfer rates when a DMA channel is programmed to use the ISA-compatible DMA bus cycle to transfer data.

Table 8-2. ISA-Compatible Transfer Rates

I/O Device Size	Transfer Rate
8-bit	1.0416MB/second
16-bit	2.0833MB/second
32-bit	4.1666MB/second

When programmed to use the ISA-compatible DMA bus cycle, a DMA channel may be used to transfer data between an ISA-compatible I/O device and memory.

The Type "A" DMA Bus Cycle

Description

When programmed to use Type "A" DMA bus cycles, a transfer is performed every six BCLK periods. Table 8 - 3 defines the duration of key signals during a Type "A" DMA bus cycle.

Table 8-3. The DMA Type "A" Bus Cycle

Event	Duration
Memory address present	6.0 BCLKs
Duration of data transfer period during a memory-to-IO transfer (CMD# active)	3.5 BCLKs
Duration of IORC# during IO-to-memory transfer	4.5 BCLKs
Duration of IOWC# during a memory-to-IO transfer	3.0 BCLKs

The duration of the key signals illustrated in table 8 - 3 give an idea as to the amount of time the memory and I/O device have to recognize that they are being addressed and to either accept or output data. Comparing this table to the tables in the sections on the other three DMA bus cycle types, it is clear that the amount of time allotted for address decode and data movement becomes increasingly shorter for the faster bus cycle types. When running Type "A" bus cycles, the DMA controller uses the W/R# line to indicate the type of memory operation, rather than the MRDC# and MWTC# lines.

Performance and Compatibility

Table 8 - 4 defines the data transfer rates when a DMA channel is programmed to use the Type "A" DMA bus cycle to transfer data.

Table 8-4. ISA-Compatible Transfer Rates

I/O Device Size	Transfer Rate
8-bit	1.388MB/second
16-bit	2.777MB/second
32-bit	5.555MB/second

When a DMA channel is programmed to use the Type "A" DMA bus cycle to transfer data, the channel may be used to transfer data between fast, EISA memory and an I/O device designed for Type "A" transfers. In addition, many older, ISA I/O devices may also work with a channel programmed for Type "A" bus cycles. This is because the Type "A" transfer does not involve a significant amount of compression compared to the ISA-compatible bus cycle. Compatibility may be determined by testing.

The Type "B" DMA Bus Cycle

Description

When programmed to use Type "B" DMA bus cycles, a transfer is performed every four BCLK periods. Table 8 - 5 defines the duration of key signals during a Type "B" DMA bus cycle.

Table 8-5. The DMA Type "B" Bus Cycle

Event	Duration
Memory address present	4.0 BCLKs
Duration of data transfer period during a memory-to-IO transfer (CMD# active)	2.5 BCLKs
Duration of IORC# during IO-to-memory transfer	3.5 BCLKs
Duration of IOWC# during a memory-to-IO transfer	2.0 BCLKs

The duration of the key signals illustrated in table 8 - 5 gives an idea as to the amount of time the memory and I/O device have to recognize that they are being addressed and to either accept or output data. Comparing this table to the tables in the sections on the other three DMA bus cycle types, it is clear that the amount of time allotted for address decode and data movement becomes

EISA DMA

increasingly shorter for the faster bus cycle types. When running Type "B" bus cycles, The DMA controller uses the W/R# line to indicate the type of memory operation, rather than the MRDC# and MWTC# lines.

Performance and Compatibility

Table 8 - 6 defines the data transfer rates when a DMA channel is programmed to use the Type "B" DMA bus cycle to transfer data.

Table 8-6. Type "B" Transfer Rates

I/O Device Size	Transfer Rate
8-bit	2.083MB/second
16-bit	4.166MB/second
32-bit	8.333MB/second

When a DMA channel is programmed to use the Type "B" DMA bus cycle to transfer data, the channel may be used to transfer data between fast, EISA memory and an I/O device designed for Type "B" transfers. In addition, some older, ISA I/O devices may also work with a channel programmed for Type "B" bus cycles. Although the Type "B" transfer involves a significant amount of compression compared to the ISA-compatible bus cycle, some ISA I/O devices may be fast enough to function correctly at this speed. Compatibility may be determined by testing.

The Type "C" DMA Bus Cycle

Description

The DMA Type "C" bus cycle is very similar to the Burst bus cycle run by a bursting EISA bus master or the main CPU. When the first bus cycle in a series is initiated, the DMA controller samples SLBURST# to determine if the addressed memory supports burst mode. In response, the controller then activates MSBURST# to indicate bursting will be used to transfer the data block. As with the other DMA bus cycle types, the controller uses the combination of DAKn# and either the IORC# or IOWC# line to address the I/O device. A byte, word or doubleword of data will be transferred every BCLK cycle.

EISA System Architecture

Performance and Compatibility

Table 8 - 7 defines the data transfer rates when a DMA channel is programmed to use the Type "B" DMA bus cycle to transfer data.

Table 8-7. Type "C" Transfer Rates

I/O Device Size	Transfer Rate
8-bit	8.33MB/second
16-bit	16.66MB/second
32-bit	33.33MB/second

When a DMA channel is programmed to use the Type "C" DMA bus cycle to transfer data, the channel may only be used to transfer data between fast, EISA memory and an I/O device designed for Type "C" transfers. No ISA I/O devices will work with a channel programmed for Type "C" bus cycles.

Summary of EISA DMA Transfer Rates

Table 8 - 8 indicates the maximum data transfer rates achievable for each DMA bus cycle type, and the expansion devices that are compatible with the bus cycle type.

Table 8-8. EISA DMA Transfer Rates

Transfer Type	DMA Cycle Type	Transfer Rate (MB/sec)	Compatibility
ISA-compatible	8-bit	1.0	all ISA
	16-bit	2.0	all ISA
Type A	8-bit	1.3	most ISA
	16-bit	2.6	most ISA
	32-bit	5.3	EISA-only
Type B	8-bit	2.0	some ISA
	16-bit	4.0	some ISA
	32-bit	8.0	EISA-only
Type C (Burst)	8-bit	8.2	EISA-only
	16-bit	16.5	EISA-only
	32-bit	33.0	EISA-only

EISA DMA

Other DMA Enhancements

Addressing Capability

The EISA DMA controller generates full 32-bit addresses, giving it the ability to transfer data to or from memory throughout the full 4GB address range.

Preemption

When a DMA channel is programmed for Type "A", Type "B", or Type "C" bus cycles, it may be preempted by the Central Arbitration Control if another device requires the use of the buses. When a channel is programmed for ISA-compatible DMA bus cycles, however, it cannot be preempted. This means that it can prevent other devices from receiving the use of the buses on a timely basis if the channel is programmed for a lengthy block or demand mode transfer. Care should therefore be exercised.

When the Central Arbitration Control detects another device that requires the use of the buses, it will remove the acknowledge from the DMA controller. The active DMA channel will release the buses within four microseconds.

Buffer Chaining

The EISA DMA controller's buffer chaining function permits the implementation of scatter write and gather read operations. A scatter write operation is one in which a contiguous block of data is read from an I/O device and is written to two or more areas of memory, or buffers. A gather read operation reads a stream of data from several blocks of memory, or buffers, and writes it to an I/O device.

The programmer writes the start address of the first memory buffer to the DMA channel and sets the channel's transfer count equal to the number of bytes, words, or doublewords to be transferred to or from the first buffer. The programmer then enables chaining mode, causing the DMA channel to load the start memory address and transfer count into another set of channel registers, known as the current registers. The programmer then writes the start address of the second memory buffer to the DMA channel and sets the channel's transfer count equal to the number of bytes, words, or doublewords to be transferred to or from the second buffer.

EISA System Architecture

When the DMA channel has exhausted the first transfer count, the channel automatically loads the current registers from the secondary registers and generates either TC or an IRQ13. If the channel was programmed by the main CPU, IRQ13 is generated. If the channel was programmed by an EISA bus master, however, TC is generated instead. The TC or IRQ13 informs the bus master or microprocessor that the first buffer transfer has been completed, the second buffer transfer is in progress and the start address and transfer count for the third buffer transfer should be written to the channel's registers. Updating these registers causes the controller to de-activate TC or IRQ13.

The channel will generate a "Transfer Complete", or TC, if the transfer count is exhausted and the channel's registers have not been reloaded.

Ring Buffers

The EISA DMA controller allows the programmer to implement a ring buffer. If enabled, the ring buffer reserves a fixed range of memory to be used for a channel. The start and end address of the ring buffer are defined by the start memory address and the start memory address plus the transfer count. As data is read from the I/O device it is written into the ring buffer in memory. When the DMA transfer has exhausted its transfer count, the channel automatically reloads the start memory address and transfer count registers and continues with the DMA transfer from the I/O device. The new data is written into memory at the start of the ring buffer, over-writing the older information that has already been read by the microprocessor. As the programmer reads information that was deposited in the ring buffer by the channel, the channel's Stop register should be updated with the memory address of the next address that has not yet been read by the microprocessor. The Stop register prevents the DMA channel from over-writing information that the microprocessor hasn't read yet.

Transfer Size

Each DMA channel can be programmed to perform either 8, 16 or 32-bit transfers.

EISA System Configuration

Chapter 9

The Previous Chapter

The previous chapter, "EISA DMA," described the bus cycle types supported by the EISA DMA controller. In addition, other EISA DMA enhancements were also described.

This Chapter

In this chapter, EISA automatic system configuration is discussed. This includes a description of the slot-specific I/O address space, the EISA product identifier, and the EISA card control ports. The EISA configuration process and board description files are also covered.

The Next Chapter

The next chapter begins Part II of the book. In Part II, the Intel EISA chip set and its relationship to the major system components is discussed.

The ISA I/O Address Space Problem

When the original IBM PC and XT were designed, IBM defined the use of the processor's 64KB I/O address space as shown in table 9 - 1.

Table 9-1. IBM PC and XT I/O Address Space Usage

I/O Address Range	Reserved For
0000h - through - 00FFh	256 locations set aside for I/O devices integrated onto the system board.
0100h - through - 03FFh	768 locations set aside for I/O expansion cards.
0400h - through - FFFFh	Reserved. Do not use.

I/O addresses above 03FFh could not be used due to the inadequate I/O address decode performed by many of the early I/O expansion cards. The card's I/O address decoder inspects A5:A9 to determine which of twenty-four, thirty-two location blocks of I/O space is currently being addressed. Figure 9 - 1

EISA System Architecture

illustrates these twenty-four address ranges. If the currently addressed I/O location is within the block of thirty-two locations assigned to the I/O expansion card, the card's logic examines address bits A0:A4 to determine if one of up to thirty-two I/O ports on the addressed expansion card is being addressed.

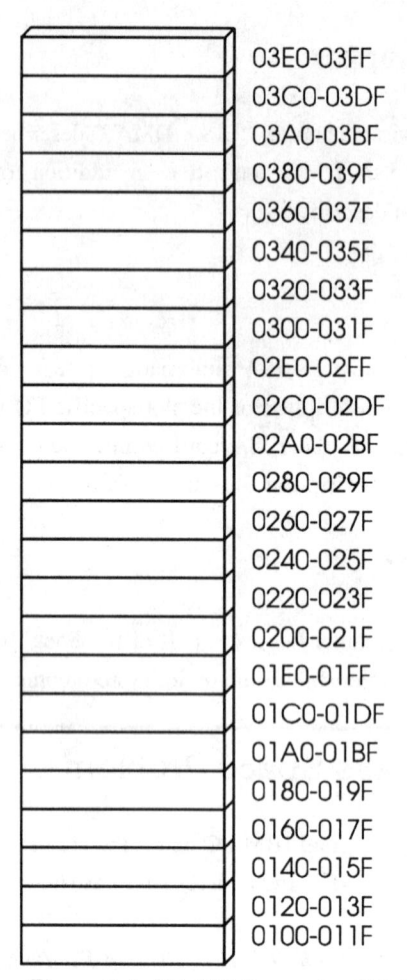

```
03E0-03FF
03C0-03DF
03A0-03BF
0380-039F
0360-037F
0340-035F
0320-033F
0300-031F
02E0-02FF
02C0-02DF
02A0-02BF
0280-029F
0260-027F
0240-025F
0220-023F
0200-021F
01E0-01FF
01C0-01DF
01A0-01BF
0180-019F
0160-017F
0140-015F
0120-013F
0100-011F
```

Figure 9-1. ISA I/O Expansion I/O Ranges

The I/O address decoders on the expansion cards for the PC, XT and AT only looked at address bits A5:A9, ignoring bits A10:A15. The I/O address range assigned for usage by expansion cards is 0100h - through 03FFh. Within the group of address bits used by expansion I/O address decoders, A5:A9, bits A9 and A8 would therefore be either 01b (0100h - through - 01FFh range), 10b (0200h - through - 02FFh range), or 11b (0300h - through - 03FFh range). When the microprocessor places any address within the expansion I/O address range on the address bus, an I/O expansion card may respond.

EISA System Configuration

As an example, assume that a machine has two expansion cards installed. One of them performs an inadequate address decode using A5:A9 and has eight registers residing at I/O ports 0100h - through - 0107h. The other card performs a full decode using A5:A15 and has four registers residing at I/O ports 0500h - through - 0503h. Now assume that the microprocessor initiates a one byte I/O read from I/O port 0500h. The address placed on the bus is shown in table 9 - 2.

Table 9-2. Example I/O Address

A15	A14	A13	A12	A11	A10	A9	A8	A7	A6	A5	A4	A3	A2	A1	A0
0	0	0	0	0	1	0	1	0	0	0	0	0	0	0	0

The board that occupies the 0500h - through - 0503h range looks at A5:A15 and determines that the address is within the 0500h - through - 051Fh block. It then looks at A0:A1 and determines that location 0500h is being addressed. Since this is an I/O read bus cycle, the card places the contents of location 0500h on the lower data path (this is an even address).

At the same time, the board that occupies the 0100h - through - 0107h range looks at A5:A9, a subset of the address seen by the other card's address decoder, and determines that the address appears to be within the 0100h - through - 011Fh block. It then looks at A0:A2 and determines that location 0100h is being addressed. Since this is an I/O read bus cycle, the card places the contents of location 0100h on the lower data path (this is an even address).

Since both cards are driving a byte of data onto the lower data path, SD0:SD7, data bus contention is occurring. This results in garbage data and possible hardware damage because two separate current sources are driving the lower data path. The problem occurs because the card residing in the 0100h - through - 0107h range looks at A8:A9 and thinks that this address is within the 0100h - through - 01FFh range. If the card were designed to perform a full address decode using A5:A15, the problem could have been avoided.

Addresses above 03FFh may be used as long as A8:A9 are always 00b, thus ensuring that the address will not appear to be in the 0100h - through - 01FFh, 0200h - through - 02FFh, or 0300h - through - 03FF ranges. Table 9 - 3 illustrates the usability or unusability of address ranges above 03FFh.

Table 9-3. Usable and Unusable I/O Address Ranges Above 03FFh

I/O Address Range	Usable or Unusable
x400h - x4FFh	usable

EISA System Architecture

x500h - x5FFh	Unusable. Appears to be 0100h - 01FFh
x600h - x6FFh	Unusable. Appears to be 0200h - 02FFh
x700h - x7FFh	Unusable. Appears to be 0300h - 03FFh
x800h - x8FFh	usable
x900h - x9FFh	Unusable. Appears to be 0100h - 01FFh
xA00h - xAFFh	Unusable. Appears to be 0200h - 02FFh
xB00h - xBFFh	Unusable. Appears to be 0300h - 03FFh
xC00h - xCFFh	usable
xD00h - xDFFh	Unusable. Appears to be 0100h - 01FFh
xE00h - xEFFh	Unusable. Appears to be 0200h - 02FFh
xF00h - xFFFh	Unusable. Appears to be 0300h - 03FFh

Note: where x = any hex digit

The next section describes how the EISA specification defines the usage of these allowable address ranges above 03FFh.

EISA Slot-Specific I/O Address Space

The EISA specification expands the number of I/O locations available to system and expansion board designers and also implements automatic configuration of both system and expansion boards.

In addition to the 256 I/O locations available for ISA system board I/O devices (from 0000h-00FFh), the EISA system board has 768 additional I/O locations available for usage. Each EISA expansion slot and each embedded EISA device has 1024 locations of slot-specific I/O address space available for use in addition to the 768 bytes of ISA I/O address space allocated to ISA expansion boards. An embedded device is an EISA I/O device that is integrated onto the motherboard. In all operational respects, it acts as if it's installed in an EISA expansion slot. Table 9 - 4 defines the I/O address assignment for the EISA system board and the expansion board slots.

Table 9-4. EISA I/O Address Assignment

I/O Address Range (hex)	Reserved For	Range Reserved For
0000 - 00FF	EISA/ISA system board I/O devices	System Board
0100 - 03FF	ISA expansion cards	ISA cards
0400 - 04FF	EISA system board I/O	System Board
0500 - 07FF	alias of ISA range; do not use	
0800 - 08FF	EISA system board I/O	System Board

EISA System Configuration

0900 - 0BFF	alias of ISA range; do not use	
0C00 - 0CFF	EISA system board I/O	System Board
0D00 - 0FFF	alias of ISA range; do not use	
1000 - 10FF	Slot 1 I/O	EISA slot one
1100 - 13FF	alias of ISA range; do not use	
1400 - 14FF	Slot 1 I/O	EISA slot one
1500 - 17FF	alias of ISA range; do not use	
1800 - 18FF	Slot 1 I/O	EISA slot one
1900 - 1BFF	alias of ISA range; do not use	
1C00 - 1CFF	Slot 1 I/O	EISA slot one
1D00 - 1FFF	alias of ISA range; do not use	
2000 - 20FF	Slot 2 I/O	EISA slot two
2100 - 23FF	alias of ISA range; do not use	
2400 - 24FF	Slot 2 I/O	EISA slot two
2500 - 27FF	alias of ISA range; do not use	
2800 - 28FF	Slot 2 I/O	EISA slot two
2900 - 2BFF	alias of ISA range; do not use	
2C00 - 2CFF	Slot 2 I/O	EISA slot two
2D00 - 2FFF	alias of ISA range; do not use	

repeated for every
X000 - XFFF range

In order to implement the slot-specific I/O address ranges illustrated in table 9 - 4, the AEN logic on the system board in an ISA system must be modified. Figure 9 - 2 illustrates the AEN decoder located on the EISA system board.

In an ISA system, the DMAC's AEN output is connected to the AEN pin on all ISA expansion slots in parallel. During non-DMA operation, AEN is low, allowing all memory and I/O devices to decode addresses normally. When the DMA controller, or DMAC, is bus master and is placing a memory address on the bus, it sets AEN, or Address Enable, high. When I/O cards detect AEN high, the DMAC is placing a memory address on the bus and the I/O cards should ignore the address. Whenever a memory card detects AEN high, it should decode the address on the bus to determine if the DMAC is addressing it.

In an EISA system, when the DMAC is bus master and is addressing memory, it sets its AEN output active, causing the system board AEN decoder to set all of its AEN outputs high. In this way, the AEN decoder emulates AEN operation in an ISA machine. No I/O devices should decode the address.

EISA System Architecture

During normal, non-DMA, memory bus cycles, M/IO# will be high, causing the system board AEN decoder to set all of its AEN outputs low, allowing all memory and I/O cards to decode addresses normally.

During normal I/O bus cycles, M/IO# will be low, enabling the system board AEN decoder to use the upper digit of the I/O address, A12:A15, to select which of its AEN outputs to set low. If either A8 or A9 is detected high, however, the I/O address is within the range of 768 locations set aside for ISA expansion I/O devices. The AEN decoder will set all of its AEN outputs low, allowing all of the installed I/O cards to decode the address. When a card's AEN line is sensed low, an EISA I/O device that uses slot-specific I/O address space should examine A8 and A9 to ensure both are zero before decoding A0:A11. If either bit is high, the bus master is addressing an ISA I/O device and the EISA I/O card should not respond.

If A8 and A9 are both zero during an I/O bus cycle, the bus master is addressing slot-specific I/O address space. In response, the AEN decoder uses A12:A15 to determine which one of its AEN outputs to set low. Only the card in the expansion slot to which the low AEN line is connected can decode and respond to the I/O address. Upon sensing its AEN line low, the card ensures that A8:A9 are zero before decoding A0:A11. Table 9 - 5 defines the action taken by the system board's AEN decoder under each set of circumstances.

EISA System Configuration

Table 9-5. AEN Decoder Action Table

DMAC's AEN	A9	A8	M/IO#	AEN Decoder Action
1	na	na	na	The DMAC drives its AEN output high when it is bus master and is placing a memory address on the address bus. The AEN decoder responds by driving all of its AEN outputs high. This prevents I/O devices from decoding memory addresses.
0	na	na	1	A device other than the DMAC is bus master and has initiated a memory bus cycle. In response, the AEN decoder sets all of its AEN outputs low. The low on AEN allows both memory and I/O devices to decode addresses.
0	0	0	0	A device other than the DMAC is bus master and has initiated an I/O bus cycle. Since A8:A9 are both zero, the bus master is addressing slot-specific I/O address space. In response, the AEN decoder decodes the high digit of the address, A12:A15, to determine which of its AEN outputs to set low. All of the decoder's other AEN outputs are set high. Only the I/O device in the expansion slot addressed by the address' high digit can then decode the I/O address.
0	0	1	0	The bus master is addressing an ISA I/O expansion device that resides within the 0100h through 01FFh range. In response, the AEN decoder sets all of its AEN outputs low. EISA I/O devices that use slot-specific I/O address space should not respond when either A8 or A9 are high.
0	1	0	0	The bus master is addressing an ISA I/O expansion device that resides within the 0200h through 02FFh range. In response, the AEN decoder sets all of its AEN outputs low. EISA I/O devices that use slot-specific I/O address space should not respond when either A8 or A9 are high.
0	1	1	0	The bus master is addressing an ISA I/O expansion device that resides within the 0300h through 03FFh range. In response, the AEN decoder sets all of its AEN outputs low. EISA I/O devices that use slot-specific I/O address space should not respond when either A8 or A9 are high.

EISA System Architecture

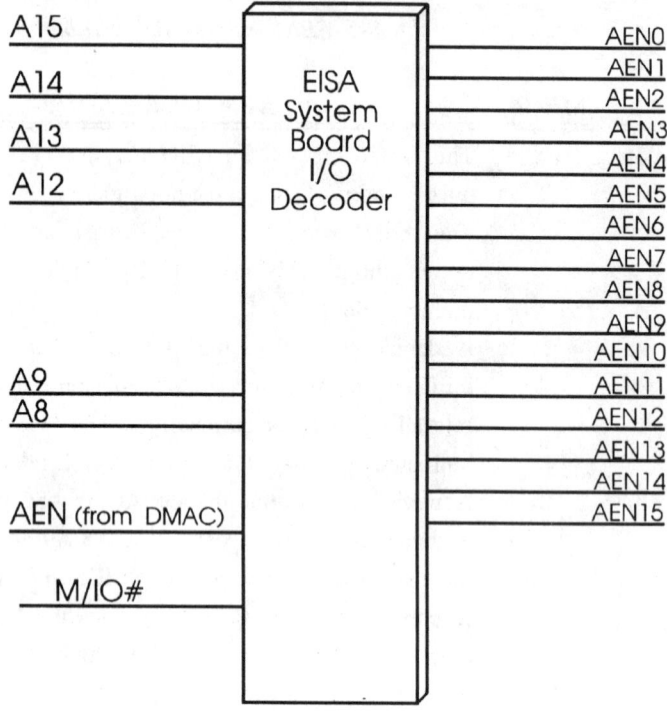

Figure 9-2. The System Board's AEN Decoder

The EISA Product Identifier

EISA expansion boards, embedded devices and system boards have a four byte product ID that can be read from I/O port addresses xC80h through xC83h, where x = 0 for the system board or the number of the expansion slot the card is installed in. For example, the system board's ID can be read from I/O addresses 0C80-0C83h and slot 1's ID can be read from 1C80-1C83h.

The first two bytes of the system board ID, read from I/O ports xC80-xC81, contain a three character manufacturer's code. The three character manufacturer code is uppercase, ASCII alpha chosen by the manufacturer and registered with the firm that distributes the EISA spec. A compressed version of the ASCII code, using just the lower five bits of each character, is used. The third byte and the high-order four bits of the fourth byte are used to specify a product identifier consisting of three hex digits. The lower four bits of the fourth byte is use to specify the product revision number. Table 9 - 6 illustrates the format of the Product ID bytes read from an expansion board. Table 9 - 7 illustrates the format of the Product ID bytes read from an EISA system board.

EISA System Configuration

To verify that an EISA expansion card is installed in a particular card slot:

- Write FFh to I/O port xC80h.
- Read one byte from xC80h.
- If the byte read equals FFh, an EISA card isn't installed in the slot. If the byte does not equal FFh and bit 7 of the byte read is zero, the card's EISA product ID can be read from xC80h-xC83h.

Table 9-6. Expansion Board Product ID Format

Location/Bits	Specify
xC80, bit 7	not used, must be 0
xC80, bits 6:2	1st compressed ASCII character of Manufacturer's ID
xC80, bits 0:1	upper two bits of 2nd compressed ASCII character of Manufacturer's ID
xC81, bits 7:5	lower three bits of 2nd compressed ASCII character of Manufacturer's ID
xC81, bits 0:4	3rd compressed ASCII character of Manufacturer's ID
xC82, bits 4:7	upper hex digit of product type
xC82, bits 0:3	middle hex digit of product type
xC83, bits 4:7	lower hex digit of product type
xC83, bits 0:3	single hex digit of product revision number

Table 9-7. EISA System Board Product ID Format

Location/Bits	Specify
0C80, bit 7	not used, must be 0
0C80, bits 6:2	1st compressed ASCII character of Manufacturer's ID
0C80, bits 0:1	upper two bits of 2nd compressed ASCII character of Manufacturer's ID
0C81, bits 7:5	lower three bits of 2nd compressed ASCII character of Manufacturer's ID
0C81, bits 0:4	3rd compressed ASCII character of Manufacturer's ID
0C82, bits 0:7	reserved for manufacturer's use
0C83, bits 3:7	reserved for manufacturer's use
0C83, bits 0:2	EISA bus version

EISA System Architecture

Expansion Card Control Bits

In an ISA machine, expansion cards are configured by setting DIP switches and/or jumpers to the desired settings. This allows the user to select options like:

- the start address of a device ROM mounted on the card
- the start address of RAM located on the card
- the IRQ line the card utilizes
- the DMA channel the card utilizes
- the I/O address range the card responds to

Setting the switches and/or jumpers allows the user to resolve conflicts between installed expansion cards. In addition, many ISA system boards have switches and/or jumpers that are used to configure the system board options.

The EISA specification replaces the switches and/or jumpers with special I/O locations. Each of these I/O locations can contain up to eight bits that may be used to select options on the system or expansion card. Each I/O location may be thought of as a pseudo DIP switch bank. These special I/O locations reside in the slot-specific I/O address space starting at xC80h and extending up to xCFFh, a total of 128 locations. The first four of these I/O locations are reserved for the card ID, while three of the eight bits in xC84h are reserved for special card functions. The remaining five bits in xC84h and locations xC85h through xCFFh are available for the implementation of card-specific option switches.

EISA System Configuration

The Expansion Card Control Bits Defined by the EISA Specification

Three of the eight bits available in port xC84h must be implemented on all EISA expansion cards. Table 9 - 8 defines these three bits.

Table 9-8. EISA Expansion Board Control Bits

Port xC84 Bit	Description
bit 0	ENABLE bit. 0 = disable card; 1 = enable card. This bit is read/writable and is mandatory.
bit 1	IOCHKERR bit. This read-only bit is used to determine if am EISA card is generating CHCHK#, causing an NMI. This bit is mandatory if the card can generate CHCHK#.
bit 2	IOCHKRST bit. This write-only bit is used to reset an expansion card. Setting it high for a minimum of 500ns causes the card to be reset. When reset, the ENABLE and IOCHKERR bits are cleared and all of the cards logic should be reset to an initialized state. If a card doesn't implement the IOCHKERR bit, the IOCHKRST bit need not be implemented.
bit 3:7	available for use in configuring the card.

EISA Configuration Process

General

Several elements are necessary in order to implement automatic system configuration in an EISA system. The system must have some way of verifying the placement and type of EISA boards in the system. This is accomplished by reading the board ID from each card slot during the POST.

Each EISA card must implement a set of one or more configuration registers to allow automatic configuration of the card each time the machine is powered on. The configuration registers are card-specific and are located in the I/O address range from xC84h through xCFFh.

The manufacturer of the system board and each of the EISA and, where possible, ISA boards should supply a configuration file for each card that describes the programmable options available on the card. Programmable options might include interrupt request lines and DMA channels to be used, size and start address of required memory space and start address of required

EISA System Architecture

I/O space. The configuration file must identify the options within each functional area: for example, the choice of interrupt request lines or DMA channels the card can be configured to use. For each possible choice, the file must describe the respective bit settings and I/O port to be written in order to choose the selected option. For ISA cards, the configuration file describes the available options and the respective DIP switch and/or jumper settings necessary to implement each selected option.

The system manufacturer must provide a configuration program that is capable of examining all of the selectable options available on each of the installed cards and of producing a conflict-free scenario. In other words, it must be capable of choosing a set of options for each card where none of the selected options conflict with the chosen option settings for any other installed ISA or EISA card. The configuration program then stores the configuration information in non-volatile memory and also makes a backup copy on diskette. The diskette may then be distributed within an organization to ensure that all machines will be configured the same way.

The EISA system board must incorporate at least 340 bytes of non-volatile memory for each expansion card slot and an additional 340 bytes for the system board configuration information. The block of non-volatile memory associated with a card slot is used to store card-specific configuration information such as the card ID and the address of and data to be written to the card's configuration registers each time the machine is powered on.

The system manufacturer must supply ROM-based BIOS routines that all configuration information to be written to and read from configuration memory (non-volatile memory).

Configuration File Naming Convention

The name of a card's configuration file consists of an exclamation point followed by the product ID and the file extension of CFG. The following are some examples of legal configuration file names:

- !DEL1233.CFG
- !CPQ5672.CFG
- !IBM9AB1.CFG

The configuration program includes a method for handling cards with duplicate product IDs. As the configuration program copies the configuration file for each card to the configuration diskette, it checks for duplicate product

EISA System Configuration

IDs. When one is found, the first character of the filename is changed from an exclamation point to the number one. If a third configuration file with the same product ID is found, its name is altered by changing the first character from an exclamation point to the number two, and so on. As an example, assume that the machine being configured has three boards with the same product ID. As the three configuration files are copied to the configuration diskette, they will be renamed as follows:

- first file name is left as !DEL1231.CFG
- second file name is altered to 1DEL1231.CFG
- third file name is altered to 2DEL1231.CFG.

The card manufacturer should always ensure that the card's configuration file name and product ID are changed to reflect the actual revision number of the card.

The Configuration Procedure

The example sequence that follows provides a guide to the configuration of an EISA system.

1. With the machine powered off, insert the configuration diskette in floppy drive A.
2. Install all EISA expansion cards. Do not install ISA cards yet.
3. Power on the machine. During the POST, the machine will attempt to read the product ID from each expansion slot in order to determine which slots have EISA cards installed.
4. When the POST is complete, the unit will boot from the configuration diskette and execute the configuration program.
5. Use the "copy configuration file" command on the configuration program's menu to copy each of the configuration files for the installed EISA cards and the yet-to-be-installed ISA cards onto the configuration diskette. During the copy process, the configuration program will automatically detect and rename the configuration files for cards with duplicate product IDs.
6. Select automatic system configuration from the menu. The configuration program will automatically generate a conflict-free scenario for both the EISA and ISA cards. The configuration program will store the EISA card product IDs, I/O configuration port addresses and the data to be written to each configuration port in non-volatile memory. Information about the ISA cards will also be stored in the slot-specific non-volatile memory areas reserved for the slots the ISA cards are to be installed in.

EISA System Architecture

7. Using the prompts generated by the configuration program, the user should set the DIP switches and/or jumpers on the ISA cards to the indicated positions.
8. Print a hardcopy of the expansion slots the ISA cards must be installed in and any command lines that may need to be entered into the operating system's startup files (such as the CONFIG.SYS and AUTOEXEC.BAT files in an MS-DOS environment).
9. Turn the system off and install the ISA cards in the expansion slots indicated by the configuration program. Refer to the hardcopy.
10. Remove the configuration program diskette from drive A: and power up the system again. The system will now boot from the hard disk.
11. Using a text editor, incorporate command lines into the operating system's startup files that were indicated by the configuration program. Refer to the hardcopy.
12. Reboot the system so the commands in the operating system's startup files will be executed.

The Configuration File Macro Language

The option information contained within a configuration file is written in a high-order macro language developed by the EISA consortium specifically for this purpose. The syntax of this language is described in detail in the EISA specification. It would be counter-productive to duplicate the entire language definition within this document. The following section provides an annotated listing of a sample configuration file.

An Example Configuration File

The following example configuration file demonstrates many, but not all, of the elements found in the typical configuration file. The text following the example explains each element.

EISA System Configuration

```
₁BOARD
   ID = "TLC0011"
   NAME = "XYZ Corp. Ethernet Board - Rev. 5"
   MFR = "XYZ Corp."
   CATEGORY = "NET"
   SLOT = EISA
   LENGTH = 330
   READID=YES

₂IOPORT(1) = 0zC94h
   INITVAL = 0000xxxx
₃IOPORT(2) = 0zC98h
   INITVAL = xxxxxxxxxxxxxxrr
₄IOPORT(3) = 0zC9Ah
   INITVAL = xxxxxxrr
₅IOPORT(4) = 0zC9Bh
   INITVAL = rrrrrxxx
₆IOPORT(5) = 0zC85h
   INITVAL = xxxxxxxx
₇IOPORT(6) = 0zC86h
   INITVAL = 0rrxxxxx
₈IOPORT(7) = 0zC86h
   INITVAL = 1rrxxxxx

₉SOFTWARE(1) = "TLCDRVR.EXE - \n If using MS-
      DOS, place the following command line in
      AUTOEXEC.BAT:\n\t\tTLCDRVR /S=n /A =n\n
      Use the following values with the /S and
      /A parameters:"
```

```
; Function description starts here
10GROUP = "Ethernet Network Interface"
   11TYPE = "NET,ETH"
12FUNCTION = "Network Interface Location"
   13CHOICE = "Set Up as Node 0"
      SUBTYPE = "LAN0"
      FREE
       INIT = SOFTWARE(1) = "/S = 1 /A = 0"
       INIT = IOPORT(5) = LOC (5-2) 0000
   CHOICE = "Set up as Node 1"
      SUBTYPE = "LAN1"
      FREE
       INIT = SOFTWARE(1) = "/S = 0 /A = 1"
       INIT = IOPORT(5) = LOC (5-2) 0001
   CHOICE = "Set Up as Node 2"
      SUBTYPE = "LAN2"
      FREE
       INIT = SOFTWARE(1) = "/S = 0 /A = 2"
       INIT = IOPORT(5) = LOC (5-2) 0010
       .
       .
       .
   CHOICE = "Set Up as Node 15"
      SUBTYPE = "LAN15"
      FREE
       INIT = SOFTWARE(1) = "/S = 0 /A = 15"
       INIT = IOPORT(5) = LOC (5-2) 1111
```

```
 ₁₄FUNCTION = "DMA and Interrupt assignment"
   ₁₅CHOICE = "System Resources"
      ₁₆;DMA channel uses Type "C" bus cycle
      ₁₇LINK
       ₁₈DMA = 5|7
         SHARE = no
         SIZE = dword
         TIMING = TYPEC
        INIT = IOPORT(5) LOC (0) 0|1

        ;interrupt is level-sensitive, shareable
       LINK
        ₁₉IRQ = 2|5
         SHARE = yes
         TRIGGER = level
        INIT = IOPORT(5) LOC (1) 0|1
      ₂₀COMBINE
       ₂₁MEMORY = 2K
         ADDRESS = 0C0000h|0D0000h|0E0000h
         MEMTYPE = oth
         WRITABLE = no
         SHARE = no
         SIZE = byte
         CACHE = yes
         DECODE = 32
        INIT=IOPORT(6)LOC(3-0) 1100|1101|1110
```

```
                ;network board local RAM
             22FUNCTION = "Local RAM initialization"
               23CHOICE = "64K RAM"
                   SUBTYPE = "64K"
                   COMBINE
                    MEMORY = "64K"
                      ADDRESS= 100000h-1F0000h STEP = 64K
                      WRITABLE = yes
                      MEMTYPE = oth
                      SIZE = dword
                      CACHE = no
                     INIT=IOPORT(7)LOC(4 3 2 1 0)00000-01111
               24CHOICE = "128K RAM"
                   SUBTYPE = "128K"
                   COMBINE
                    MEMORY = "128K"
                      ADDRESS = 100000h-1F0000h STEP = 64K
                      WRITABLE = yes
                      MEMTYPE = oth
                      SIZE = dword
                      CACHE = no
                     INIT=IOPORT(7)LOC(4 3 2 1 0)10000-11111
             25ENDGROUP
```

```
             ;serial port section
           26FUNCTION = "Serial Port"
             27TYPE = "COM,ASY"
             28CHOICE = "COM1"
                SUBTYPE = "COM1"
                FREE
                 IRQ = 4
                   SHARE = yes
                   TRIGGER = level
                 PORT = 3F8h-3FFh
                   SHARE = no
                   SIZE = byte
                 INIT = IOPORT(1) LOC (3-0) 0000
                 INIT=IOPORT(2)LOC (15-2) 00000011111100
                 INIT = IOPORT(3) LOC (7-2) 110000
                 INIT = IOPORT(4) LOC (2-0) 010
             29CHOICE = "COM2"
                SUBTYPE = "COM2"
                FREE
                 IRQ = 3
                   SHARE = yes
                   TRIGGER = level
                 PORT = 2F8h-2FFh
                   SHARE = no
                   SIZE = byte
                 INIT = IOPORT(1) LOC (3-0) 0000
                 INIT=IOPORT(2)LOC (15-2) 00000011111100
                 INIT = IOPORT(3) LOC (7-2) 110000
                 INIT = IOPORT(4) LOC (2-0) 000

             30CHOICE = "Serial Port Disable"
                SUBTYPE = "Port Disable"
                DISABLE = yes
                FREE
                 INIT = IOPORT(4) LOC (0) 0
```

EISA System Architecture

Explanation of the Example Configuration File

Each of the numbered sections that follow provides an explanation of the section of the example configuration file with the corresponding subscripted number.

1. Every configuration file must include the board identification block. The BOARD statement identifies the beginning of the block. The ID statement contains the product ID consisting of the three character manufacturer's code, the three digit board type and the one digit revision number. The NAME field contains text that describes the board. The MFR field contains the full name of the board manufacturer. The CATEGORY field contains a three character designator that identifies the basic board type. Table 9 - 9 provides a listing of the available categories. The SLOT statement identifies the type of slot the board requires. If the SLOT statement is missing, the configuration program assumes that the board requires a 16-bit ISA slot. The LENGTH statement specifies the length of the board in millimeters. The READID statement identifies whether the board has a product ID that can be read from I/O ports xC80h-xC83h.

2. The IOPORT(1) statement associates the variable name IOPORT(1) with I/O port address xC94h. The INITVAL statement identifies the source of each of the bits within the specified I/O port. In this example statement, the xxxx indicates that bits 0:3 are supplied by the configuration program based on the configuration chosen. The 0000 in bits 4:7 indicates that these bits are always zero.

3. The IOPORT(2) statement associates the variable name IOPORT(2) with I/O port addresses xC98h and xC99h. The INITVAL statement identifies the source of each of the bits within the specified I/O port. In this example statement, the bit field is sixteen bits wide, indicating that this is a 16-bit I/O port. Bits 0:1 have an "rr" designation, meaning that they are read-only bits. The x's in bits 2:15 indicate that they are supplied by the configuration program based on the configuration chosen.

4. The IOPORT(3) statement associates the variable name IOPORT(3) with I/O port address xC9Ah. The INITVAL statement identifies the source of each of the bits within the specified I/O port. In this example statement, the bit field is eight bits wide, indicating that this is an 8-bit I/O port. Bits 0:1 have an "rr" designation, meaning that they are read-only bits. The x's in

EISA System Configuration

bits 2:7 indicate that they are supplied by the configuration program based on the configuration chosen.

5. The IOPORT(4) statement associates the variable name IOPORT(4) with I/O port address xC9Bh. The INITVAL statement identifies the source of each of the bits within the specified I/O port. In this example statement, the bit field is eight bits wide, indicating that this is an 8-bit I/O port. Bits 3:7 have an "r" designation, meaning that they are read-only bits. The x's in bits 0:2 indicate that they are supplied by the configuration program based on the configuration chosen.

6. The IOPORT(5) statement associates the variable name IOPORT(5) with I/O port address xC85h. The INITVAL statement identifies the source of each of the bits within the specified I/O port. In this example statement, the bit field is eight bits wide, indicating that this is an 8-bit I/O port. The x's in bits 0:7 indicate that they are supplied by the configuration program based on the configuration chosen.

7. The IOPORT(6) statement associates the variable name IOPORT(6) with I/O port address xC86h. The INITVAL statement identifies the source of each of the bits within the specified I/O port. In this example statement, the bit field is eight bits wide, indicating that this is an 8-bit I/O port. Bit seven is always zero. Bits 5:6 have an "r" designation, meaning that they are read-only bits. The x's in bits 0:4 indicate that they are supplied by the configuration program based on the configuration chosen.

8. The IOPORT(7) statement associates the variable name IOPORT(7) with I/O port address xC86h. The INITVAL statement identifies the source of each of the bits within the specified I/O port. In this example statement, the bit field is eight bits wide, indicating that this is an 8-bit I/O port. Bit seven is always one. Bits 5:6 have an "r" designation, meaning that they are read-only bits. The x's in bits 0:4 indicate that they are supplied by the configuration program based on the configuration chosen.

9. The SOFTWARE(1) statement provides the end user with instructions regarding a customized command line to be written into operating system startup files like AUTOEXEC.BAT and/or CONFIG.SYS. Customization of the command line is based on selections made during the configuration process. The text located within the quotes will be displayed for the end user and may be printed out as well. The "\n" will cause the configuration program to output a "new line" to the screen, while the "\t" represents a tab.

EISA System Architecture

10. The GROUP statement block begins with the GROUP statement and ends with the ENDGROUP statement. The option choices for board functions that may be logically grouped are placed within the GROUP block. In this example, the network card being described contains both a network interface and a serial port. All of the card's functions related to the network interface are grouped together.

11. The TYPE and SUBTYPE identifiers are used by device drivers to identify, set up and operate a device that is compatible with the device driver. In the example, NET indicates it is a network interface and ETH indicates that it is an Ethernet network interface.

12. The FUNCTION statement provides the name of the functional area to be configured. In this example, it is the location of the network interface on the network.

13. The statements within a CHOICE block define the option settings for a given choice. The first CHOICE block specifies the most desired choice, with subsequent choices in order to preference. In the example, the first CHOICE block defines the settings if the network interface board is to be configured as node 0 on the network. If this choice is made, the SUBTYPE field is set to "LAN0" to supply additional information to the card's software driver. The elements with a free-form group, defined by the FREE statement, have no functional relationship to each other. The first INIT statement declares that the text string "/S = 1 /A = 0" will be appended to the text in the SOFTWARE(1) variable if the first choice is selected. In addition, the second INIT statement declares that bits 2:5 of the I/O port specified in the variable IOPORT(5), port xC85h, must be set to zero to configure the network interface card as node 0 on the network.

14. The next functional area to be configured is the assignment of the interrupt request line, DMA channel and the start address of the card's device ROM.

15. There is only one CHOICE block within this functional area.

16. This is a comment line.

17. The elements of a LINK group have a direct relationship to each other. The first LINK block contains statement relating to the DMA channel selection and programming. The second LINK block contains statements relating to the selection and programming of an interrupt request line.

EISA System Configuration

18. The DMA statement offers a choice of DMA channel five or seven. The vertical line between the two numbers is the logical "or" symbol. The SHARE statement declares the DMA channel as not shareable. The SIZE statement declares the DMA channel as handling doubleword, or 32-bit, transfers. The TIMING statement declares that the selected DMA channel must be programmed to use Type "C" bus cycles. The INIT statement declares that bit zero of IOPORT(5), port xC85h, must be set to zero to select DMA channel five or to one to select DMA channel seven.

19. The second LINK block contains statements relating to the selection and programming of an interrupt request line. It allows a choice of IRQ two or five, the selected IRQ input must be programmed as a shareable, level-sensitive interrupt request line, and IOPORT(5), port xC85h, bit one must be set to zero to select IRQ2, or to one to select IRQ5.

20. The elements of a combined group have an indirect relationship to each other.

21. The MEMORY statement identifies the start of a memory description block. This block describes a block of memory 2K in size. The ADDRESS statement provides a choice of one of three possible start addresses for the memory block. The three possible start addresses are 0C0000h, 0D0000h, or 0E0000h. The MEMTYPE field identifies whether the memory block is normal system memory (SYS), expanded memory (EXP), a LIM page frame (VIR), or memory space used for memory-mapped I/O or bank-switched memory (OTH for other). OTH is primarily intended for memory-mapped I/O devices such as network cards. This memory block is declared not writable (WRITABLE = no), meaning it is ROM memory. The memory block may not be shared with another device (SHARE = no). It is 8-bit memory (SIZE = byte). It is safe to cache information from this area of memory (CACHE = yes). All 32 address lines are decoded by the board (DECODE = 32). To implement the selected memory start address, IOPORT(6), port xC86h, bits 0:3, must be set to Ch (1100), Dh (1101), or Eh(1110).

22. The next functional area to be configured is the RAM memory residing on the network interface card.

23. The first CHOICE block defines the configuration if the network interface card has 64K of RAM memory installed. Its SUBTYPE is declared as 64K for the use of the network interface driver. If this choice is made, the

MEMORY block statement declares the memory as 64K in size. Its start address may begin on any one of sixteen possible address boundaries within the 1M range between 100000h and 1FFFFFh and the must start at an address divisible by 64K. It is declared as writable, meaning it is RAM memory that can be both written to and read from. It is declared with a MEMTYPE of OTH. It is a 32-bit device and the selected memory address range is declared as non-cacheable. If this choice is made, IOPORT(7), port xC86h, bits 0:4 must be set to a value between 0 0000 and 0 1111, depending on the start address selected.

24. The statements within the second CHOICE block will be executed if the network interface card has 128K of RAM memory installed. The setup is the same as that with 64K of RAM installed except for the SUBTYPE declaration and the value to be written to IOPORT(7), port xC86h. If this choice is made, IOPORT(7), port xC86h, bits 0:4 must be set to a value between 1 0000 and 1 1111, depending on the start address selected.

25. The ENDGROUP statement marks the end of the network interface portion of the configuration information. The remaining configuration information relates to the serial port.

26. The next functional area to be configured is the serial port logic residing on the network interface card.

27. For the benefit of the device driver software, the SUBTYPE is declared as "COM,ASY", meaning asynchonous communications port.

28. There are three possible configuration choices for the serial port: COM1, COM2, or disabled. For the COM1 choice, the following selections are made: the serial port will use IRQ4 and it will be programmed as a shareable, level-triggered IRQ input; it will respond to port addresses 03F8h - 03FFh; and its I/O ports may not be shared by another device and they are 8-bit ports. Bits 0:3 of IOPORT(1), port xC94h, will be set to zeros. Bits 0:1 and 8:15 of IOPORT(2), ports xC98h and xC99h, will be set to zeros, while bits 2:7 will be set to ones. Bits 2:5 of IOPORT(3), port xC9Ah, will be set to zeros, while bits 6:7 will be set to ones. Bits 0 and 2 of IOPORT(4), port xC9Bh, will be set to zero, while bit 1 is set to one.

29. For the COM2 choice, the selections made are the same as COM1, except: the serial port will use IRQ3; and it will respond to port addresses 02F8h - 02FFh. Bits 0:2 of IOPORT(4), port xC9Bh, will be set to zero.

EISA System Configuration

30. If the serial port is to be disabled, bit 0 of IOPORT(4), port xC9Bh, is set to zero and the SUBTYPE is set to disabled for the driver.

Table 9-9. Category List

Category Name	Description
COM	communications device
KEY	keyboard
MEM	memory board
MFC	multifunction board
MSD	mass storage device
NET	network board
NPX	numeric coprocessor
OSE	operating system/ environment
OTH	other
PAR	parallel port
PTR	pointing device
SYS	system board
VID	video board

Part II:

The Intel 82350DT Chip Set

The EISA System Buses

Chapter 10

Prior To This Chapter

In the previous chapter, automatic system configuration was described.

In This Chapter

This chapter describes the major buses found in virtually all EISA systems. This includes the host, EISA, ISA and X buses.

The Next Chapter

The next chapter, "The Bridge, Translator, Pathfinder and Toolbox," describes the major functions provided by the EISA chip set.

Introduction

Refer to figure 10 - 1. EISA systems may consist of a number of buses including:

- host bus
- EISA bus
- X-bus
- local*

* Only in systems that include a look-through cache subsystem will the processor have its own local bus.

111

EISA System Architecture

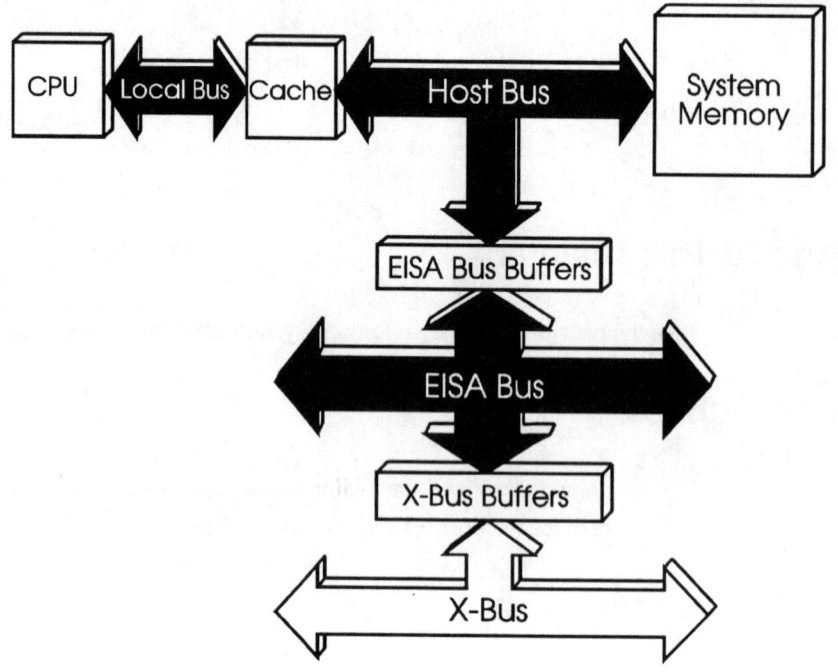

Figure 10-1. Buses typically found in EISA systems

The Host Bus

Virtually all EISA systems are shipped with an integral CPU. This CPU may be integrated onto the system board itself or may reside on a special, CPU daughtercard that installs in a special connector on the system board. This is referred to as the host CPU. The host CPU's local address, data and control buses comprise the host bus. Typically, devices that the CPU requires fast access to would be placed on the host bus. These would include devices like:

- system board RAM memory
- numeric coprocessor
- local cache controller and cache memory
- non-cacheable access, or NCA, logic
- advanced video controller
- other I/O devices requiring fast access to the CPU

If the host CPU resides on a daughtercard, the CPU's local cache controller, cache memory, NCA logic and numeric coprocessor will typically reside on the CPU card.

112

The EISA System Buses

The EISA/ISA Bus

Since the ISA bus is a subset of the EISA bus, any reference to the EISA bus in this book is a reference to the ISA bus and its EISA extensions. The ISA bus is discussed in detail in the MindShare book entitled, *The ISA System Architecture*. The EISA extensions to the ISA bus are described earlier in this book.

The X Bus

The ability of the microprocessor to drive data onto the data bus and the address onto the address bus is limited by the power of its output drivers. When the microprocessor is writing data to any external memory or I/O device, the data is driven out onto the processor's local data bus. If the local data bus is fanned out and connected to too many external devices, the drive capability of the microprocessor's output drivers may be exceeded and the data driven onto the data bus becomes corrupted. The local data bus is connected to the external data bus transceivers pictured in figure 10 - 2.

During a write operation, the Bus Control logic allows the appropriate data bus transceiver to pass data from the processor's local data bus onto the system data, or SD, bus. The output drive capability of the transceiver is substantially greater than that of the processor's internal drivers, allowing the SD bus to fan out to more places. The SD bus is connected to all of the ISA expansion slots. In addition, many devices that may be written to are physically located on the system board itself. However, it would exceed the output drive capability of the data bus transceivers to fan out the SD bus to all of the devices integrated onto the system board as well as to all of the expansion slots.

To solve this problem, the SD bus is passed through another transceiver onto the XD, or extended data, bus. The X data bus transceiver redrives the data onto the XD bus during writes, permitting the data to be fanned out the devices residing on the XD bus. The devices integrated onto the system board are connected to the X data bus.

When a write is in progress, the Bus Control logic sets up the data bus transceivers to pass data from the microprocessor's local data bus onto the SD bus and also enables the X data bus transceiver to pass data from the SD bus to the XD bus. When a read is in progress, the Bus Control logic sets up the X

EISA System Architecture

data bus transceiver to pass data from the XD to the SD bus and sets up the data bus transceivers to pass data from the SD to the microprocessor's local data bus. It should be noted that the XD bus is just a buffered version of the ISA bus's SD bus.

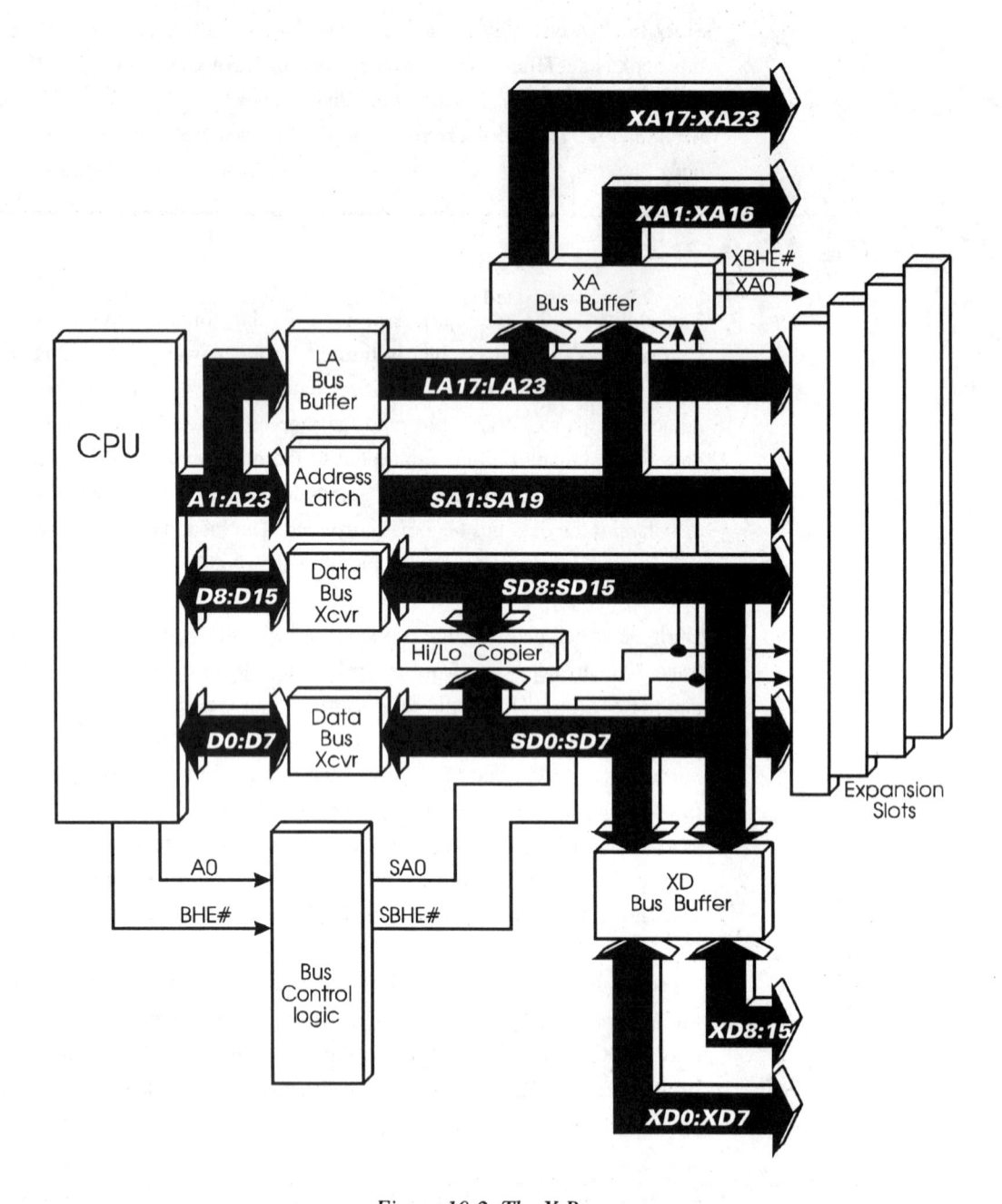

Figure 10-2. The X Bus

The same fanout problem exists on the processor's address bus. The address generated by the microprocessor is driven onto the processor's local address

The EISA System Buses

bus. In an ISA machine, it then passes through the LA bus buffer, the Address Latch and the Bus control logic onto the ISA address bus. The ISA address bus consists of LA17:LA23, SA0:SA19 and SBHE#. The redrive capability of the LA bus buffer, the Address Latch and the Bus Control logic permits the address information to be fanned out to all of the ISA expansion slots. In addition to the ISA devices installed in expansion slots, however, the address information must also be fanned out to the addressable devices that are integrated onto the system board. This would exceed the drive capability of the LA bus buffer, the Address Latch and the Bus Control logic. To allow additional fanout, the ISA address information is passed through a buffer onto the XA bus. The buffer's redrive capability permits the XA address to be fanned out to all the devices integrated onto the system board. In other words, the devices integrated onto the system board are connected to the XA and XD buses, a buffered version of the ISA address bus.

The Bridge, Translator, Pathfinder and Toolbox

Chapter 11

The Previous Chapter

The previous chapter introduced the buses around which all EISA systems are constructed. They are the host, EISA, ISA and X buses.

In This Chapter

This chapter provides a description of the major functions performed by the EISA chip set. It acts as the bridge between the host and EISA buses. It translates addresses and other bus cycle information into a form understood by all of the host, EISA and ISA devices in a system. When necessary, it performs data bus steering to ensure data travels over the correct paths between the current bus master and the currently addressed device. It incorporates a toolbox including all of the standard support logic necessary in any EISA machine. It should be noted that the ISA bus is a subset of the EISA bus. For this reason, all references to the EISA bus in this publication (or any other) refer to both the ISA bus and the Extended ISA bus (EISA).

The Next Chapter

The next chapter, "The Intel 82350DT EISA Chip Set," provides an introduction to Intel's version of the EISA chip set.

The Players

When a device requires the use of the buses to communicate with another device in the system, it requests the use of the buses from the Central Arbitration Control, or CAC. Upon being granted ownership of the buses, the bus master initiates the bus cycle by addressing the target device, or slave.

The Bridge

Upon sensing the start of the bus cycle, the EISA chip set must begin to aid in the communication process. Acting as a bridge, the EISA chip set must allow the address generated by the bus master to propagate onto all of the system

EISA System Architecture

buses so all of the devices in the system have an opportunity to determine if they are currently being addressed. In this section, this function is referred to as bridging. This term isn't part of the EISA specification, but is employed here to reinforce the visual image of the process being described. Table 11 - 1 defines the circumstances under which the EISA chip set must act as a bridge. Figure 11 - 1 illustrates the relationship of the bridge to the three buses. At the start of a bus cycle, neither the current bus master nor the EISA chip set knows which bus the target slave is located on. For this reason, the EISA chip set always propagates addresses generated by the host CPU onto the EISA and X-buses. Conversely, it always propagates addresses by an EISA or ISA bus master onto the host and X-buses.

Table 11-1. Situations Requiring Address Bridging

Bus Master Type	Slave Type	Action Required
Host CPU	host slave	No bridging required.
Host CPU	EISA slave	Address must be passed from the host bus to the EISA bus.
Host CPU	ISA expansion slave	Address must be passed from the host bus onto the ISA bus.
Host CPU	ISA X-bus slave	Address must be passed from the host bus onto the ISA bus and then onto the X-bus.
EISA Bus Master	host slave	Address must be passed from the EISA bus to the host bus.
EISA Bus Master	EISA slave	No bridging required.
EISA Bus Master	ISA expansion slave	No bridging required.
EISA Bus Master	ISA X-bus slave	Address must be passed from the EISA bus to the X-bus.
ISA Bus Master	host slave	Address must be passed from the ISA bus to the host bus.
ISA Bus Master	EISA slave	No bridging required.
ISA Bus Master	ISA expansion slave	No bridging required.
ISA Bus Master	ISA X-bus slave	Address must be passed from the ISA bus to the X-bus.

The Bridge, Translator, Pathfinder and Toolbox

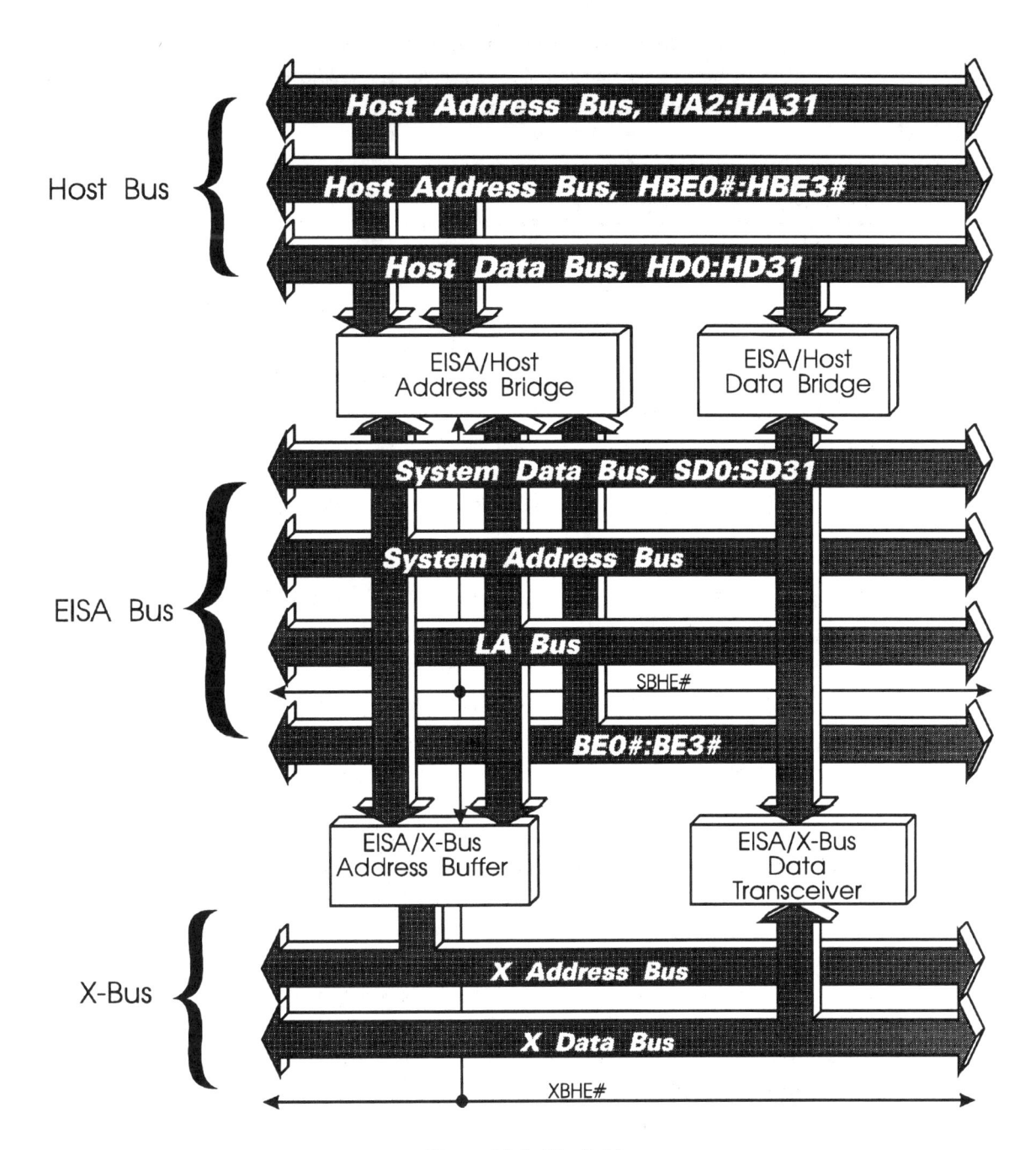

Figure 11-1. The Bridge

EISA System Architecture

In addition, under some circumstances the data being transferred between the bus master and the slave must be allowed to pass from one system bus to another. Table 11 - 2 defines these situations.

Table 11-2. Situations Requiring Data Bridging

Bus Master Type	Slave Type	Action Required
Host CPU	host slave	No bridging required.
Host CPU	EISA slave	On a read, data must be passed from the EISA data bus to the host data bus. On a write, data must be passed from the host data bus to the EISA data bus.
Host CPU	ISA expansion slave	On a read, data must be passed from the EISA data bus to the host data bus. On a write, data must be passed from the host data bus to the EISA data bus.
Host CPU	ISA X-bus slave	On a read, data must be passed from the X data bus to the ISA data bus and then from the ISA data bus to the host data bus. On a write, data must be passed from the host data bus to the ISA data bus and then to the X data bus.
EISA Bus Master	host slave	On a read, data must be passed from the host data bus onto the EISA data bus. On a write, data must be passed from the EISA data bus to the host data bus.
EISA Bus Master	EISA slave	No bridging required.
EISA Bus Master	ISA expansion slave	No bridging required.
EISA Bus Master	ISA X-bus slave	On a read, data must be passed from the X data bus to the EISA data bus. On a write, data must be passed from the EISA data bus to the X data bus.
ISA Bus Master	host slave	On a read, data must be passed from the host data bus to the ISA data bus. On a write, data must be passed from the ISA data bus to the host data bus.
ISA Bus Master	EISA slave	No bridging required.
ISA Bus Master	ISA expansion slave	No bridging required.
ISA Bus Master	ISA X-bus slave	On a read, data must be passed from the X data bus to the ISA data bus. On a write, data must be passed from the ISA data bus to the X data bus.

The Bridge, Translator, Pathfinder and Toolbox

The Translator

Address Translation

The EISA chip set must translate the address being generated by the bus master to a form that is understood by the slave devices on all three buses. Table 11-3 defines the different forms that devices on the three buses expect to see the address.

Table 11-3. Address Translation Table

Bus Master Type	Address Generated	Address Expected by 8-bit ISA Slave	Address Expected by 16-bit ISA Slave	Address Expected by 16-bit EISA Slave	Address Expected by 32-bit EISA Slave	Address Expected by 32-bit Host Slave
Host CPU	A2:31 + BE0:3#	SA0:19	SA0:23 + SBHE#	LA2:31 + BE0:3#	LA2:31 + BE0:3#	A2:31 + BE0:3#
16-bit EISA Bus Master	LA2:31 + BE0:3#	SA0:19	SA0:23 + SBHE#	LA2:31 + BE0:3#	LA2:31 + BE0:3#	A2:31 + BE0:3#
32-bit EISA Bus Master	LA2:31 + BE0:3#	SA0:19	SA0:23 + SBHE#	LA2:31 + BE0:3#	LA2:31 + BE0:3#	A2:31 + BE0:3#
16-bit ISA Bus Master	SA0:23 + SBHE#	SA0:19	SA0:23 + SBHE#	LA2:31 + BE0:3#	LA2:31 + BE0:3#	A2:31 + BE0:3#

When an EISA bus master or the host CPU is performing a bus cycle, the EISA chip set must convert the bus master's byte enable outputs, BE0#:BE3#, to the correct setting on the A0, A1 and BHE# signal lines. When an ISA bus master is performing a bus cycle, A0, A1 and BHE# must be converted to the correct setting on the byte enable lines.

Command Line Translation

Each of the three types of bus masters, EISA, ISA and host CPU, uses a specific set of signal lines to indicate the address time and data time periods and the type of bus cycle in progress. Conversely, each of the three types of slaves recognizes the same respective set of signals indicating address time, data time and the bus cycle type. When a bus master initiates a bus cycle, the EISA chip set must convert the bus master's signal set to those recognized by the other two slave types. This enables any bus master type to communicate with devices of any other type. Table 11-4 indicates the signal lines used by each of the three bus master and slave types to indicate address time, data time and the bus cycle type.

EISA System Architecture

Table 11-4. Command Lines

Device Type	Address Time Signal	Data Time Signal	Bus Cycle Type Indicators
EISA	START#	CMD#	M/IO# and W/R#
ISA	BALE	SMRDC#, SMWTC#, MRDC#, MWTC#, IORC#, IOWC#	SMRDC#, SMWTC#, MRDC#, MWTC#, IORC#, IOWC#
Host	ADS#	end of ADS# until READY# sampled active	W/R#, M/IO# and D/C#

The Pathfinder

Under some circumstances, data path steering is necessary. When a bus master is communicating with a slave using a data path or paths that the slave is incapable of using, the data bus steering logic must be activated. During a read bus cycle, the data bus steering logic ensures that the returning data arrives at the bus master on the correct data path(s). During a write bus cycle, the data bus steering logic ensures that the data being written by the bus master is routed to the data path(s) that the slave expects to receive the data on. In an EISA machine, the data bus steering function is provided by the EISA chip set. Table 11 - 5 defines the situations when data bus steering is necessary. A more detailed description of data bus steering may be found in the MindShare publication entitled, "The ISA System Architecture." The 32-bit bus master or a 16-bit EISA bus master indicates the data path(s) to be used during a bus cycle using its byte enable outputs, BE0#:BE3#. A 16-bit bus ISA bus master uses A0 and BHE# to indicate the data path(s) that will be used during a bus cycle. The addressed slave indicates the data path(s) it is connected to by asserting IO16#, M16#, EX16# or EX32#. If IO16#, M16# or EX16# is activated by the addressed slave, it is a 16-bit device and is connected to data paths 0 and 1. If the addressed slave activates EX32#, it is a 32-bit device and is connected to all four data paths. If none of these lines are activated, the addressed slave is an 8-bit device and is connected only to path 0.

The Bridge, Translator, Pathfinder and Toolbox

Table 11-5. Situations Requiring Data Bus Steering

Bus Master Type	Slave Type	Bus Cycle Type	Steering Action Required
32-bit	8-bit	write	When a 32-bit bus master is writing a single byte to an 8-bit device over paths 1, 2, or 3, the data bus steering logic must copy the byte down to path 0 so it can get to the 8-bit device. When a 32-bit bus master is writing multiple bytes to an 8-bit device in a single bus cycle, the data bus steering logic must route the data to path 0 one byte at a time. As each byte is routed to the lower data path, the address seen by the 8-bit device must be incremented by the steering logic and the MWTC# or IOWC# line must be turned off and then on again to trick the 8-bit device into thinking another bus cycle has been initiated.
32-bit	8-bit	read	When a 32-bit bus master is reading a single byte from an 8-bit device over path 1, 2, or 3, the data bus steering logic must copy the byte from path 0 to the path the bus master expects to receive the byte on. When a 32-bit bus master is attempting to read multiple bytes from an 8-bit device in a single bus cycle, the 8-bit device can only return one byte at a time. The steering logic must address each byte individually, copy it to the proper data path and latch it in a latching data bus transceivers until all of the requested bytes have been retrieved. As each byte is routed to and latched by the proper data bus transceiver, the address seen by the 8-bit device must be incremented by the steering logic and the MRDC# or IORC# line must be turned off and then on again to trick the 8-bit device into thinking another bus cycle has been initiated.
32-bit	16-bit	write	When a 32-bit bus master is writing one or two bytes to a 16-bit device over paths 2 or 3, the data bus steering logic must copy the byte or bytes to path 0 and/or path 1 so they can get to the 16-bit device.
32-bit	16-bit	read	When a 32-bit bus master is reading one or two bytes from a 16-bit device over paths 2 or 3, the data bus steering logic must copy the byte or bytes from path 0 and/or path 1 to path 2 and/or path 3 so they are received by the bus master over the expected data path(s).
32-bit	32-bit	read or write	none

16-bit	8-bit	write	When a 16-bit bus master is writing a single byte to an 8-bit device over path 1, the data bus steering logic must copy the byte down to path 0 so it can get to the 8-bit device. When a 16-bit bus master is writing two bytes to an 8-bit device in a single bus cycle, the data bus steering logic must route the data to path 0 one byte at a time. As each byte is routed to the lower data path, the address seen by the 8-bit device must be incremented by the steering logic and the MWTC# or IOWC# line must be turned off and then on again to trick the 8-bit device into thinking another bus cycle has been initiated.
16-bit	16-bit	read or write	none
16-bit	32-bit	write	When a 16-bit bus master is writing one or two bytes to either of the last two locations in a doubleword in a single bus cycle, the steering logic must copy the byte or bytes to path 2 and/or path 3 so the data will be routed to the proper location(s) within the addressed doubleword.
16-bit	32-bit	read	When a 16-bit bus master is reading one or two bytes from either of the last two locations in a doubleword in a single bus cycle, the steering logic must route the byte or bytes from path 2 and/or path 3 to path 0 and/or path 1 so the data will be received over the proper path(s).

The Toolbox

In addition to providing the bridge, translation and data bus steering functions, the EISA chip set includes a toolbox with all of the basic support elements necessary to the proper function of any EISA system. These include:

- Two modified Intel 8259A Programmable Interrupt Controllers in a master/slave configuration.
- Two modified Intel 8237 DMA Controllers in a master/slave configuration.
- The Refresh Logic.
- The Central Arbitration Control.
- Five Programmable Timers.
- The NMI control logic.

Detailed descriptions of interrupts, DMA, refresh, the timers and the NMI control logic can be found in the MindShare publication entitled, "The ISA

The Bridge, Translator, Pathfinder and Toolbox

System Architecture." Information regarding the EISA-specific-enhancements to the interrupt, DMA, refresh and the NMI control logic can be found earlier in this publication. Information regarding the Central Arbitration Control can be found earlier in this publication. A description of the Intel 82357 Integrated Systems Peripheral, or ISP, can be found in the next chapter. The ISP, part of the Intel EISA chip set, contains all of the above-mentioned logic elements.

The Intel 82350DT EISA Chip Set

Chapter 12

The Previous Chapter

The previous chapter described the major functions performed by an EISA chip set.

In This Chapter

This chapter provides an introduction to the Intel 82350DT EISA chip set. The focus is on the 82358DT EISA Bus Controller, or EBC, the 82357 Integrated Systems Peripheral, or ISP, and the 82352 EISA Bus Buffers, or EBBs.

Introduction

This chapter is not intended as a substitute for the Intel publication that describes the 82350DT EISA chip set. It is intended as a companion to the Intel document, providing an introduction to the roles each component plays in a typical EISA system. Only the crucial chip set components are represented here: the EBC, the address EBB, the data EBB and the ISP. For detailed information, refer to the Intel document entitled, "82350DT EISA Chip Set," order number 290377-002. The EBC can be configured to run in three different types of environments:

- with the host interface unit interfaced directly to the host CPU subsystem. This is referred to as the 82350 environment.
- with the host interface unit interfaced to the host bus through the Intel 82359 DRAM controller. This is referred to as the 82350DT/enhanced environment.
- with the host interface unit interfaced to a buffered bus. The buffered bus, in turn, is connected to the Intel 82359 DRAM controller, which is connected to the host bus. This is referred to as the 82350DT/buffered environment.

This chapter describes operation of the EISA chip set configured for the 82350 environment.

EISA System Architecture

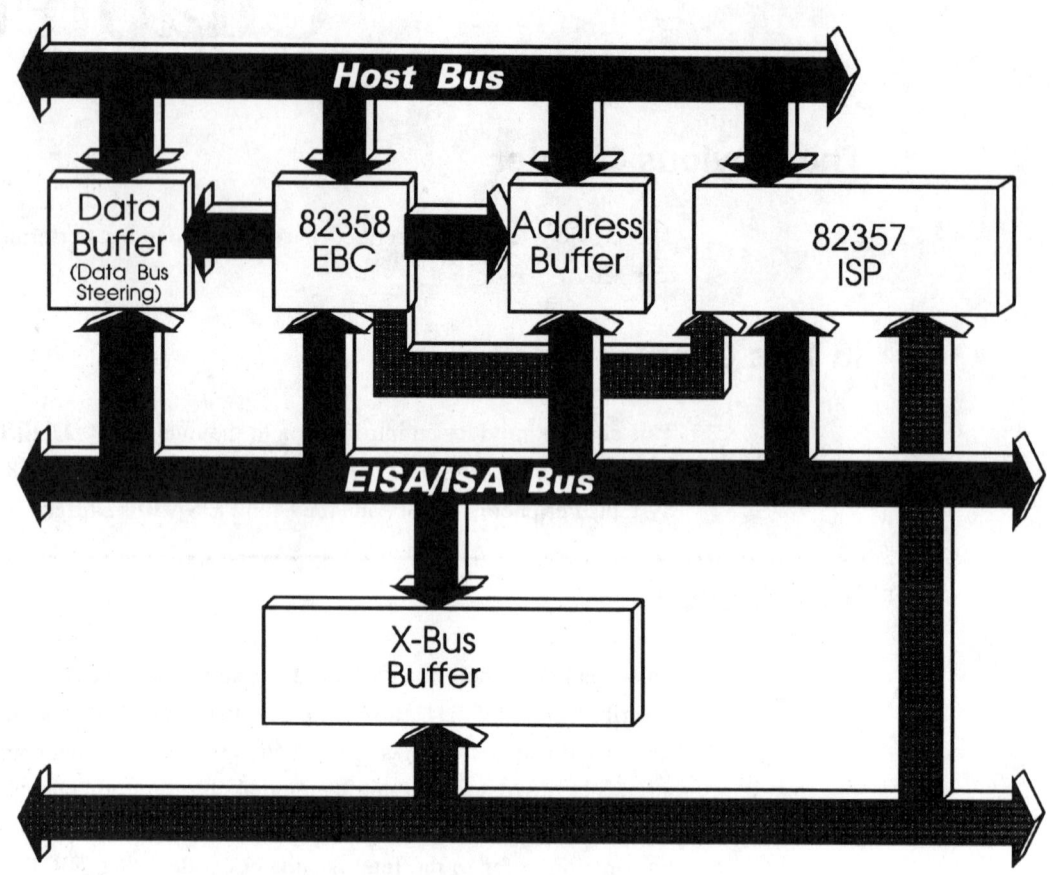

Figure 12 - 1 illustrates the relationship of the Intel EBC, ISP, Data Buffer and Address Buffer to the host, EISA/ISA and X-buses in the 82350 environment.

Figure 12-1. The Intel EISA Chip Set

The 82358DT EISA Bus Controller (EBC) and the 82352 EISA Bus Buffers

General

The EBC is pictured in figure 12 - 2. Together with the Data and Address EBBs, the EBC provides the bridging, translation and data bus steering functions described in the previous chapter. The following sections describe each of the functional areas that comprise the EBC.

The Intel 82350DT EISA Chip Set

CPU Selection

These four inputs to the EBC indicate the host CPU type and its bus frequency. Table 12 - 1 defines the valid settings for these inputs. If the host CPU is integrated onto the system board, these pins should be permanently strapped to the appropriate state. When the host CPU resides on a plug-in card, however, the four CPU signals should be set to the appropriate state when the CPU card is inserted. This allows automatic configuration of the EBC to match the CPU card installed in the machine. CPU input patterns not specified in table 12 - 1 are reserved for future use.

Table 12-1. CPU Type/Frequency

CPU3	CPU2	CPU1	CPU0	**CPU Type/Frequency**
1	0	1	0	32-bits, 2x clock, 25MHz 80386
1	0	1	1	32-bits, 2x clock, 33MHz 80386
1	1	0	0	32-bits, 1x clock, 25MHz 80486
1	1	0	1	32-bits, 1x clock, 33MHz 80486

EISA System Architecture

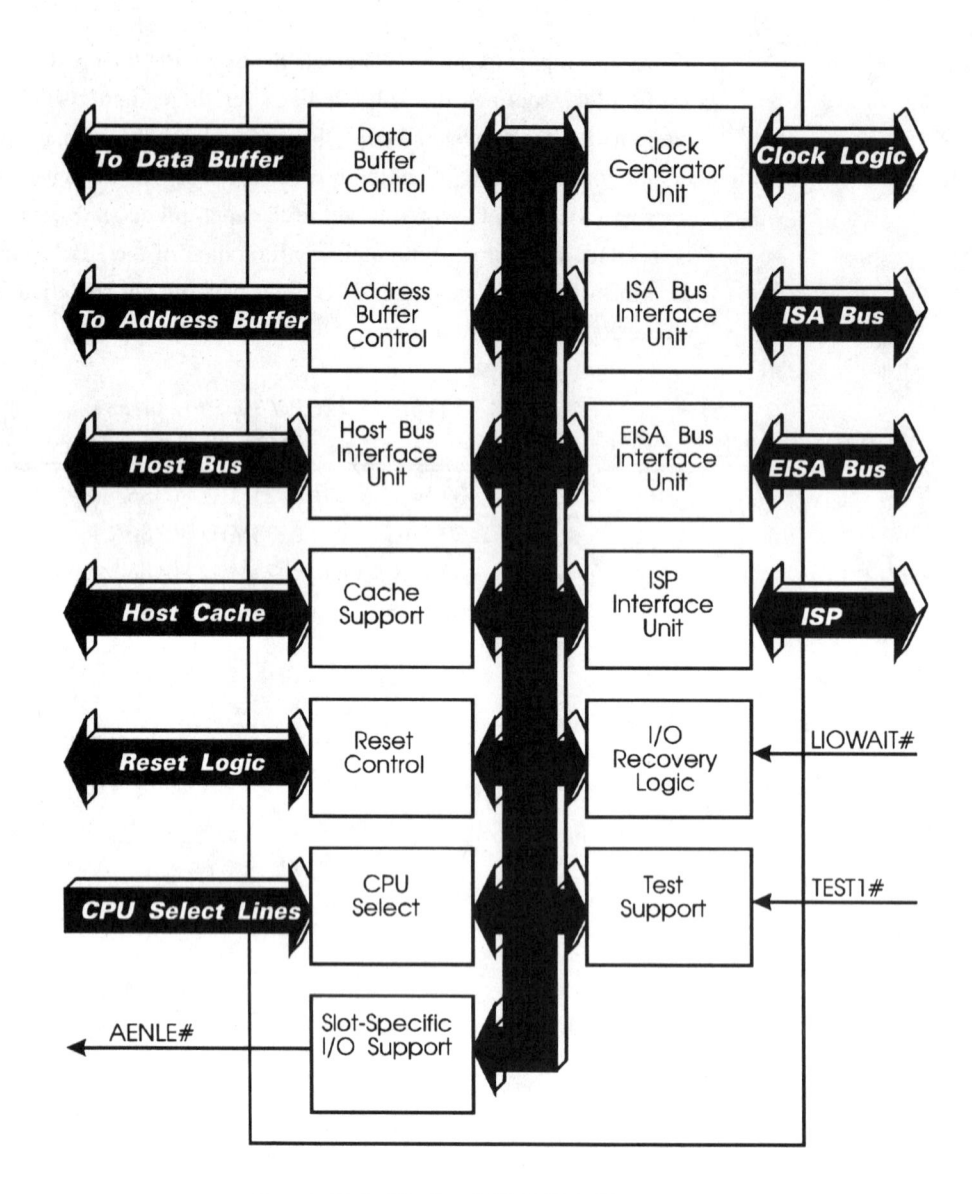

Figure 12-2. The Intel 82358DT EBC

The Intel 82350DT EISA Chip Set

Data Buffer Control and the 82352 EISA Bus Buffer (EBB)

General

The EBC Data Buffer Control block pictured in figure 12 - 2 uses a group of EBC output signals to:

- control the data transceivers when routing data between the host and EISA buses.
- perform data bus steering when necessary, utilizing the latches and data bus transceivers.

These transceivers and latches are located in the 82352 EISA Bus Buffer, or EBB, pictured in figure 12 - 3. Table 12 - 2 defines the EBC output signals used to control the data EBB.

Table 12-2. EBC Output Signals Used to Control the Data EBB

Signal	Pin	Description
SDCPYEN01#	4	Enables the data EBB's steering transceiver between EISA data paths zero and one. The direction of copy is defined by the state of the SDCPYUP signal. If SDCPYUP is low, the byte on EISA data path one is copied to EISA data path zero. If SDCPYUP is high, the byte on EISA data path zero is copied to EISA data path one.
SDCPYEN02#	5	Enables the data EBB's steering transceiver between EISA data paths zero and two. The direction of copy is defined by the state of the SDCPYUP signal. If SDCPYUP is low, the byte on EISA data path two is copied to EISA data path zero. If SDCPYUP is high, the byte on EISA data path zero is copied to EISA data path two.
SDCPYEN03#	6	Enables the data EBB's steering transceiver between EISA data paths zero and three. The direction of copy is defined by the state of the SDCPYUP signal. If SDCPYUP is low, the byte on EISA data path three is copied to EISA data path zero. If SDCPYUP is high, the byte on EISA data path zero is copied to EISA data path three.

EISA System Architecture

Signal	Pin	Description
SDCPYEN13#	7	Enables the data EBB's steering transceiver between EISA data paths one and three. The direction of copy is defined by the state of the SDCPYUP signal. If SDCPYUP is low, the byte on EISA data path three is copied to EISA data path one. If SDCPYUP is high, the byte on EISA data path one is copied to EISA data path three.
SDCPYUP	8	See SDCPYEN01# description.
SDHDLE3#	10	When activated by the EBC, causes the data EBB to latch the data byte on EISA data path three.
SDHDLE2#	11	When activated by the EBC, causes the data EBB to latch the data byte on EISA data path two.
SDHDLE1#	12	When activated by the EBC, causes the data EBB to latch the data byte on EISA data path one.
SDHDLE0#	13	When activated by the EBC, causes the data EBB to latch the data byte on EISA data path zero.
SDOE2#	14	When activated by the EBC, causes the data EBB to drive the two previously latched bytes onto EISA data paths two and three.
SDOE1#	16	When activated by the EBC, causes the data EBB to drive the previously latched byte onto EISA data path one.
SDOE0#	17	When activated by the EBC, causes the data EBB to drive the previously latched byte onto EISA data path zero.
HDSDLE1#	18	When activated by the EBC, causes the data EBB to latch four bytes from the host data bus.
HDOE1#	20	When activated by the EBC, causes the data EBB to drive the two bytes latched into the path two and three latches onto paths two and three of the host data bus.
HDOE0	22	When activated by the EBC, causes the data EBB to drive the two bytes latched into the path zero and one latches onto paths zero and one of the host data bus.

The Intel 82350DT EISA Chip Set

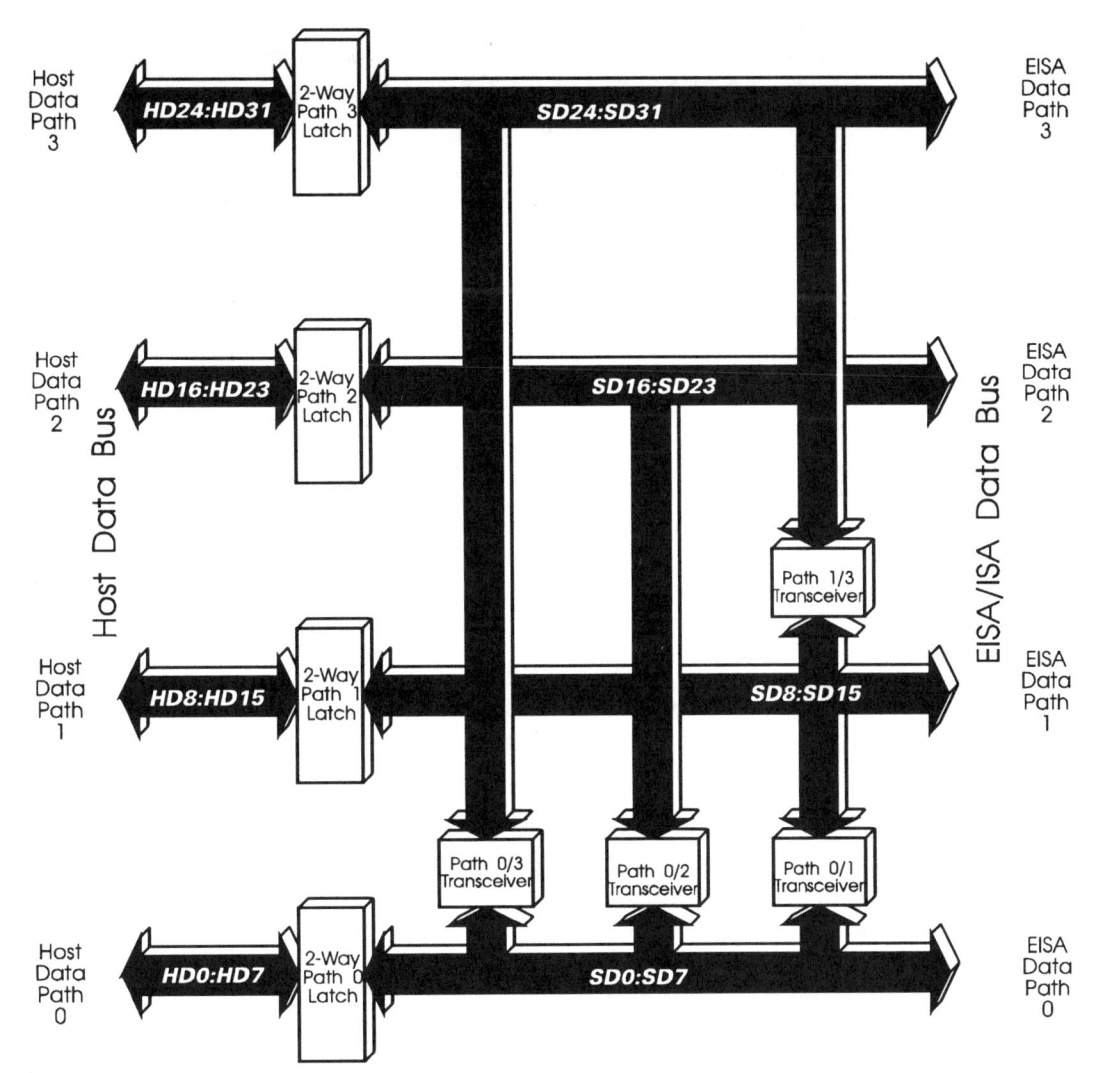

Figure 12-3. The Data EISA Bus Buffer, or EBB

Transfer Between a 32-bit EISA Bus Master and an 8-bit ISA Slave

Two examples are described in the following paragraphs: a 32-bit read from an 8-bit ISA slave; and a 32-bit write to an 8-bit ISA slave. Refer to figure 12 - 4 during the discussion.

In the first example, the bus master is initiating a 32-bit read from an 8-bit ISA slave. The 32-bit bus master begins the bus cycle by placing the doubleword address on LA2:LA31, setting M/IO# to the appropriate state, and activating all four byte enable lines, BE0#:BE3#. The bus master sets the

W/R# bus cycle definition line low to indicate a read is in progress and activates the START# signal to indicate that the bus cycle has begun.

At the end of address time, which is one BCLK cycle in duration, the 32-bit bus master deactivates START#, the EBC activates CMD# and the bus master samples the EX32# line to see if a 32-bit EISA slave is responding. When the bus master is addressing an 8 or 16-bit ISA, a 16-bit EISA slave, or an 8 or 16-bit host slave, EX32# will not be returned active. Since an 8-bit ISA slave is being addressed in this example, EX32# is not sampled active by the bus master. At the end of address time, the EBC also samples EX32#, as well as EX16#, M16# and IO16# to determine the size and type of slave device that is responding. Since none of these four signals are sampled active, the EBC determines that the bus master is currently addressing an 8-bit ISA slave. Upon determining that the addressed slave is not connected to all four data paths, the bus master assumes that the EBC and EBB will take care of any data bus steering that may be necessary to accomplish the transfer. In order to let the EBC and EBB use the buses for steering, the bus master disconnects from the four data paths, the byte enable lines and the START# signal at midpoint of data time. The bus master continues to drive the doubleword address onto LA2:LA31, however, as well as M/IO# and W/R#. The bus master then samples the state of the EX32# line at the end of each data time until it is sampled active. During this period of time, data bus steering is being performed by the EBC and EBB.

The EBC converts the M/IO# and W/R# settings to an active level on either the IORC#, SMRDC# or MRDC# bus cycle definition line on the ISA portion of the bus. The EBC also converts the active level on the byte enable lines to zeros on SA0 and SA1 and a low on SBHE#. The addressed 8-bit ISA slave responds to the read and drives the byte from the addressed location onto the lower data path, SD0:SD7. The EBC monitors NOWS# and CHRDY to determine when the slave is ready to end the transfer and then latches the byte into the path zero latch in the data EBB using the EBC's SDHDLE0# output signal. The EBC deactivates CMD#.

Having completed the transfer of the first of the four bytes, the EBC increments the address by setting SA0 to a one, SA1 to a zero and SBHE# active. The EBC then tricks the addressed slave into thinking a new bus cycle has begun by generating START# again, followed by CMD#. When the EBC senses the changes on START# and CMD#, it turns the ISA command line off (SMRDC#, SMWTC#, IORC# or IOWC#) and then on again, causing the 8-bit ISA device to think another bus cycle has begun. The 8-bit ISA slave then drives the byte from the currently addressed location onto data path zero,

SD0:SD7. The EBC again monitors NOWS# and CHRDY to determine when the slave is ready to end the transfer. The EBC then copies the byte to data path one and latches it into the data EBB's path one data latch. This is accomplished by activating the EBC's SDCPYEN01# and SDCPYUP output signals to copy the byte from path zero to path one and then latching the byte into the path one latch in the data EBB using the EBC's SDHDLE1# output signal. The first two of the four requested data bytes are now latched into the data EBB.

The EBC again increments the address by setting SA0 to a zero, SA1 to a one and SBHE# active. The EBC again tricks the addressed slave into thinking a new bus cycle has begun by generating START#, followed by CMD#, causing the appropriate ISA command line to be deactivated and then activated again. The 8-bit ISA slave then drives the byte from the currently addressed location onto data path zero, SD0:SD7. The EBC again monitors NOWS# and CHRDY to determine when the slave is ready to end the transfer. The EBC then copies the byte to data path two and latches it into the data EBB's path two data latch. This is accomplished by activating the EBC's SDCPYEN02# and SDCPYUP output signals to copy the byte from path zero to path two and then latching the byte into the path two latch in the data EBB using the EBC's SDHDLE2# output signal. The first three of the four requested data bytes are now latched into the data EBB.

The EBC again increments the address by setting SA0 and SA1 high and SBHE# active. The EBC again tricks the addressed slave into thinking a new bus cycle has begun by generating START#, followed by CMD#, causing the appropriate ISA command line to be deactivated and then activated again. The 8-bit ISA slave then drives the byte from the currently addressed location onto data path zero, SD0:SD7. The EBC again monitors NOWS# and CHRDY to determine when the slave is ready to end the transfer. The EBC then copies the byte to data path three and latches it into the data EBB's path three data latch. This is accomplished by activating the EBC's SDCPYEN03# and SDCPYUP output signals to copy the byte from path zero to path three and then latching the byte into the path three latch in the data EBB using the EBC's SDHDLE3# output signal. All four of the requested data bytes are now latched into the data EBB.

Using its SDOE0#, SDOE1# and SDOE2# outputs, the EBC now commands the data EBB to drive the four latched bytes onto the four data paths. The EBC activates the EX32# and EX16# lines at the midpoint of the current data time to signal the end of data bus steering. At the trailing-edge of the current data time, the 32-bit EISA bus master samples EX32# active, indicating that the

EISA System Architecture

necessary steering has been completed. The bus master can begin to drive the address for the next bus cycle onto the buses at the midpoint of the next data time. The current bus cycle completes at the end of this last data time. Since this is a read bus cycle, the bus master reads the four bytes from the four data paths when the EBC deactivates CMD#, ending the bus cycle.

In the second example, the bus master is initiating a 32-bit write to an 8-bit ISA slave. The 32-bit bus master begins the bus cycle by placing the doubleword address on LA2:LA31, setting M/IO# to the appropriate state, and activating all four byte enable lines, BE0#:BE3#. The bus master sets the W/R# bus cycle definition line high to indicate a write is in progress and activates the START# signal to indicate that the bus cycle has begun. At the midpoint of address time, the bus master begins to drive the four bytes onto the four EISA data paths.

At the end of address time, which is one BCLK cycle in duration, the following events occur:

- the 32-bit bus master deactivates START# and the EBC activates CMD#.
- Using its four SDHDLEx# outputs, the EBC causes the data EBB to latch the four data bytes being driven onto the four EISA data paths by the bus master.
- The bus master samples the EX32# line to see if a 32-bit EISA slave is responding.

When the bus master is addressing an 8 or 16-bit ISA, a 16-bit EISA slave, or an 8 or 16-bit host slave, EX32# will not be returned active. Since an 8-bit ISA slave is being addressed in this example, EX32# is not sampled active by the bus master. At the end of address time, the EBC also samples EX32#, as well as EX16#, M16# and IO16# to determine the size and type of slave device that is responding. Since none of these four signals are sampled active, the EBC determines that the bus master is currently addressing an 8-bit ISA slave. Upon determining that the addressed slave is not connected to all four data paths, the bus master assumes that the EBC and EBB will take care of any data bus steering that may be necessary to accomplish the transfer. In order to let the EBC and EBB use the buses for steering, the bus master disconnects from the four data paths, the byte enable lines and the START# signal at midpoint of data time. The bus master continues to drive the doubleword address onto LA2:LA31, however, as well as M/IO# and W/R#. The bus master then samples the state of the EX32# line at the end of each data time until it is

The Intel 82350DT EISA Chip Set

sampled active. During this period of time, data bus steering is being performed by the EBC and EBB.

The EBC converts the M/IO# and W/R# settings to an active level on either the IOWC#, SMWTC# or MWTC# bus cycle definition line on the ISA portion of the bus. The EBC also converts the active level on the byte enable lines to zeros on SA0 and SA1 and a low on SBHE#. Using its SDOE0# output, the EBC causes the data EBB to drive the byte latched in its path zero latch onto EISA data path zero. The addressed 8-bit ISA slave responds to the write and accepts the byte from the lower data path, SD0:SD7. The EBC monitors NOWS# and CHRDY to determine when the slave is ready to end the transfer. The EBC deactivates CMD# and SDOE0#, causing the data EBB to cease driving the byte onto EISA data path zero.

Having completed the transfer of the first of the four bytes, the EBC increments the address by setting SA0 to a one, SA1 to a zero and SBHE# active. The EBC then tricks the addressed slave into thinking a new bus cycle has begun by generating START# again, followed by CMD#. This causes the appropriate ISA command line to be deactivated and then activated again. Using its SDCPYUP, SDCPYEN01# and SDOE1# output signals, the EBC causes the data EBB to drive the byte latched in its path one latch onto path one and copies it down to EISA data path zero. The 8-bit ISA slave then accepts the byte from EISA data path zero, SD0:SD7. The EBC again monitors NOWS# and CHRDY to determine when the slave is ready to end the transfer. The first two of the four data bytes have been written to the target 8-bit ISA slave. The EBC deactivates CMD#, SDCPYEN01# and SDOE1#, causing the data EBB to cease driving the byte onto EISA data path one and turning off the EBB's copy transceiver.

The EBC again increments the address by setting SA0 to a zero, SA1 to a one and SBHE# active. The EBC again tricks the addressed slave into thinking a new bus cycle has begun by generating START#, followed by CMD#, causing the appropriate ISA command line to be deactivated and then activated again. Using its SDCPYUP, SDCPYEN02# and SDOE2# output signals, the EBC causes the data EBB to drive the byte latched in its path two latch onto path two and copies it down to EISA data path zero. The 8-bit ISA slave then accepts the byte from EISA data path zero, SD0:SD7. The EBC again monitors NOWS# and CHRDY to determine when the slave is ready to end the transfer. The first three of the four data bytes have been written to the target 8-bit ISA slave. The EBC deactivates CMD#, SDCPYEN02# and SDOE2#, causing the data EBB to cease driving the byte onto EISA data path two and turning off the EBB's copy transceiver.

EISA System Architecture

The EBC again increments the address by setting SA0 and SA1 high and SBHE# active. The EBC again tricks the addressed slave into thinking a new bus cycle has begun by generating START#, followed by CMD#, causing the appropriate ISA command line to be deactivated and then activated again. Using its SDCPYUP, SDCPYEN03# and SDOE2# output signals, the EBC causes the data EBB to drive the byte latched in its path three latch onto path three and copies it down to EISA data path zero. The 8-bit ISA slave then accepts the byte from EISA data path zero, SD0:SD7. The EBC again monitors NOWS# and CHRDY to determine when the slave is ready to end the transfer. All four of the requested data bytes have now been written to the target 8-bit ISA slave. The EBC deactivates CMD#, SDCPYEN03# and SDOE2#, causing the data EBB to cease driving the byte onto EISA data path three and turning off the EBB's copy transceiver.

The EBC activates the EX32# and EX16# lines at the midpoint of the current data time to signal the end of data bus steering. At the trailing-edge of the current data time, the 32-bit EISA bus master samples EX32# active, indicating that the necessary steering has been completed. The bus master can begin to drive the address for the next bus cycle onto the buses at the midpoint of the next data time. The current bus cycle completes at the end of this last data time. Since this is a write bus cycle, the bus master ends the bus cycle when the EBC deactivates CMD#.

The Intel 82350DT EISA Chip Set

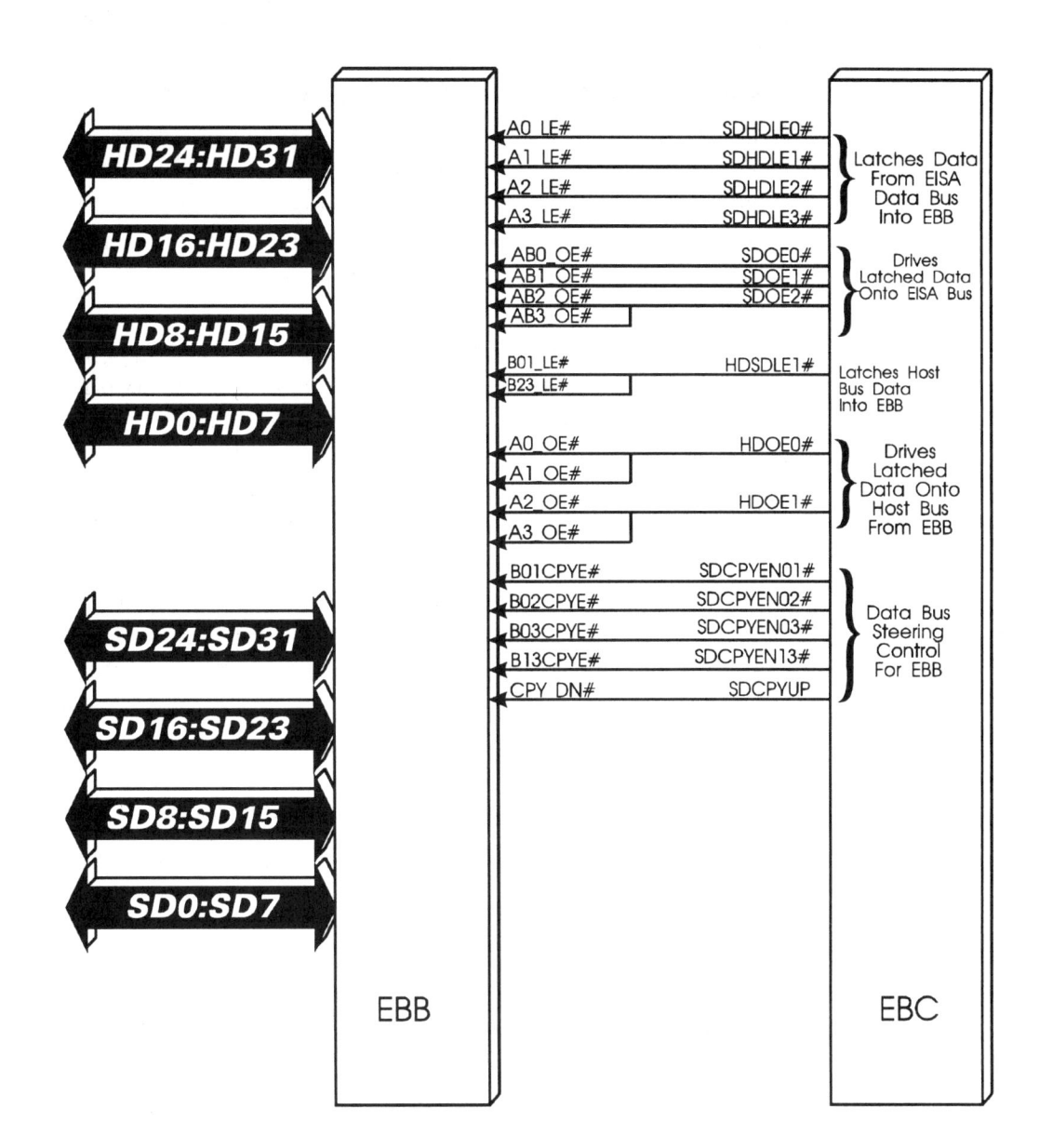

Figure 12-4. Linkage Between the EBC and the Data EBB

EISA System Architecture

Transfer Between a 32-bit EISA Bus Master and a 16-bit ISA Slave

Two examples are described in the following paragraphs: a 32-bit read from the 16-bit ISA slave; and a 32-bit write to a 16-bit ISA slave. Refer to figure 12 - 4 during the discussion.

In the first example, the bus master is initiating a 32-bit read from a 16-bit ISA slave. The 32-bit bus master begins the bus cycle by placing the doubleword address on LA2:LA31, setting M/IO# to the appropriate state, and activating all four byte enable lines, BE0#:BE3#. The bus master sets the W/R# bus cycle definition line low to indicate a read is in progress and activates the START# signal to indicate that the bus cycle has begun.

The EBC determines that a 32-bit EISA bus master has initiated the bus cycle using the criteria in table 12 - 3. HHLDA, Host Hold Acknowledge, is inactive, indicating that the host CPU is not the bus master. EXMASTER# is active and MASTER16# is inactive, indicating that a 32-bit EISA bus master is using the buses.

Table 12-3. EBC's Bus Type Determination Criteria

HHLDA	REFRESH#	EXMASTER#	MASTER16#	EMSTR16#	MSBURST#	Bus Master Type
0	1	1	1	1	1	32-bit host CPU
1	0	1	1	x	1	Refresh
1	1	0	1	1	1	32-bit EISA
1	1	0	1	1	0	32-bit EISA burst
1	1	0	pulse	1	0	downshift 32-bit EISA burst
1	1	0	0	1	1	16-bit EISA
1	1	0	0	1	0	16-bit EISA burst
1	1	1	0	0	1	16-bit ISA
1	1	1	1	1	1	DMA
1	1	1	1	1	0	DMA burst

At the end of address time, which is one BCLK cycle in duration, the 32-bit bus master deactivates START#, the EBC activates CMD# and the bus master samples the EX32# line to see if a 32-bit EISA slave is responding. When the bus master is addressing an 8 or 16-bit ISA, a 16-bit EISA slave, or an 8 or 16-bit host slave, EX32# will not be returned active. Since a 16-bit ISA slave is being addressed in this example, EX32# is not sampled active by the bus master. At the end of address time, the EBC also samples EX32#, as well as EX16#, M16# and IO16# to determine the size and type of slave device that is responding. Since either M16# or IO16# is sampled active, the EBC determines that the bus master is currently addressing a 16-bit ISA slave. Upon determining that the addressed slave is not connected to all four data paths, the bus master assumes that the EBC and EBB will take care of any data bus steering that may be necessary to accomplish the transfer. In order to let the EBC and EBB use the buses for steering, the bus master disconnects from the four data paths, the byte enable lines and the START# signal at midpoint of data time. The bus master continues to drive the doubleword address onto LA2:LA31, however, as well as M/IO# and W/R#. The bus master then samples the state of the EX32# line at the end of each data time until it is sampled active. During this period of time, data bus steering is being performed by the EBC and EBB.

The EBC converts the M/IO# and W/R# settings to an active level on either the IORC#, SMRDC# or MRDC# bus cycle definition line on the ISA portion of the bus. The EBC also converts the active level on the byte enable lines to zeros on SA0 and SA1 and a low on SBHE#. The low on SA0 and SBHE# indicates to the addressed 16-bit ISA slave that a 16-bit transfer is in progress. The addressed 16-bit ISA slave responds to the read and drives the byte from the even-addressed location onto the EISA data path zero, SD0:SD7, and the byte from the odd-addressed location onto EISA data path one, SD8:SD15. The EBC monitors NOWS# and CHRDY to determine when the slave is ready to end the transfer and then latches the two bytes into the path zero and path one latches in the data EBB using the EBC's SDHDLE0# and SDHDLE1# output signals. The EBC deactivates CMD#.

Having completed the transfer of the first two of the four bytes, the EBC increments the address by setting SA0 to a zero, SA1 to a one and SBHE# active. The EBC then tricks the addressed slave into thinking a new bus cycle has begun by generating START# again, followed by CMD#, causing the appropriate ISA command line to be deactivated and then activated again. The 16-bit ISA slave then drives the byte from the even-addressed location onto EISA data path zero, SD0:SD7, and the byte from the odd-addressed location onto EISA data path one. The EBC again monitors NOWS# and CHRDY to determine when the slave is ready to end the transfer. The EBC then copies the two bytes on paths zero and one to data paths two and three and latches them into the data EBB's path two and three data latches. This is accomplished by activating the EBC's SDCPYEN02#, SDCPYEN13# and SDCPYUP output signals to copy the byte from path zero to path two, the byte from path one to path three, and then latching the bytes into the path two and three latches in the data EBB using the EBC's SDHDLE2# and SDHDLE3# output signals. All four of the requested data bytes are now latched into the data EBB.

EISA System Architecture

Using its SDOE0#, SDOE1# and SDOE2# outputs, the EBC now commands the data EBB to drive the four latched bytes onto the four data paths. The EBC activates the EX32# and EX16# lines at the midpoint of the current data time to signal the end of data bus steering. At the trailing-edge of the current data time, the 32-bit EISA bus master samples EX32# active, indicating that the necessary steering has been completed. The bus master can begin to drive the address for the next bus cycle onto the buses at the midpoint of the next data time. The current bus cycle completes at the end of this last data time. Since this is a read bus cycle, the bus master reads the four bytes from the four data paths when the EBC deactivates CMD#, ending the bus cycle.

In the second example, the bus master is initiating a 32-bit write to a 16-bit ISA slave. The 32-bit bus master begins the bus cycle by placing the doubleword address on LA2:LA31, setting M/IO# to the appropriate state, and activating all four byte enable lines, BE0#:BE3#. The bus master sets the W/R# bus cycle definition line high to indicate a write is in progress and activates the START# signal to indicate that the bus cycle has begun. At the midpoint of address time, the bus master begins to drive the four bytes onto the four EISA data paths.

At the end of address time, which is one BCLK cycle in duration, the following events occur:

- the 32-bit bus master deactivates START# and the EBC activates CMD#.
- Using its four SDHDLEx# outputs, the EBC causes the data EBB to latch the four data bytes being driven onto the four EISA data paths by the bus master.
- The bus master samples the EX32# line to see if a 32-bit EISA slave is responding.

When the bus master is addressing an 8 or 16-bit ISA, a 16-bit EISA slave, or an 8 or 16-bit host slave, EX32# will not be returned active. Since a 16-bit ISA slave is being addressed in this example, EX32# is not sampled active by the bus master. At the end of address time, the EBC also samples EX32#, as well as EX16#, M16# and IO16# to determine the size and type of slave device that is responding. Since either M16# or IO16# is sampled active, the EBC determines that the bus master is currently addressing a 16-bit ISA slave. Upon determining that the addressed slave is not connected to all four data paths, the bus master assumes that the EBC and EBB will take care of any data bus steering that may be necessary to accomplish the transfer. In order to let the

# The Intel 82350DT EISA Chip Set

EBC and EBB use the buses for steering, the bus master disconnects from the four data paths, the byte enable lines and the START# signal at midpoint of data time. The bus master continues to drive the doubleword address onto LA2:LA31, however, as well as M/IO# and W/R#. The bus master then samples the state of the EX32# line at the end of each data time until it is sampled active. During this period of time, data bus steering is being performed by the EBC and EBB.

The EBC converts the M/IO# and W/R# settings to an active level on either the IOWC#, SMWTC# or MWTC# bus cycle definition line on the ISA portion of the bus. The EBC also converts the active level on the byte enable lines to zeros on SA0 and SA1 and a low on SBHE#. Using its SDOE0# and SDOE1# outputs, the EBC causes the data EBB to drive the bytes latched in its path zero and one latches onto EISA data paths zero and one. The addressed 16-bit ISA slave responds to the write and accepts the two bytes from the EISA data paths zero and one, SD0:SD7 and SD8:SD15. The EBC monitors NOWS# and CHRDY to determine when the slave is ready to end the transfer. The EBC deactivates CMD#, SDOE0# and SDOE1#, causing the data EBB to cease driving the two bytes onto EISA data paths zero and one.

The EBC increments the address by setting SA0 to a zero, SA1 to a one and SBHE# active. The EBC tricks the addressed slave into thinking a new bus cycle has begun by generating START#, followed by CMD#, causing the appropriate ISA command line to be deactivated and then activated again. Using its SDCPYUP, SDCPYEN02#, SDCPYEN13# and SDOE2# output signals, the EBC causes the data EBB to drive the two bytes latched in its path two and three latches onto paths two and three and copies them down to EISA data paths zero and one. The 16-bit ISA slave then accepts the two bytes from EISA data paths zero and one, SD0:SD7 and SD8:SD15. The EBC again monitors NOWS# and CHRDY to determine when the slave is ready to end the transfer. All four of the four data bytes have been written to the target 16-bit ISA slave. The EBC deactivates CMD#, SDCPYEN02#, SDCPYEN13# and SDOE2#, causing the data EBB to cease driving the two bytes onto EISA data paths two and three and turning off the EBB's two copy transceivers.

The EBC activates the EX32# and EX16# lines at the midpoint of the current data time to signal the end of data bus steering. At the trailing-edge of the current data time, the 32-bit EISA bus master samples EX32# active, indicating that the necessary steering has been completed. The bus master can begin to drive the address for the next bus cycle onto the buses at the midpoint of the next data time. The current bus cycle completes at the end of this last

EISA System Architecture

data time. Since this is a write bus cycle, the bus master ends the bus cycle when the EBC deactivates CMD#.

Transfer Between a 32-bit EISA Bus Master and a 16-bit EISA Slave

Two examples are described in the following paragraphs: a 32-bit read from the 16-bit EISA slave; and a 32-bit write to a 16-bit EISA slave. Refer to figure 12 - 4 during the discussion.

In the first example, the bus master is initiating a 32-bit read from a 16-bit EISA slave. The 32-bit bus master begins the bus cycle by placing the doubleword address on LA2:LA31, setting M/IO# to the appropriate state, and activating all four byte enable lines, BE0#:BE3#. The bus master sets the W/R# bus cycle definition line low to indicate a read is in progress and activates the START# signal to indicate that the bus cycle has begun.

At the end of address time, which is one BCLK cycle in duration, the 32-bit bus master deactivates START#, the EBC activates CMD# and the bus master samples the EX32# line to see if a 32-bit EISA slave is responding. When the bus master is addressing an 8 or 16-bit ISA, a 16-bit EISA slave, or an 8 or 16-bit host slave, EX32# will not be returned active. Since a 16-bit EISA slave is being addressed in this example, EX32# is not sampled active by the bus master. At the end of address time, the EBC also samples EX32#, as well as EX16#, M16# and IO16# to determine the size and type of slave device that is responding. Since EX16# is sampled active, the EBC determines that the bus master is currently addressing a 16-bit EISA slave. Upon determining that the addressed slave is not connected to all four data paths, the bus master assumes that the EBC and EBB will take care of any data bus steering that may be necessary to accomplish the transfer. In order to let the EBC and EBB use the buses for steering, the bus master disconnects from the four data paths, the byte enable lines and the START# signal at midpoint of data time. The bus master continues to drive the doubleword address onto LA2:LA31, however, as well as M/IO# and W/R#. The bus master then samples the state of the EX32# line at the end of each data time until it is sampled active. During this period of time, data bus steering is being performed by the EBC and EBB.

The active level on BE0# and BE1# indicates to the addressed 16-bit EISA slave that a 16-bit transfer is in progress involving the first two locations in the currently addressed doubleword. The addressed 16-bit EISA slave responds to the read and drives the byte from the even-addressed location onto the EISA data path zero, SD0:SD7, and the byte from the odd-addressed location onto

The Intel 82350DT EISA Chip Set

EISA data path one, SD8:SD15. The EBC monitors EXRDY to determine when the slave is ready to end the transfer and then latches the two bytes into the path zero and path one latches in the data EBB using the EBC's SDHDLE0# and SDHDLE1# output signals. The EBC deactivates CMD#.

The EBC now addresses the last two bytes in the addressed doubleword by activating BE2# and BE3# and deactivating BE0# and BE1#. The EBC then tricks the addressed slave into thinking a new bus cycle has begun by generating START# again, followed by CMD#. The 16-bit EISA slave then drives the byte from the even-addressed location onto EISA data path zero, SD0:SD7, and the byte from the odd-addressed location onto EISA data path one. The EBC again monitors EXRDY to determine when the slave is ready to end the transfer. The EBC then copies the two bytes on paths zero and one to data paths two and three and latches them into the data EBB's path two and three data latches. This is accomplished by activating the EBC's SDCPYEN02#, SDCPYEN13# and SDCPYUP output signals to copy the byte from path zero to path two, the byte from path one to path three, and then latching the bytes into the path two and three latches in the data EBB using the EBC's SDHDLE2# and SDHDLE3# output signals. All four of the requested data bytes are now latched into the data EBB.

Using its SDOE0#, SDOE1# and SDOE2# outputs, the EBC now commands the data EBB to drive the four latched bytes onto the four data paths. The EBC activates the EX32# and EX16# lines at the midpoint of the current data time to signal the end of data bus steering. At the trailing-edge of the current data time, the 32-bit EISA bus master samples EX32# active, indicating that the necessary steering has been completed. The bus master can begin to drive the address for the next bus cycle onto the buses at the midpoint of the next data time. The current bus cycle completes at the end of this last data time. Since this is a read bus cycle, the bus master reads the four bytes from the four data paths when the EBC deactivates CMD#, ending the bus cycle.

In the second example, the bus master is initiating a 32-bit write to a 16-bit EISA slave. The 32-bit EISA bus master begins the bus cycle by placing the doubleword address on LA2:LA31, setting M/IO# to the appropriate state, and activating all four byte enable lines, BE0#:BE3#. The bus master sets the W/R# bus cycle definition line high to indicate a write is in progress and activates the START# signal to indicate that the bus cycle has begun. At the midpoint of address time, the bus master begins to drive the four bytes onto the four EISA data paths.

EISA System Architecture

At the end of address time, which is one BCLK cycle in duration, the following events occur:

- the 32-bit bus master deactivates START# and the EBC activates CMD#.
- Using its four SDHDLEx# outputs, the EBC causes the data EBB to latch the four data bytes being driven onto the four EISA data paths by the bus master.
- The bus master samples the EX32# line to see if a 32-bit EISA slave is responding.

When the bus master is addressing an 8 or 16-bit ISA, a 16-bit EISA slave, or an 8 or 16-bit host slave, EX32# will not be returned active. Since a 16-bit EISA slave is being addressed in this example, EX32# is not sampled active by the bus master. At the end of address time, the EBC also samples EX32#, as well as EX16#, M16# and IO16# to determine the size and type of slave device that is responding. Since EX16# is sampled active, the EBC determines that the bus master is currently addressing a 16-bit EISA slave. Upon determining that the addressed slave is not connected to all four data paths, the bus master assumes that the EBC and EBB will take care of any data bus steering that may be necessary to accomplish the transfer. In order to let the EBC and EBB use the buses for steering, the bus master disconnects from the four data paths, the byte enable lines and the START# signal at midpoint of data time. The bus master continues to drive the doubleword address onto LA2:LA31, however, as well as M/IO# and W/R#. The bus master then samples the state of the EX32# line at the end of each data time until it is sampled active. During this period of time, data bus steering is being performed by the EBC and EBB.

The active level on BE0# and BE1# indicates to the addressed 16-bit EISA slave that a 16-bit transfer is in progress involving the first two locations in the currently addressed doubleword. Using its SDOE0# and SDOE1# outputs, the EBC causes the data EBB to drive the bytes latched in its path zero and one latches onto EISA data paths zero and one. The addressed 16-bit EISA slave responds to the write and accepts the two bytes from the EISA data paths zero and one, SD0:SD7 and SD8:SD15. The EBC monitors EXRDY to determine when the slave is ready to end the transfer. The EBC deactivates CMD#, SDOE0# and SDOE1#, causing the data EBB to cease driving the two bytes onto EISA data paths zero and one.

The EBC now addresses the last two bytes in the addressed doubleword by activating BE2# and BE3# and deactivating BE0# and BE1#. The EBC tricks the addressed slave into thinking a new bus cycle has begun by generating

START#, followed by CMD#. Using its SDCPYUP, SDCPYEN02#, SDCPYEN13# and SDOE2# output signals, the EBC causes the data EBB to drive the two bytes latched in its path two and three latches onto paths two and three and copies them down to EISA data paths zero and one. The 16-bit EISA slave then accepts the two bytes from EISA data paths zero and one, SD0:SD7 and SD8:SD15. The EBC again monitors EXRDY to determine when the slave is ready to end the transfer. All four of the four data bytes have been written to the target 16-bit EISA slave. The EBC deactivates CMD#, SDCPYEN02#, SDCPYEN13# and SDOE2#, causing the data EBB to cease driving the two bytes onto EISA data paths two and three and turning off the EBB's two copy transceivers.

The EBC activates the EX32# and EX16# lines at the midpoint of the current data time to signal the end of data bus steering. At the trailing-edge of the current data time, the 32-bit EISA bus master samples EX32# active, indicating that the necessary steering has been completed. The bus master can begin to drive the address for the next bus cycle onto the buses at the midpoint of the next data time. The current bus cycle completes at the end of this last data time. Since this is a write bus cycle, the bus master ends the bus cycle when the EBC deactivates CMD#.

Transfer Between a 32-bit EISA Bus Master and a 32-bit EISA Slave

Two examples are described in the following paragraphs: a 32-bit read from the 32-bit EISA slave; and a 32-bit write to a 32-bit EISA slave. Refer to figure 12 - 4 during the discussion.

In the first example, the bus master is initiating a 32-bit read from a 32-bit EISA slave. The 32-bit bus master begins the bus cycle by placing the doubleword address on LA2:LA31, setting M/IO# to the appropriate state, and activating all four byte enable lines, BE0#:BE3#. The bus master sets the W/R# bus cycle definition line low to indicate a read is in progress and activates the START# signal to indicate that the bus cycle has begun.

At the end of address time, which is one BCLK cycle in duration, the 32-bit bus master deactivates START#, the EBC activates CMD# and the bus master samples the EX32# line to see if a 32-bit EISA slave is responding. When the bus master is addressing an 8 or 16-bit ISA, a 16-bit EISA slave, or an 8 or 16-bit host slave, EX32# will not be returned active. Since a 32-bit EISA slave is being addressed in this example, EX32# is sampled active by the bus master. At the end of address time, the EBC also samples EX32#, as well as EX16#,

M16# and IO16# to determine the size and type of slave device that is responding. Since EX32# is sampled active, the EBC determines that the bus master is currently addressing a 32-bit EISA slave. Upon determining that the addressed slave is connected to all four data paths, the bus master recognizes that the EBC and EBB will not have to perform data bus steering.

The active level on all four byte enable lines indicates to the addressed 32-bit EISA slave that a 32-bit transfer is in progress involving all four locations in the currently addressed doubleword. The addressed 32-bit EISA slave responds to the read and drives the four bytes onto their respective EISA data paths. The bus master monitors EXRDY to determine when the slave is ready to end the transfer and latches the four bytes when the EBC deactivates CMD#.

In the second example, the bus master is initiating a 32-bit write to a 32-bit EISA slave. The 32-bit EISA bus master begins the bus cycle by placing the doubleword address on LA2:LA31, setting M/IO# to the appropriate state, and activating all four byte enable lines, BE0#:BE3#. The bus master sets the W/R# bus cycle definition line high to indicate a write is in progress and activates the START# signal to indicate that the bus cycle has begun. At the midpoint of address time, the bus master begins to drive the four bytes onto the four EISA data paths.

At the end of address time, which is one BCLK cycle in duration, the following events occur:

- the 32-bit bus master deactivates START# and the EBC activates CMD#.
- The bus master samples the EX32# line to see if a 32-bit EISA slave is responding.

When the bus master is addressing an 8 or 16-bit ISA, a 16-bit EISA slave, or an 8 or 16-bit host slave, EX32# will not be returned active. Since a 32-bit EISA slave is being addressed in this example, EX32# is sampled active by the bus master. At the end of address time, the EBC also samples EX32#, as well as EX16#, M16# and IO16# to determine the size and type of slave device that is responding. Since EX32# is sampled active, the EBC determines that the bus master is currently addressing a 32-bit EISA slave. Upon determining that the addressed slave is connected to all four data paths, the bus master recognizes that the EBC and EBB will not have to perform data bus steering.

The active level on the four byte enable lines indicates to the addressed 32-bit EISA slave that a 32-bit transfer is in progress involving all four locations in the currently addressed doubleword. The addressed 32-bit EISA slave responds to the write and accepts the four bytes from EISA data paths zero through three. The bus master monitors EXRDY to determine when the slave is ready to end the transfer. Since this is a write bus cycle, the bus master ends the bus cycle when the EBC deactivates CMD#.

Transfer Between a 32-bit EISA Bus Master and an 32-bit Host Slave

It should be noted that all host bus slaves are 32-bit devices. In this example, assume that a 32-bit EISA bus master initiates a bus cycle to read two bytes of data from an 32-bit host slave. Assume also that they are the first two bytes in the addressed doubleword. The 32-bit EISA bus master begins the bus cycle by placing the doubleword address on LA2:LA31, setting M/IO# to the appropriate state, and activating byte enable lines BE0# and BE1#. The bus master sets the W/R# bus cycle definition line low to indicate a read is in progress and activates the START# signal to indicate that the bus cycle has begun.

The EBC determines that a 32-bit EISA bus master has initiated the bus cycle using the criteria in table 12 - 3. HHLDA, Host Hold Acknowledge, is inactive, indicating that the host CPU is not the bus master. EXMASTER# is active and MASTER16# is inactive, indicating that a 32-bit EISA bus master is using the buses. The EBC determines that a host slave is responding by sampling either HLOCMEM# or HLOCIO# active. Having already determined that the bus cycle was initiated by an EISA bus master, the EBC generates EX32# to inform the bus master that a 32-bit device is responding.

At the end of address time, which is one BCLK cycle in duration, the 32-bit bus master deactivates START#, the EBC activates CMD# and the bus master samples the EX32# line to see if a 32-bit EISA slave is responding. When the bus master is addressing an 8 or 16-bit ISA, a 16-bit EISA slave, or an 8 or 16-bit host slave, EX32# will not be returned active. Since a 32-bit slave is being addressed in this example, EX32# is sampled active by the bus master. Upon determining that the addressed slave is connected to all four data paths, the bus master recognizes that the EBC and EBB will not have to perform data bus steering.

The EBC propagates the state of the EISA byte enable lines through to the host byte enable lines, HBE0#:HBE3#. The active level on byte enable lines HBE0# and HBE1# indicates to the addressed 32-bit host slave that a 16-bit transfer is in progress involving the first two locations in the currently addressed doubleword. The addressed 32-bit host slave responds to the read and drives the two requested bytes onto their respective EISA data paths, HD0:HD7 and HD8:HD15. The EBC causes the data EBB to latch the two bytes by activating its HDSDLE1# output. It then gates the two latched bytes onto paths zero and one of the EISA data bus by activating its SDOE0# and SDOE1# outputs.

The bus master monitors EXRDY to determine when the slave is ready to end the transfer and then latches the two bytes when the EBC deactivates CMD#.

Transfer Between a 16-bit EISA Bus Master and an 8-bit ISA Slave

This example assumes that a 16-bit EISA bus master is writing two bytes to the first two locations of a doubleword located within an 8-bit ISA slave. When the 16-bit EISA bus master initiates a bus cycle, it performs the following functions:

- drives the MASTER16# line active to inform the EBC that a 16-bit bus master has initiated the bus cycle.
- drives the doubleword address onto LA2:LA31 and sets the M/IO# line to the appropriate state.
- drives the START# signal active.
- sets W/R# and the byte enable lines to the appropriate states.
- During a write transfer, the bus master starts to drive data onto EISA data path zero and/or path one at the midpoint of address time.

At the trailing-edge of address time, the bus master deactivates START# and the EBC activates CMD# to indicate the beginning of data time. The bus master samples EX16# and EX32# to determine if the currently addressed device is attached to at least the lower two data paths. Since this example assumes that the bus master is addressing an 8-bit ISA slave, neither EX16# nor EX32# will be sampled active. Upon determining that the addressed slave is not connected to the lower two EISA data paths, the bus master assumes that the EBC and EBB will take care of any data bus steering that may be necessary to accomplish the transfer. Using its SDHDLE0# and SDHDLE1# outputs, the EBC causes the data EBB to latch the two bytes being driven onto EISA data paths zero and one by the bus master.

In order to let the EBC and EBB use the buses for steering, the bus master disconnects from the two data paths, the byte enable lines and the START# signal at the midpoint of data time. The bus master continues to drive the

The Intel 82350DT EISA Chip Set

doubleword address onto LA2:LA31, however, as well as M/IO# and W/R#. The bus master then samples the state of the EX16# line at the end of each data time until it is sampled active. During this period of time, data bus steering is being performed by the EBC and EBB.

When the EBC determines that an ISA device is responding, the EBC converts M/IO# and W/R# to an active level on one of the following ISA bus cycle definition signals:

- IORC#
- IOWC#
- MRDC#
- MWTC#
- SMRDC#
- SMWTC#

In this example, either the IOWC#, MWTC# or SMWTC# line would be activated by the EBC. The EBC also converts the setting on the EISA byte enable lines to the appropriate setting on SA0, SA1 and SBHE#. In this case, the active level on BE0# and BE1# would be converted to a low on SA0, SA1 and SBHE# on the ISA address bus, indicating that the bus master is addressing an even location and the next sequential odd location and will use the lower two data paths to transfer the two bytes. When the bus master has disconnected from the data bus, START# and the byte enable lines at the midpoint of data time, the EBC initiates the necessary data bus steering.

Using its SDOE0# output, the EBC causes the data byte latched into the data EBB's path zero latch to be driven onto path zero, SD0:SD7. This byte is written into the even-addressed location within the target 8-bit ISA slave. The EBC monitors NOWS# and CHRDY to determine when the slave is ready to end the transfer. The EBC then deactivates CMD# and SDOE0#, causing the data EBB to cease driving the byte onto EISA data path zero.

Having completed the transfer of the first of the four bytes, the EBC increments the address by setting SA0 to a one, SA1 to a zero and SBHE# active. The EBC then tricks the addressed slave into thinking a new bus cycle has begun by generating START# again, followed by CMD#, causing the appropriate ISA command line to be deactivated and then activated again. Using its SDCPYUP, SDCPYEN01# and SDOE1# output signals, the EBC causes the data EBB to drive the byte latched in its path one latch onto path one and copies it down to EISA data path zero. The 8-bit ISA slave then accepts the byte from EISA data path zero, SD0:SD7. The EBC again monitors

EISA System Architecture

NOWS# and CHRDY to determine when the slave is ready to end the transfer. Both data bytes have now been written to the target 8-bit ISA slave. The EBC deactivates CMD#, SDCPYEN01# and SDOE1#, causing the data EBB to cease driving the byte onto EISA data path one and turning off the EBB's copy transceiver.

The EBC activates the EX32# and EX16# lines at the midpoint of the current data time to signal the end of data bus steering. At the trailing-edge of the current data time, the 16-bit EISA bus master samples EX16# active, indicating that the necessary steering has been completed. The bus master can begin to drive the address for the next bus cycle onto the buses at the midpoint of the next data time. The current bus cycle completes at the end of this last data time. Since this is a write bus cycle, the bus master ends the bus cycle when the EBC deactivates CMD#.

Transfer Between a 16-bit EISA Bus Master and a 16-bit ISA Slave

This example assumes that a 16-bit EISA bus master is reading two bytes from the last two locations of a doubleword located within a 16-bit ISA slave. When the 16-bit EISA bus master initiates a bus cycle, it performs the following functions:

- drives the MASTER16# line active to inform the EBC that a 16-bit bus master has initiated the bus cycle.
- drives the doubleword address onto LA2:LA31 and sets the M/IO# line to the appropriate state.
- drives the START# signal active.
- sets W/R# and the byte enable lines to the appropriate states. In this example, W/R# is set low, indicating a read, and BE2# and BE3# are set active.

At the trailing-edge of address time, the bus master deactivates START# and the EBC activates CMD# to indicate the beginning of data time. The bus master samples EX16# and EX32# to determine if the currently addressed device is at least attached to the lower two data paths and supports EISA bus cycle timing. Since this example assumes that the bus master is addressing a 16-bit ISA slave, neither EX16# nor EX32# will be sampled active. The EBC will, however, sample either M16# or IO16# active indicating a 16-bit ISA slave is responding. Upon determining that the addressed slave is not capable of responding to EISA bus cycle timing, the bus master assumes that the EBC and EBB will take care of any data bus steering that may be necessary to accomplish the transfer. In this particular example, a 16-bit EISA bus master is communicating with a 16-bit ISA slave. Since both devices are connected to EISA data paths zero and one, no steering is actually necessary. The bus master, however, having no indication as to whether the addressed ISA slave is an 8 or 16-bit device, assumes that steering may be necessary and surrenders the data bus, byte enable lines and START# to the EBC's control. This is done at the midpoint of data time. The bus master continues to drive the doubleword address onto LA2:LA31, however, as well as M/IO# and W/R#. The bus master then samples the state of the EX16# line at the end of each data time until it is sampled active. During this period of time, data bus steering is being performed by the EBC and EBB.

When the EBC determines that an ISA device is responding, the EBC converts M/IO# and W/R# to an active level on one of the following ISA bus cycle definition signals:

- IORC#
- IOWC#
- MRDC#
- MWTC#
- SMRDC#
- SMWTC#

In this example, either the IORC#, MRDC# or SMRDC# line would be activated by the EBC. The EBC also converts the setting on the EISA byte enable lines to the appropriate setting on SA0, SA1 and SBHE#. In this case, the active level on BE2# and BE3# would be converted to a low on SA0, and SBHE# and a high on SA1 on the ISA address bus, indicating that the bus master is addressing an even location and the next sequential odd location and will use the lower two data paths to transfer the two bytes.

The 16-bit ISA device returns the two requested data bytes on EISA data paths zero and one and the EBC activates EX16# to inform the bus master that it may resume control of the bus cycle. The EBC monitors NOWS# and CHRDY to determine when the slave is ready to end the transfer. The EBC then deactivates CMD# and the bus master reads the two bytes from EISA data paths zero and one when CMD# goes inactive.

EISA System Architecture

Transfer Between a 16-bit EISA Bus Master and a 16-bit EISA Slave

This example assumes that a 16-bit EISA bus master is reading two bytes from the last two locations of a doubleword located within a 16-bit EISA slave. When the 16-bit EISA bus master initiates a bus cycle, it performs the following functions:

- drives the MASTER16# line active to inform the EBC that a 16-bit bus master has initiated the bus cycle.
- drives the doubleword address onto LA2:LA31 and sets the M/IO# line to the appropriate state.
- drives the START# signal active.
- sets W/R# and the byte enable lines to the appropriate states. In this example, W/R# is set low, indicating a read, and BE2# and BE3# are set active.

At the trailing-edge of address time, the bus master deactivates START# and the EBC activates CMD# to indicate the beginning of data time. The bus master samples EX16# and EX32# to determine if the currently addressed device is at least attached to the lower two data paths and supports EISA bus cycle timing. Since this example assumes that the bus master is addressing a 16-bit EISA slave, EX16# will be sampled active. The EBC will also sample EX16# active, indicating a 16-bit EISA slave is responding. Upon determining that the addressed slave is capable of responding to EISA bus cycle timing, the bus master assumes that no data bus steering will be necessary to accomplish the transfer. In this particular example, a 16-bit EISA bus master is communicating with a 16-bit EISA slave. Since both devices are connected to EISA data paths zero and one, no steering is necessary.

Using the active level on BE2# and BE3# to determine the requested bytes, the 16-bit EISA device returns the two requested data bytes on EISA data paths zero and one. The EBC monitors EXRDY to determine when the slave is ready to end the transfer. The EBC then deactivates CMD# and the bus master reads the two bytes from EISA data paths zero and one when CMD# goes inactive.

The Intel 82350DT EISA Chip Set

Transfer Between a 16-bit EISA Bus Master and a 32-bit EISA Slave

This example assumes that a 16-bit EISA bus master is reading two bytes from the last two locations of a doubleword located within a 32-bit EISA slave. When the 16-bit EISA bus master initiates a bus cycle, it performs the following functions:

- drives the MASTER16# line active to inform the EBC that a 16-bit bus master has initiated the bus cycle.
- drives the doubleword address onto LA2:LA31 and sets the M/IO# line to the appropriate state.
- drives the START# signal active.
- sets W/R# and the byte enable lines to the appropriate states. In this example, W/R# is set low, indicating a read, and BE2# and BE3# are set active.

At the trailing-edge of address time, the bus master deactivates START# and the EBC activates CMD# to indicate the beginning of data time. The bus master samples EX16# and EX32# to determine if the currently addressed device is at least attached to the lower two data paths and supports EISA bus cycle timing. Since this example assumes that the bus master is addressing a 32-bit EISA slave, EX32# will be sampled active. The EBC will also sample EX32# active, indicating a 32-bit EISA slave is responding. Upon determining that the addressed slave is capable of responding to EISA bus cycle timing, the bus master assumes that no data bus steering will be necessary to accomplish the transfer. In this particular example, a 16-bit EISA bus master is communicating with a 32-bit EISA slave. Since both devices are connected to EISA data paths zero and one, no steering is necessary.

Using the active level on BE2# and BE3# to determine the requested bytes, the 32-bit EISA device returns the two requested data bytes on EISA data paths two and three. Since the 16-bit EISA bus master expects to receive the two bytes back on EISA data paths zero and one, the EBC must command the data EBB to copy the two bytes from paths two and three to paths zero and one. This is accomplished by the EBC setting its SDCPYEN02# and SDCPYEN13# outputs active and its SDCPYUP output low.

The 16-bit EISA bus master monitors EXRDY to determine when the slave is ready to end the transfer. The EBC then deactivates CMD# and the bus master

EISA System Architecture

reads the two bytes from EISA data paths zero and one when CMD# goes inactive.

Transfer Between a 16-bit ISA Bus Master and an 8-bit ISA Slave

When the 16-bit ISA bus master initiates a bus cycle, the Central Arbitration Control in the ISP chip activates its EMSTR16# output to inform the EBC that a 16-bit ISA bus master is running a bus cycle. In addition, the ISA bus master sets MASTER16# active to indicate that it is a 16-bit bus master. The bus master places the address on SA0:SA19, SBHE# and LA17:LA23. The EBC commands the address EBB to bridge this address over to the EISA address bus on LA2:LA31 and the EBC converts SA0, SA1 and SBHE# to the correct setting on the EISA byte enable lines.

In this example, assume the 16-bit ISA bus master is performing a two byte write to an 8-bit ISA slave. The least significant bit of the address, SA0, would therefore be zero and SBHE# would be low to address the even address and the next sequential odd address as well. The bus master begins to drive the two bytes of data onto SD0:SD7 and SD8:SD15 halfway through address time and activates either the IOWC#, MWTC# or SMWTC# ISA bus cycle definition line during data time. The EBC and the 16-bit ISA bus master recognize that an 8-bit ISA slave is responding by sampling EX16#, EX32#, M16#, IO16#, HLOCMEM# and HLOCIO# inactive. Since there is no way to get an ISA bus master to temporarily float the data bus so the EBC and data EBB can perform the two necessary transfers, it is up to the ISA bus master to recognize that it is attempting to perform a 16-bit transfer with an 8-bit device and handle the multiple transfers itself.

The ISA bus master monitors NOWS# and CHRDY to determine when the 8-bit ISA slave is ready to end the transfer of the first byte over EISA data path zero. It then ceases to drive the first byte onto path zero and copies the second byte from path one, SD8:SD15, to path zero, SD0:SD7. In addition, the ISA bus master increments the address by setting SA0 to a one and tricks the slave into thinking a second bus cycle has been initiated by momentarily turning off the write command line (IOWC#, MWTC# or SMWTC#) and then reactivating it. The slave accepts the second byte. The master once again monitors NOWS# and CHRDY to determine when the slave is ready to end the bus cycle. This completes the two byte transfer to the 8-bit ISA slave.

The Intel 82350DT EISA Chip Set

Transfer Between a 16-bit ISA Bus Master and a 16-bit ISA Slave

When the 16-bit ISA bus master initiates a bus cycle, the Central Arbitration Control in the ISP chip activates its EMSTR16# output to inform the EBC that a 16-bit ISA bus master is running a bus cycle. In addition, the ISA bus master sets MASTER16# active to indicate that it is a 16-bit bus master. The bus master places the address on SA0:SA19, SBHE# and LA17:LA23. The EBC commands the address EBB to bridge this address over to the EISA address bus on LA2:LA31 and the EBC converts SA0, SA1 and SBHE# to the correct setting on the EISA byte enable lines.

In this example, assume the 16-bit ISA bus master is performing a two byte write to a 16-bit ISA slave. The least significant bit of the address, SA0, would therefore be zero and SBHE# would be low to address the even address and the next sequential odd address as well. The bus master begins to drive the two bytes of data onto SD0:SD7 and SD8:SD15 halfway through address time and activates either the IOWC#, MWTC# or SMWTC# ISA bus cycle definition line during data time. The EBC and the 16-bit ISA bus master recognize that a 16-bit ISA slave is responding when it samples EX16#, EX32#, M16#, IO16#, HLOCMEM# and HLOCIO# and senses either M16# or IO16# active.

The ISA bus master monitors NOWS# and CHRDY to determine when the 16-bit ISA slave is ready to end the transfer of the two bytes over EISA data paths zero and one. This completes the two byte transfer to the 16-bit ISA slave.

Transfer Between a 16-bit ISA Bus Master and a 16-bit EISA Slave

When the 16-bit ISA bus master initiates a bus cycle, the Central Arbitration Control in the ISP chip activates its EMSTR16# output to inform the EBC that a 16-bit ISA bus master is running a bus cycle. In addition, the ISA bus master sets MASTER16# active to indicate that it is a 16-bit bus master. The bus master places the address on SA0:SA19, SBHE# and LA17:LA23. The EBC commands the address EBB to bridge this address over to the EISA address bus on LA2:LA31 and the EBC converts SA0, SA1 and SBHE# to the correct setting on the EISA byte enable lines.

In this example, assume the 16-bit ISA bus master is performing a two byte write to a 16-bit EISA slave. The least significant bit of the address, SA0, would therefore be zero and SBHE# would be low to address the even address

EISA System Architecture

and the next sequential odd address as well. The EBC translates this to an active level on BE0# and BE1#. The EBC sets START# active during address time for the benefit of EISA slaves. The bus master begins to drive the two bytes of data onto SD0:SD7 and SD8:SD15 halfway through address time and activates either the IOWC#, MWTC# or SMWTC# ISA bus cycle definition line during data time. At the end of address time, the EBC sets CMD# active to indicate that it is data transfer time. The EBC converts the active ISA bus cycle line to the correct setting on the EISA bus cycle definition lines, M/IO# and W/R#. The EBC recognizes that a 16-bit EISA slave is responding when it samples EX16#, EX32#, M16#, IO16#, HLOCMEM# and HLOCIO# and senses EX16# active. If a memory bus cycle is in progress, the active level on EX16# is converted to an active level on M16#. If an I/O bus cycle is in progress, the active level on EX16# is converted to an active level on IO16#. This informs the ISA bus master that it is conversing with a 16-bit device and data bus steering is therefore unnecessary.

If the addressed EISA slave requires additional time to complete the transfer, it deactivates EXRDY until it is ready. The EBC converts EXRDY to CHRDY for the benefit of the ISA bus master. The ISA bus master monitors NOWS# and CHRDY to determine when the 16-bit EISA slave is ready to end the transfer of the two bytes over EISA data paths zero and one. This completes the two byte transfer to the 16-bit EISA slave.

Transfer Between a 16-bit ISA Bus Master and a 32-bit EISA Slave

In this example, assume that a 16-bit ISA bus master is writing two bytes of data to the second word of a doubleword within a 32-bit EISA slave. The bus master activates MASTER16# to inform the EBC that it is a 16-bit bus master. The Central Arbitration Control in the ISP chip activates EMSTR16# to inform the EBC that a 16-bit ISA bus master is performing a bus cycle.

The bus master places the address on SA0:SA19, SBHE# and LA17:LA23. SA1 is set high, SA0 low and SBHE# low. The EBC activates START# during address time. EBC bridges this address across to the EISA address bus, LA2:LA31, and converts SA0, SA1 and SBHE# to an active level on BE2# and BE3#. The EBC converts the active level on IOWC#, MWTC# or SMWTC# to the corresponding setting on the EISA bus cycle definition lines, M/IO# and W/R#. The EBC also deactivates START# and activates CMD# at the beginning of data transfer time. The bus master drives the two bytes onto EISA data paths zero and one.

The Intel 82350DT EISA Chip Set

Using its SDCPYEN02#, SDCPYEN13# and SDCPYUP outputs, the EBC causes the data EBB to copy the two bytes on paths zero and one to paths two and three. The addressed 32-bit EISA slave is expecting to receive the two bytes on the upper two data paths. The EBC monitors the EXRDY line to determine when the 32-bit EISA slave is ready to end the bus cycle. It then deactivates CMD#. The EISA slave latches the two data bytes from EISA data paths two and three when CMD goes high at the end of the bus cycle.

Transfer Between a 32-bit Host CPU and a 32-bit Host Slave

All host bus I/O and memory devices are 32-bit devices. The EBC recognizes that the host CPU is performing a bus cycle when HHLDA, Host Hold Acknowledge, is inactive and HADS0# and HADS1# are set active. The HADSx# lines are connected to the CPU's Host Address Status output. The host CPU places the address on HA2:HA31 and sets the host byte enable lines, HBE0#:HBE3#, to the appropriate state. The EBC causes the address EBB to broadcast the address onto the EISA and ISA address buses. The host CPU indicates the type of bus cycle on HM/IO#, HW/R# and HD/C#. When the host slave recognizes that it is being addressed, it activates either HLOCIO# (host local IO) or HLOCMEM# (host local memory).

Since the host CPU is communicating with a 32-bit slave on its own bus, the EBC and the data EBB do not become involved in the bus cycle. In other words, the data is not bridged over to the EISA/ISA bus.

Transfer Between a 32-bit Host CPU and an 8-bit ISA Slave

The EBC recognizes that the host CPU is performing a bus cycle when HHLDA, Host Hold Acknowledge, is inactive and HADS0# and HADS1# are set active. The HADSx# lines are connected to the CPU's Host Address Status output. The host CPU places the address on HA2:HA31 and sets the host byte enable lines, HBE0#:HBE3#, to the appropriate state. The EBC causes the address EBB to broadcast the address onto the ISA and EISA address buses as well. In this example, assume that the host CPU is writing two bytes to the 8-bit ISA slave over host data paths one and two. This means that the host CPU is setting BE1# and BE2# active. SA0 is set high, while SA1 and SBHE# are set low. The host CPU indicates the type of bus cycle on HM/IO#, HW/R# and HD/C#.

EISA System Architecture

Since an 8-bit ISA slave is being addressed, the EBC samples inactive levels on M16#, IO16#, EX16#, EX32#, HLOCIO# and HLOCMEM#. The EBC latches the two bytes into the path one and two latches in the data EBB using its HDSDLE1# output. It then outputs the two bytes onto the EISA data bus by activating its SDOE1# and SDOE2# outputs. The data byte on EISA data path one is copied down to path zero when the EBC activates its SDCPYEN01# output and sets SDCPYUP low. The EBC monitors NOWS# and CHRDY to determine when the ISA slave is ready to end the byte transfer. The EBC turns off SDCPYEN01# and SDOE1# to turn off the copy transceiver and the cause the path one latch in the data EBB to stop outputting the first data byte.

Having completed the transfer of the first byte, the EBC then increments the address on the ISA address bus by setting SA1 and SBHE# high and SA0 low. The ISA slave is tricked into thinking another bus cycle is initiated by the EBC momentarily turning off the IOWC# or MWTC# line and then reactivating it. The EBC uses its SDCPYEN02# and SDCPYUP outputs to copy the second data byte from EISA data path two to path zero. The EBC again monitors NOWS# and CHRDY to determine when the ISA slave is ready to end the byte transfer. The EBC turns off SDCPYEN02# and SDOE2# to turn off the copy transceiver and the cause the path two latch in the data EBB to stop outputting the second data byte.

Both bytes have now been transferred to the 8-bit ISA slave. The EBC now activates HRDYO#, host ready output, to tell the host CPU that it's ok to end the bus cycle.

Transfer Between a 32-bit Host CPU and a 16-bit ISA Slave

The EBC recognizes that the host CPU is performing a bus cycle when HHLDA, Host Hold Acknowledge, is inactive and HADS0# and HADS1# are set active. The HADSx# lines are connected to the CPU's Host Address Status output. The host CPU places the address on HA2:HA31 and sets the host byte enable lines, HBE0#:HBE3#, to the appropriate state. The EBC causes the address EBB to broadcast the address onto the ISA and EISA address buses as well. In this example, assume that the host CPU is writing two bytes to a 16-bit ISA slave over host data paths two and three. This means that the host CPU is setting BE2# and BE3# active. SA1 is set high, while SA0 and SBHE# are set low. The host CPU indicates the type of bus cycle on HM/IO#, HW/R# and HD/C#.

Since a 16-bit ISA slave is being addressed, the EBC samples an active level on M16# or IO16#. The EBC latches the two bytes into the path two and three latches in the data EBB using its HDSDLE1# output. It then outputs the two bytes onto the EISA data bus by activating its SDOE2# output. The data bytes on EISA data paths two and three are copied down to paths zero and one when the EBC activates its SDCPYEN02# and SDCPYEN13# outputs and sets SDCPYUP low. The EBC monitors NOWS# and CHRDY to determine when the ISA slave is ready to end the transfer. The EBC turns off SDCPYEN02#, SDCPYEN13# and SDOE2# to turn off the copy transceiver and the cause the path two and three latches in the data EBB to stop outputting the two data bytes.

Both bytes have now been transferred to the 16-bit ISA slave. The EBC now activates HRDYO#, host ready output, to tell the host CPU that it's ok to end the bus cycle.

Transfer Between a 32-bit Host CPU and a 16-bit EISA Slave

The EBC recognizes that the host CPU is performing a bus cycle when HHLDA, Host Hold Acknowledge, is inactive and HADS0# and HADS1# are set active. The HADSx# lines are connected to the CPU's Host Address Status output. The host CPU places the address on HA2:HA31 and sets the host byte enable lines, HBE0#:HBE3#, to the appropriate state. The EBC causes the address EBB to broadcast the address onto the ISA and EISA address buses as well. In this example, assume that the host CPU is writing two bytes to a 16-bit EISA slave over host data paths two and three. This means that the host CPU is setting BE2# and BE3# active. The EBC activates BE2# and BE3# on the EISA address bus. The host CPU indicates the type of bus cycle on HM/IO#, HW/R# and HD/C#.

Since a 16-bit EISA slave is being addressed, the EBC samples an active level on EX16#. The EBC latches the two bytes into the path two and three latches in the data EBB using its HDSDLE1# output. It then outputs the two bytes onto the EISA data bus by activating its SDOE2# output. The data bytes on EISA data paths two and three are copied down to paths zero and one when the EBC activates its SDCPYEN02# and SDCPYEN13# outputs and sets SDCPYUP low. The EBC monitors EXRDY to determine when the EISA slave is ready to end the transfer. The EBC turns off SDCPYEN02#, SDCPYEN13# and SDOE2# to turn off the copy transceiver and the cause the path two and three latches in the data EBB to stop outputting the two data bytes.

Both bytes have now been transferred to the 16-bit EISA slave. The EBC now activates HRDYO#, host ready output, to tell the host CPU that it's ok to end the bus cycle.

Transfer Between a 32-bit Host CPU and a 32-bit EISA Slave

The EBC recognizes that the host CPU is performing a bus cycle when HHLDA, Host Hold Acknowledge, is inactive and HADS0# and HADS1# are set active. The HADSx# lines are connected to the CPU's Host Address Status output. The host CPU places the address on HA2:HA31 and sets the host byte enable lines, HBE0#:HBE3#, to the appropriate state. The EBC causes the address EBB to broadcast the address onto the ISA and EISA address buses as well. In this example, assume that the host CPU is writing four bytes to a 32-bit EISA slave using all four host data paths. This means that the host CPU is setting all four host byte enable lines, HBE0#:HBE3#, active. The EBC activates BE0#:BE3# on the EISA address bus. The host CPU indicates the type of bus cycle on HM/IO#, HW/R# and HD/C#.

Since a 32-bit EISA slave is being addressed, the EBC samples an active level on EX32#. The EBC latches the four bytes into the data EBB's data latches using its HDSDLE1# output. It then outputs the four bytes onto the EISA data bus by activating its SDOE0#, SDOE1# and SDOE2# outputs. The EBC monitors EXRDY to determine when the EISA slave is ready to end the transfer. The EBC turns off SDOE0#, SDOE1# and SDOE2# to cause the four data EBB data latches to stop outputting the four data bytes.

All four bytes have now been transferred to the 32-bit EISA slave. The EBC now activates HRDYO#, host ready output, to tell the host CPU that it's ok to end the bus cycle.

Address Buffer Control and the 82352 EISA Bus Buffer (EBB)

Under the control of the EBC, the address EBB ensures that the address generated by the current bus master is seen by every host, EISA and ISA slave in the system. Along with the address the state of the M/IO# bus cycle definition line must be propagated onto the EISA and host address buses so EISA and host slaves can discern memory addresses from I/O addresses. Table 12 - 4 defines the EBC output signals used to control the address EBB. Figure 12 - 5 provides a functional view of the address EBB and illustrates the linkage

The Intel 82350DT EISA Chip Set

between the EBC and the address EBB. The figure also illustrates the direction of address flow through the three latching transceivers when the host CPU, an ISA master or an EISA master is the bus master. Table 12 - 5 shows the state of each of the EBC's address EBB control lines when each type of master is running a bus cycle. Entries designated as "transparent" indicate that the latch control line is left active for the entire bus cycle, causing the respective latching transceiver to be transparent.

Table 12-4. EBC Output Signals Used to Control the Address EBB

Signal	Description
HALAOE#	When set active by the EBC, causes the address EBB's upper and lower Host/EISA Latching Transceivers to output the previously latched host address onto the EISA LA bus. LA2:LA23 and LA24#:LA31#.
HALE#	When set active by the EBC, causes the address EBB's upper and lower Host/EISA Latching Transceivers to latch the address on the EISA LA bus, LA2:LA31.
LASAOE#	When set active by the EBC, causes the address EBB's EISA/ISA Latching Transceiver to output the previously LA address onto the SA bus, SA2:SA19.
LAHAOE#	When set active by the EBC, causes the address EBB's upper and lower Host/EISA Latching Transceivers to output the previously latched EISA address onto the host address bus, HA2:HA31.
LALE#	When set active by the EBC, causes the address EBB's upper and lower Host/EISA Latching Transceivers to latch the address on the host address bus, HA2:HA31.
SALAOE#	When set active by the EBC, causes the address EBB's EISA/ISA Latching Transceiver to output the previously latched SA address onto LA bus, bits LA2:LA16.
SALE#	When set active by the EBC, causes the address EBB to latch the address on LA2:LA19 into the EISA/ISA Latching Transceiver.

Table 12-5. Address EBB Control Line States

Current Bus Master Type

Control Line	Host CPU	EISA	ISA	DMA	Refresh
HALAOE#	active	inactive	inactive	active	active
HALE#	transparent	transparent	transparent	transparent	transparent
LASAOE#	active	active	inactive	active	active
LAHAOE#	inactive	active	active	inactive	inactive
LALE#	pulsed to latch HA bus	na	na	transparent	transparent

| SALAOE# | inactive | inactive | active | inactive | inactive |
| SALE# | pulsed to latch LA into SA latch | pulsed to latch LA into SA latch | transparent | pulsed to latch LA into SA latch | pulsed to latch LA into SA latch |

Host CPU Bus Master

Refer to tables 12 - 5 and 12 - 4 and figure 12 - 5 while reading this description. When the host CPU is bus master, the address on the host address bus, HA2:HA31, and the state of the HM/IO# bus cycle definition line must be propagated onto the EISA address bus, consisting of LA2:LA23, LA24#:LA31# and M/IO#, and the lower part of the ISA address bus, SA2:SA19.

The pulse on LALE# causes the address EBB to latch the address from the host bus. The active on HALAOE# and the steady active on HALE# gates latched host address onto the EISA address bus, LA2:LA23 and LA24#:LA31#. It should be noted that the upper Host/EISA Latching Transceiver inverts address bits 24:31. The pulse on SALE# latches LA2:LA19 into the EISA/ISA Latching Transceiver, while the active on LASAOE# allows it to output the latched address onto the SA bus, SA2:SA19.

EISA Bus Master

Refer to tables 12 - 5 and 12 - 4 and figure 12 - 5 while reading this description. When an EISA master is the bus master, the address on the EISA address bus, LA2:LA23 and LA24#:LA31#, and the state of the M/IO# bus cycle definition line must be propagated onto the host address bus, consisting of HA2:HA31 and HM/IO#, and onto the lower part of the ISA address bus, SA2:SA19.

The active on LAHAOE# and the steady active on HALE# allows the address on the EISA address bus to flow onto the host address bus. The pulse on SALE# causes the lower part of the EISA address, LA2:LA19, to be latched into the EISA/ISA latching transceiver, while the active on LASAOE# allows the latched LA address to be driven onto the SA bus, SA2:SA19.

ISA Bus Master

Refer to tables 12 - 5 and 12 - 4 and figure 12 - 5 while reading this description. When an ISA master is the bus master, the address on the ISA address bus, SA2:SA19 and LA17:LA23, must be propagated onto the host address bus, HA2:HA31, and onto the lower part of the EISA address bus,

LA2:LA23. Since ISA bus masters do not use LA24#:LA31#, pull-up resistors force these lines inactive when an ISA bus master is placing an address on the address bus.

The steady active state of SALE# and the active state of SALAOE# allows the portion of the ISA address on SA2:SA16 to flow through the EISA/ISA latching transceiver onto the lower part of the EISA address bus, LA2:LA16. The ISA bus master places address bits 17:23 directly onto LA17:LA23 of the EISA/ISA address bus. The active on LAHAOE# and the steady active state of HALE# permits the address on the EISA address bus, LA2:LA23 and LA24#:LA31#, to flow through onto the host address bus, HA2:HA31. The ones on LA24#:LA31# are inverted by the upper Host/EISA latching transceiver before being driven onto HA24:HA31.

Refresh Bus Master

Refer to tables 12 - 5 and 12 - 4 and figure 12 - 5 while reading this description. The Refresh logic is located in the ISP chip. When the Refresh logic becomes bus master and drives the next sequential row address onto the host address bus, the row address must be propagated onto the EISA and ISA addresses buses as well.

The active state of HALAOE# and the steady active state of LALE# allows the row address to flow from the host address bus, HA2:HA31, to the EISA address bus, LA2:LA31. The pulse on SALE# latches the row address into the EISA/ISA latching transceiver and the active state of LASAOE# causes the row address to be driven onto the SA bus, SA2:SA19. The Refresh logic in the ISP also sets the HM/IO# bus cycle definition line high to indicate that a memory row address is on the bus. The EBC passes the state of the host bus HM/IO# line to the EISA M/IO# line.

DMA Bus Master

Refer to tables 12 - 5 and 12 - 4 and figure 12 - 5 while reading this description. The DMA controllers are located in the ISP chip and output a memory address onto the host address bus, HA2:HA31, when a DMA channel becomes bus master. The HM/IO# line is also set high by the ISP to indicate that a memory address is present on the bus. The EBC must command the address EBB to pass the memory address and the state of HM/IO# onto the EISA address bus, LA2:LA23 and LA24#:LA31# plus M/IO#, and onto the ISA address bus, consisting of SA2:SA19 and LA17:LA23.

EISA System Architecture

The active state of HALAOE# and the steady active state of LALE# allows the memory address on the host address bus, HA2:HA31, to flow through the upper and lower Host/EISA latching transceivers onto the EISA data bus, LA2:LA23 and LA24#:LA31#. The pulse on SALE# latches the memory address on the host address bus, HA2:HA31, into the EISA/ISA latching transceiver and the active state of LASAOE# allows the transceiver to drive it onto the SA bus, SA2:SA19.

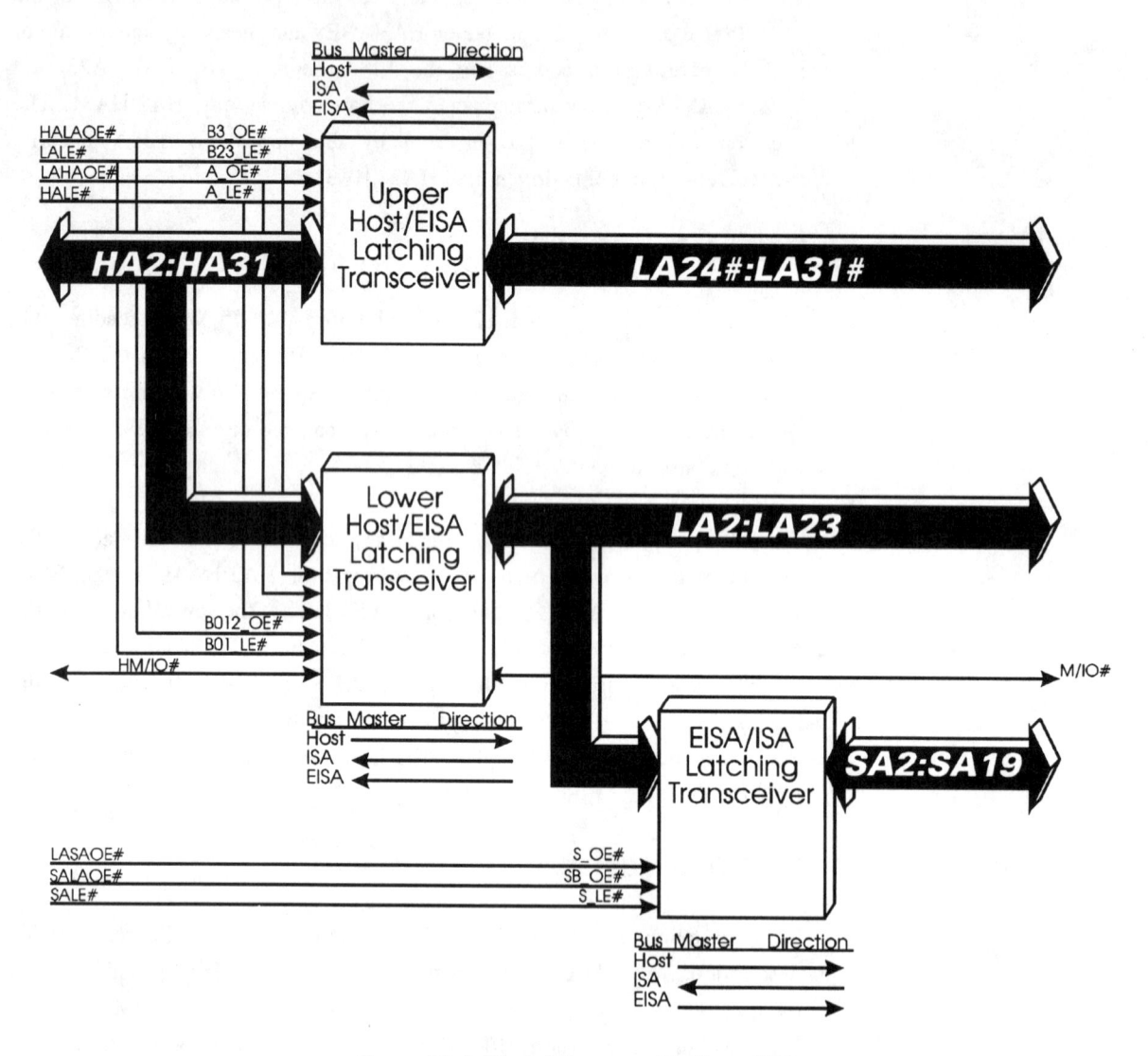

Figure 12-5. Block Diagram of Address EBB

The Host Bus Interface Unit

The host bus interface unit pictured in figure 12 - 2 observes bus cycles initiated by the host CPU. If neither HLOCMEM# nor HLOCIO# are sensed

The Intel 82350DT EISA Chip Set

active, the host bus master is addressing a slave on the EISA or ISA bus. In this case, the host bus interface unit commands either the EISA or ISA interface unit in the EBC to run a bus cycle. The host bus interface unit awaits completion of the bus cycle and sends ready to the host CPU. Table 12 - 6 provides a description of the host bus interface signals. The description of these signals assumes that the EBC is configured for the 82350 environment. To configure the EBC for the 82350 environment, two conditions must be met:

- The AMODE input must be strapped low.
- The HNA#/SBMODE# input is sampled on the leading-edge of the SPWROK input. To select the 82350 configuration, it must be sampled high.

Table 12-6. Host Interface Unit Signal Descriptions

Signal	Direction	Description
AMODE	input	Address Mode. Configures the EBC for 82350 mode when strapped low; for 82350DT mode when strapped high.
HBE0#:HBE3#	input/output	Host Byte Enables. When the host CPU is bus master, these inputs define the target location(s) within the addressed doubleword. The EBC's ISA interface unit converts them to SA0, SA1 and SBHE# on the ISA address bus, while the EBC's EISA interface unit converts them to BE0#:BE3# on the EISA address bus. When an EISA bus master has initiated a bus cycle, the state of the BE0#:BE3# lines on the EISA address bus are output onto the HBE0#:HBE3# lines on the host address bus. When an ISA bus master has initiated a bus cycle, the state of the SA0, SA1 and SBHE# lines on the ISA address bus are converted and output onto the HBE0#:HBE3# lines on the host address bus.
HADS0# and HADS1#	input	Host Address Status 0 and 1. The host CPU or the host cache controller's ADS# output is connected to the HADS0# input. ADS# indicates that it is address time and a valid address and bus cycle definition are present on the host bus. Some cache controllers perform more than one fetch in order to fill a cache line. In this case, the cache controller generates HADS0# when it initiates the bus cycle for the first fetch. This triggers an state machine that generates HADS1# when it initiates any subsequent bus cycles for the remaining fetches. Internally, these two input signals are "anded" together.
HNA#	output	Host Next Address. In a system with a 386 host CPU, this output is used to tell the 386 whether it can output the address for the next bus cycle early.

EISA System Architecture

Signal	Type	Description
HD/C#	input/output	Host Data or Control. Used as inputs when the host CPU is bus master, as outputs when a device other than the host CPU is bus master. In combination with HW/R# and HM/IO#, defines the bus cycle type.
HW/R#	input/output	Host Write or Read. See HD/C#.
HM/IO#	input/output	Host Memory or I/O. See HD/C#.
HLOCK#	input	Host Lock. This input is connected to the host CPU's LOCK# output. Will be active when the host CPU is locking multiple bus cycles together to prevent other bus masters from requesting the buses until lock goes inactive.
HRDYI#	input	Host Ready Input. The host interface unit monitors this signal to determine when a host-initiated bus cycle has completed.
HRDYO#	output	Host Ready Output. When the host CPU is accessing an EISA or ISA slave, the host interface unit activates HRDYO# to signal the end of the bus cycle to the host CPU.
HERDYO#	output	Host Early Ready Output. This is an earlier version of HRDYO# to be used with higher speed host CPUs that require more setup time.
HHOLD	output	Host Hold Request. When the Central Arbitration Control in the ISP chip must grant the buses to a device other than the host CPU, it must first take the buses away from the host CPU. To do this, the ISP activates DHOLD. DHOLD causes the EBC's host interface unit, in turn, to activate HHOLD to seize the host bus from the host CPU. In response, the host CPU surrenders the buses and activates HHLDA, Host Hold Acknowledge. The EBC then activates DHLDA to inform the Central Arbitration Control in the ISP that it may grant the buses to another device.
HHLDA	input	Host Hold Acknowledge. See HHOLD.
HLOCMEM#	input	Host Local Memory. This signal is set active by the memory address decode logic when memory residing on the host bus is being addressed. If the current bus master is the host CPU, this means that the EBC does not have to activate the data EBB or run a bus cycle on the ISA or EISA bus.
HLOCIO#	input	Host Local I/O. Host Local Memory. This signal is set active by the I/O address decode logic when an I/O device residing on the host bus is being addressed. If the current bus master is the host CPU, this means that the EBC does not have to activate the data EBB or run a bus cycle on the ISA or EISA bus.

The Intel 82350DT EISA Chip Set

HGT16M#	input	Host Greater Than 16MB. This signal is only driven by the ISP chip during DMA bus cycles. If the DMA channel is generating a memory address below 16MB (00000000h - 00FFFFFFh), HGT16M# is high and the ISA interface unit will generate MRDC# or MWTC#. For addresses above 16MB, the MRDC# or MWTC# signals are not generated. This is necessary because some DMA devices use the ISA memory command signals to start a bus cycle early.
PWEN#	input	Posted Write Enable. If sampled active at the beginning of a host CPU memory write bus cycle to an EISA or ISA memory slave, the EBC's host interface unit causes the EBC's Data Buffer Control logic to latch the write data into the data EBB. The host interface unit then activates the HRDYO# signal to let the host CPU end the memory write bus cycle. The EBC's host interface unit, in conjunction with either the ISA or EISA interface unit, then writes the posted data to the target ISA or EISA memory slave. This feature allows single host memory writes to EISA or ISA memory to complete quickly.
HSTRETCH#	input	Host Bus Stretch#. This input can be used by host bus slaves during EISA/ISA or DMA bus master cycles to stretch the low part of BCLK during CMD# (data time). This has the effect of stalling the EISA/ISA master without adding BCLK wait states.
HKEN#	input	Host Cache Enable. When sampled active, indicates that the host CPU is requesting a cache line fill operation.

The ISA Bus Interface Unit

The ISA interface unit pictured in figure 12 - 2 observes bus cycles initiated by ISA bus masters. The ISA bus interface unit awaits completion of the bus cycle. If either the host CPU or an EISA bus master is addressing an ISA slave, the ISA interface unit runs a bus cycle. When the bus cycle on the ISA bus is completed, EXRDY or HRDYO# is sent to the EISA or host bus master to terminate the bus cycle. Table 12 - 7 provides a description of the ISA interface signals. For a complete description of the ISA bus, refer to the MindShare publication entitled *ISA System Architecture*.

EISA System Architecture

Table 12-7. ISA Interface Unit Signal Descriptions

Signal	Direction	Description
BALE	output	Bus Address Latch Enable. During an ISA bus cycle, BALE is set high at the midpoint of address time and dropped low at the end of address time. The address is gated from the LA bus to the SA bus when BALE goes high and is latch when BALE goes low at the end of address time.
SA0, SA1, BHE#	input/output	Least-significant part of the ISA address bus. These are inputs when the bus cycle is being run by an ISA bus master and outputs when the bus cycle is being run by an EISA or host master.
IORC#	input/output	The I/O Read Command line. Generated by an ISA bus master when it is performing an I/O read bus cycle. When an EISA or host bus master is performing an I/O read bus cycle, the EBC's ISA interface unit generates this signal.
IOWC#	input/output	The I/O Write Command line. Generated by an ISA bus master when it is performing an I/O write bus cycle. When an EISA or host bus master is performing an I/O write bus cycle, the EBC's ISA interface unit generates this signal.
MRDC#	input/output	The Memory Read Command line. Generated by an ISA bus master when it is performing a memory read bus cycle. When an EISA or host bus master is performing a memory read bus cycle, the EBC's ISA interface unit generates this signal.
MWTC#	input/output	The Memory Write Command line. Generated by an ISA bus master when it is performing a memory write bus cycle. When an EISA or host bus master is performing a memory write bus cycle, the EBC's ISA interface unit generates this signal.
SMRDC#	output	Standard Memory Read Command line. The EBC's ISA interface unit generates this signal when any bus master is reading from memory space in the 00000000h - 000FFFFFh range. A memory address decoder located in the ISP chip generates GT1M# whenever it detects a memory address in this range, causing the ISP interface unit to generate either SMRDC# or SMWTC#.

The Intel 82350DT EISA Chip Set

SMWTC#	output	Standard Memory Write Command line. The EBC's ISA interface unit generates this signal when any bus master is writing to memory space in the 00000000h - 000FFFFFh range. A memory address decoder located in the ISP chip generates GT1M# whenever it detects a memory address in this range, causing the ISP interface unit to generate either SMRDC# or SMWTC#.
IO16#	input/output	IO Size 16. Generated by a 16-bit ISA I/O slave when addressed by a bus master. Set active by the EBC's ISA interface unit when an ISA bus master is addressing a host I/O slave (HLOCIO# sampled active). EISA slaves that support ISA bus masters must assert IO16# as well as EX16# or EX32# when addressed.
M16#	input	Memory Size 16. Generated by a 16-bit ISA memory slave when addressed by a bus master.
NOWS#	input	No Wait States. An ISA slave may generate NOWS# when it has decoded its address and a read or write command line has been activated. When set active by the slave, it conditions the default ready timer (in the ISA interface unit) to set ready active at the end of the current BCLK. It is used to shorten the number of wait states appended to a bus cycle by the default ready timer.
CHRDY	input/output	Channel Ready. If an ISA slave requires more time to complete a bus cycle than allowed by the default ready timer, it may set the CHRDY line low. This prevents the default ready timer from timing out until the slave is ready to end the bus cycle. When the slave is ready to end the bus cycle, it sets CHRDY active again, permitting the default ready timer to time out.
REFRESH#	input	Generated by the Refresh logic in the ISP chip when the Refresh logic is bus master and is performing a refresh bus cycle.
MASTER16#	input	16-bit Bus Master. Generated by either ISA or 16-bit EISA bus master when it initiates a bus cycle.

EISA System Architecture

The EISA Bus Interface Unit

The EISA interface unit pictured in figure 12 - 2 observes bus cycles initiated by EISA bus masters. The EISA bus interface unit awaits completion of the bus cycle. If either the host CPU or an ISA bus master is addressing an EISA slave, the EISA interface unit runs a bus cycle. Table 12 - 8 provides a description of the EISA interface signals. For a complete description of the EISA bus, refer to earlier sections of this publication.

Table 12-8. EISA Interface Unit Signal Descriptions

Signal	Direction	Description
BE0#:BE3#	input/output	Byte Enable lines. Set to the appropriate states during a bus cycle initiated by an EISA bus master. When an ISA master initiates a bus cycle, the EBC's EISA interface unit converts SA0, SA1 and SBHE# to the corresponding setting on the BE lines. When the host CPU initiates a bus cycle, the state of the host byte enables lines, HBE0#:HBE3#, are passed onto the EISA byte enable lines by the EBC.
M/IO#	input/output	Memory or I/O bus cycle definition line. Generated by an EISA master or by the EBC when the host CPU or an ISA master is performing a bus cycle.
W/R#	input/output	Write or Read bus cycle definition line. Generated by an EISA master or by the EBC when the host CPU or an ISA master is performing a bus cycle.
LOCK#	output	Generated by the EBC when the host CPU is bus master and has asserted HLOCK# to the EBC. An active level on the EISA LOCK# line prevents other bus masters from requesting the buses until LOCK# goes away.
START#	input/output	Set active by an EISA bus master when it initiates a bus cycle and deactivated at the end of address time. Controlled by the EBC when an ISA master or the host CPU is performing a bus cycle to signal the start of the bus cycle on the EISA bus. Also controlled by the EBC during DMA transfers and under some conditions requiring data bus steering.
CMD#	output	Command. Set active by the EBC at the start of data time and kept active until the end of the bus cycle.

The Intel 82350DT EISA Chip Set

EXRDY	input/output	EISA Ready. Set inactive by the currently addressed EISA slave if it requires more time to complete a bus cycle. Controlled by the EBC when an EISA bus master is addressing an ISA or host slave and under some conditions when data bus steering is necessary.
MSBURST#	input/output	Master Burst. Generated by an EISA or host master (through the EBC) when the addressed slave has indicated it supports burst bus cycles by asserting SLBURST#. Set active by the EISA master or the EBC at the midpoint of the first data time and sampled by the slave at the end of the first data time.
SLBURST#	input	Slave Burst. Used by the currently addressed EISA slave to indicate it supports burst bus cycles. Sampled by the master at the end of address time.
EX32#	input/output	EISA Size 32. Generated by the currently addressed slave if it is a 32-bit EISA slave. Generated by the EBC at the end of data bus steering to signal return of bus cycle control to the EISA bus master. Also generated by the EBC if an EISA bus master addresses a host slave (HLOCMEM# or HLOCIO# sampled active be EBC).
EX16#	input/output	EISA Size 16. Generated by the currently addressed slave if it is a 16-bit EISA slave. Generated by the EBC at the end of data bus steering to signal return of bus cycle control to the EISA bus master. Also generated by the EBC if an EISA bus master addresses a host slave (HLOCMEM# or HLOCIO# sampled active be EBC).

Cache Support

The EBC provides two output signals to support bus snooping. HSSTRB# is used in 386/82385 host CPU systems, while QHSSTRB# is used in 486 host CPU systems. These signals indicate to a system cache controller that a bus master is writing to system memory. The RDE#, or Ready Delay Enable, input instructs the cache support unit in the EBC to add a wait state by delaying HERDYO# and HRDYO# during a host to EISA/ISA read to allow increased cache SRAM write data setup time during cache read miss bus cycles.

EISA System Architecture

Reset Control

Table 12 - 9 describes the signals associated with the EBC's Reset Control unit (see figure 12 - 2).

Table 12-9. The EBC's Reset Control Interface Signals

Signal	Direction	Description
RST	out	System Reset. Remains active until 10 microseconds after SPWROK goes active. Resets major system components to a known state.
RSTCPU	out	Reset Host CPU. Driven active when: power isn't stable (SPWROK inactive); a shutdown bus cycle is detected on the host bus; or RSTAR# is sensed active. See RSTAR# description. RSTCPU resets just the host CPU.
RST385	out	Reset 385 cache controller. Driven active under the same conditions as RSTCPU. Resets the host bus cache controller, clearing all tag valid bits. In other words, the cache is flushed.
RSTAR#	in	Restart. Generated under software control by: issuing a CPU reset command to the keyboard controller; or toggling the fast hot reset bit in the PS/2 compatibility port at I/O port 92h. Used by 286-specific code to reset the 286 and return it to real mode from protected mode.
SPWROK	in	System Power OK. Provided as an output from the power supply. When inactive, the Reset Control unit sets RSTCPU, RST385 and RST active.

Slot-Specific I/O Support

During I/O bus cycles, the EBC generates a pulse on the signal AENLE#, AEN Latch Enable. This is used by the AEN logic to latch the active AENx line. For more information on slot-specific I/O support and AEN decode, refer to the chapter entitled, "EISA System Configuration."

The Clock Generator Unit

Table 12 - 10 provides a description of the signals related to the EBC's Clock Generator unit.

The Intel 82350DT EISA Chip Set

Table 12-10. EBC's Clock Generation Unit Signal Description

Signals	Direction	Description
HCLKCPU	in	Host CPU Clock.
BCLK	out	BCLK is generated by dividing the HCLKCPU input clock by a factor determined by the CPU0:CPU3 inputs. For a 25MHz 386 or 486 host CPU, the BCLK frequency will be 8.33MHz. For a 33MHz 386 or 486, the BCLK frequency will be 8.25MHz.
CLKKB	out	The EBC's Clock Generation unit provides an output clock for the keyboard controller. Its frequency is derived by dividing the HCLKCPU input by a factor determined by the CPU0:CPU3 inputs. If the host CPU is a 25MHz 386, the CLKKB output frequency will be 10MHz. If the host CPU is a 25MHz 486, the CLKKB output frequency will be 8.33MHz. If the host CPU is a 33MHz 386 or 486, the CLKKB output frequency will be 11MHz.
BCLKIN	in	Bus Clock input. Allows the EBC to monitor the BCLK signal.

I/O Recovery

The ISA bus's default ready timer built into the EBC automatically forces accesses to 8 or 16-bit ISA I/O devices to append one wait state to the bus cycle. If a delay of longer than one wait state is desired, the signal LIOWAIT#, Long I/O Wait, may be asserted to provide a maximum of eleven wait states when accessing 8-bit ISA I/O slaves or three wait states when accessing 16-bit ISA I/O slaves.

Testing

Normally pulled high with an external pullup resistor, an active level on the TEST1# input causes the EBC to float all of its outputs except BCLK. This allows a board tester to gain control of all of the output signal lines for testing purposes.

The ISP Interface Unit

The ISP interface unit provides the interconnect between the EBC and the ISP chip. For a description of the signals involved, refer to the next section.

The 82357 Integrated System Peripheral (ISP)

Introduction

The majority of the logic contained within the Integrated System Peripheral, or ISP, was described in detail earlier in this publication and in the MindShare publication entitled, "The ISA System Architecture." The information presented here is intended as a summary of the functions present in the ISP. Where applicable, signals indigenous to the ISP are described. Figure 12 - 6 provides a detailed view of the major logic blocks contained within the ISP.

The Intel 82350DT EISA Chip Set

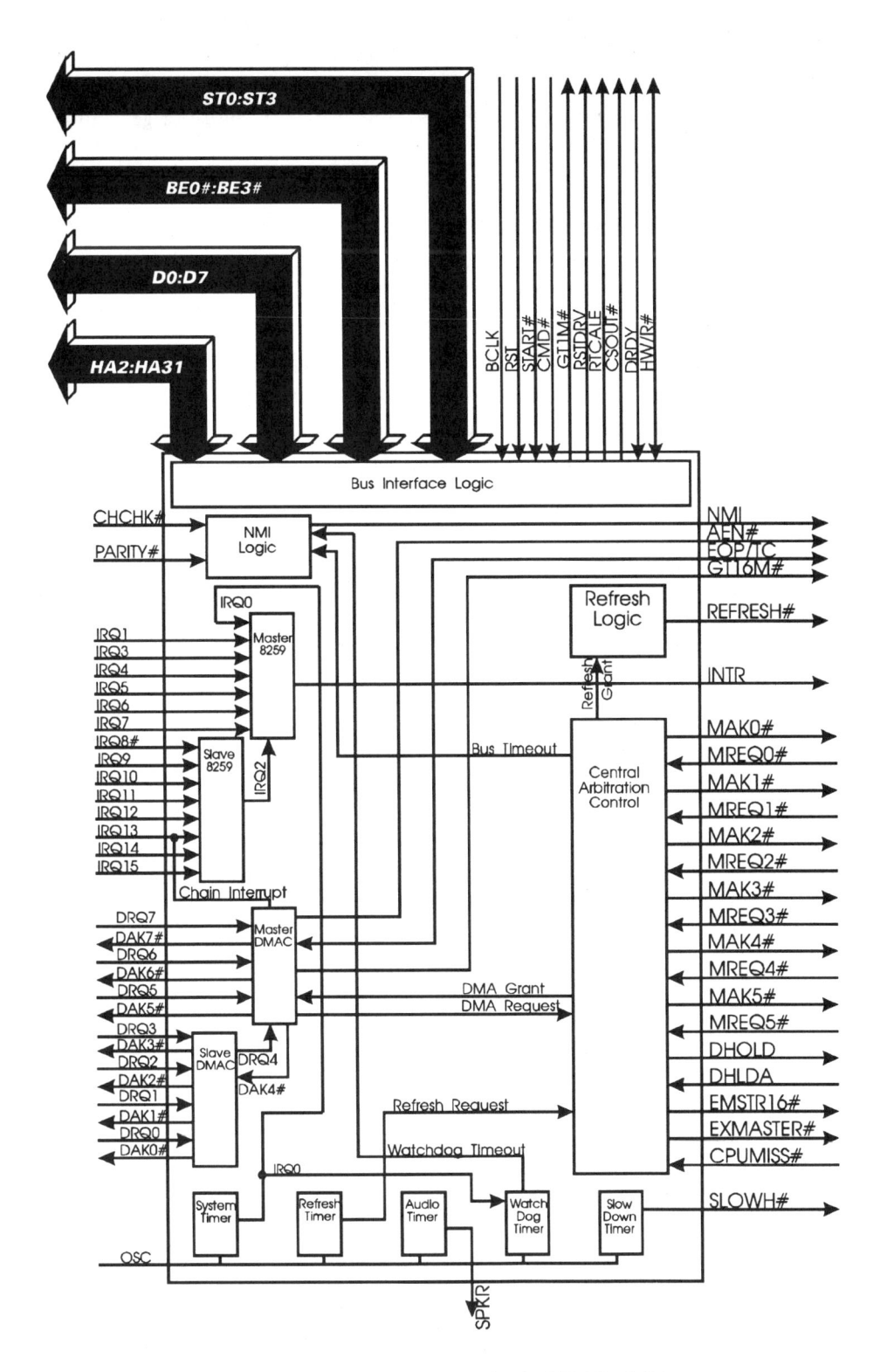

Figure 12-6. The ISP Block Diagram

EISA System Architecture

NMI Logic

In an EISA system, there are four possible hardware causes for generation of NMI to the host CPU:

- A Channel Check, or CHCHK#, from an ISA or EISA card reporting a catastrophic failure.
- A system board RAM parity error (PARITY#).
- A Watchdog Timer timeout because an applications program has disable interrupt recognition for an extended period of time.
- A bus Timeout from the Central Arbitration Control because the current bus master has refused to yield the buses within the allowed period of time (8 microseconds for an EISA bus master or 2.5 microseconds for a DMA channel).

The programmer may also force the NMI logic to generate an NMI by writing to I/O port 0462h with any data.

Interrupt Controllers

The ISP contains two modified Intel 8259A Programmable Interrupt Controllers in a master/slave configuration. Together, they provide a total of fifteen interrupt request lines. Eleven of these are attached to the EISA/ISA card slots, while the remainder are reserved for special system board functions. The Interrupt Acknowledge input to the ISP is conspicuous by its absence. When a bus master other than the DMAC or the Refresh logic is bus master, the ST2 signal line is an input to the ISP and it performs the interrupt acknowledge function. Whenever the EBC detects an interrupt acknowledge bus cycle on the host bus, it sets ST2 low to signal interrupt acknowledge to the interrupt controllers in the ISP.

Two new registers have been added to allow individual programming of each interrupt request input as level-sensitive or edge-triggered. They are referred to as the ELCR, or Edge/Level Control registers. The master interrupt controller's ELCR resides at I/O port 4D0h, while the slave's resides at I/O port 04D1h. Bit zero in the master's ELCR corresponds to the IRQ0 input, while bit seven corresponds to the IRQ7 input. Bit zero in the slave's ELCR corresponds to the IRQ8 input, while bit seven corresponds to the IRQ15 input. A zero in a bit position sets up the respective IRQ input to recognize positive, edge-triggered interrupt requests (non-shareable). A one in a bit position sets the IRQ input up

The Intel 82350DT EISA Chip Set

to recognize active low, level-sensitive interrupt requests (shareable). In both ELCR registers, bit 0 must be a zero.

DMA Controllers

The ISP contains two enhanced Intel 8237 DMA Controllers in a master slave configuration. Together, they provide a total of seven DMA channels. DMA channels five through seven may be used by 16-bit I/O devices, while channels zero through three are reserved for 8-bit I/O devices. Each of the DMA channels can be programmed to utilize the following EISA-specific features:

- 8, 16 or 32-bit transfers
- ISA compatible, Type "A", Type "B" or Type "C" bus cycles.
- buffer chaining
- ring buffer

Detailed information on programming the DMA controllers can be found in the Intel 82350DT EISA Chip Set manual.

When a DMA channel becomes bus master, the ISP depends on the EBC to run the bus cycle for the DMA channel. The EBC generates START#, CMD#, IORC# and IOWC#. When a DMA channel becomes bus master, the type of bus cycle to run is indicated by the ISP's ST0:ST3 outputs. Table 12 - 11 defines the ST0:ST3 output settings for the different types of DMA bus cycle types.

Table 12-11. Type of DMA Bus Cycle In Progress

ST3	ST2	ST1	ST0	DMA Bus Cycle Type
0	0	0	0	8-bit ISA compatible
0	0	0	1	8-bit Type "A"
0	0	1	0	8-bit Type "B"
0	0	1	1	8-bit Type "C"
0	1	0	0	16-bit ISA compatible
0	1	0	1	16-bit Type "A"
0	1	1	0	16-bit Type "B"
0	1	1	1	16-bit Type "C"
1	0	0	0	32-bit ISA compatible
1	0	0	1	32-bit Type "A"
1	0	1	0	32-bit Type "B"
1	0	1	1	32-bit Type "C"
1	1	x	x	DMA controller Idle

EISA System Architecture

System Timers

The ISP contains five programmable system timers necessary to the proper operation of any EISA machine. All of these timers derive their timing from the ISP's OSC input signal of 1.19318MHz.

- The System Timer is programmed during the POST to output a pulse onto IRQ0 once every 55ms.
- The Refresh Timer is programmed during the POST to output a Refresh Request to the Central Arbitration Control once every 15.09 microseconds.
- The Audio Timer is programmed by an applications program to yield the desired output frequency on the SPKR output to the speaker driver on the system board.
- The Watchdog Timer may be utilized by multitasking operating systems to detect a cessation of interrupt servicing. The Watchdog Timer counts unserviced IRQ0 output pulses from the System Timer. When its initial count is exhausted, the Watchdog Timer generates a Watchdog Timeout to the NMI logic, causing it to generate NMI to the host CPU.
- The Slowdown Timer allows the programmer to make the host CPU appear to run slower to facilitate the proper operation of game software and some copy protection schemes. The Slowdown Timer and all of the other timers are described in the MindShare publication entitled, "The ISA System Architecture."

Central Arbitration Control

The ISP incorporates the Central Arbitration Control, or CAC. The operation of the CAC is described earlier in this publication. In the event of a Bus Timeout (when a bus master refuses to yield control of the buses within a time limit), an NMI is generated to the host CPU. In order to force the errant bus master off the bus, the CAC sets the ISP's RSTDRV output active to reset the bus master. The buses are then granted to the host CPU so it can service the NMI. In the NMI interrupt service routine, the programmer may read the contents of the Bus Master Status Latch at I/O port 0464h to determine the identity of the faulty bus master card. Bits zero through five in this register indicate which EISA bus master card was last granted the buses. Bit zero corresponds to the bus master in EISA card slot one, while bit five corresponds

The Intel 82350DT EISA Chip Set

to the bus master in EISA card slot six. Bits six and seven in this register aren't used.

Refresh Logic

The Refresh Logic is contained in the ISP. It arbitrates for the buses once every 15.09 microseconds when the Refresh Timer sets the internal signal Refresh Request active. The CAC uses an internal Refresh Grant line to grant the buses to the Refresh Logic. At that time, the Refresh logic sets the ISP's REFRESH# output active. The Refresh logic drives the row address onto the host address bus, HA2:HA31.

Miscellaneous Interface Signals

Table 12 - 12 defines ISP signals not defined elsewhere.

Table 12-12. Miscellaneous ISP Signals

Signal	Direction	Description
CPUMISS#	in	Generated by the host CPU logic, it indicates that the host CPU or its related cache controller requires the use of the buses to run a bus cycle. This is an input to the Central Arbitration Control.
EXMASTER#	out	EISA Master. Generated by the Central Arbitration Control when the buses are granted to an EISA bus master. This output is connected to the EBC so it will know whether an EISA bus master is performing a bus cycle.
EMSTR16#	out	Early 16-bit Bus Master. Set active by the Central Arbitration Control if the buses are granted to a 16-bit ISA bus master. This output is connected to the EBC so it will know whether an ISA bus master is performing a bus cycle.
DHOLD	out	Hold Request. When the Central Arbitration Control is going to grant the buses to a device other than the host CPU, it must first force the host CPU to relinquish control of the buses. The ISP sets its DHOLD output active to the EBC. The EBC, in turn, sets HHOLD (Host Hold Request) active. HHOLD is connected to either the host CPU's (in a cacheless system) or the host cache controller's HOLD line. This forces the host off the bus. In response, the host sets HHLDA, Host Hold Acknowledge, active to the EBC. The EBC, in turn, sets its DHLDA output active to the ISP to inform the CAC that the host is off the bus.

EISA System Architecture

DHLDA	in	Hold Acknowledge. See DHOLD description.
GT16M#	out	Greater Than 16MB. Generated by the DMA logic in the ISP if the active DMA channel is driving a memory address greater than 16MB (address greater than 00FFFFFFh) onto the host address bus, HA2:HA31. GT16M# is sent to the EBC's ISA interface unit, where it determines whether the MRDC# or the MWTC# will be set active during the DMA bus cycle. See description of HGT16M# in table 12 - 6.
EOP/TC	in/out	End-of-Process or Transfer Complete. Generated by the DMA controller at the end of a DMA transfer when the transfer count has been exhausted. The TC signal is connected to all EISA/ISA slots. When TC is detected by the I/O device associated with the DMA channel, the I/O device will respond by setting its respective IRQ line active to signal the end of the transfer. EISA I/O cards may also generate TC to the DMA controller to prematurely terminate a transfer (e.g., in the case of an error). TC also is used to inform Bus Masters when to reprogram the DMA address buffer when buffer chaining is used. This only pertains to bus masters that program the DMA channel for buffer chaining.
AEN#	out	Address Enable. Generated by the DMA controller whenever a DMA channel is bus master and is driving a memory address onto the host address bus, HA2:HA31. For more information, refer to the chapter entitled, "EISA Automatic Configuration."
DRDY	in/out	When an ISA bus master is accessing one of the registers within the ISP, this acts as the ready line and is connected externally to the CHRDY signal. When a DMA channel is bus master, DRDY acts as the ready input from the I/O slave associated with the active DMA channel. This permits the I/O slave to lengthen a bus cycle until it is ready to complete it.
CSOUT#	out	Chip-Select Out. Whenever any bus master accesses any of the ISP's internal registers, the signal CSOUT# is set active. It should act as an enable for an external data bus buffer between the ISP and data EBB. The direction of the buffer is dictated by whether a read or a write transaction is in progress.

RTCALE	out	Real-Time Clock Address Latch Enable. Any write to the Real-Time Clock chip's address port at I/O address 0070h will cause RTCALE to be set active. This signal informs the RTC chip that a CMOS RAM address is present on the data bus and should be latched.
GT1M#	out	Greater Than 1MB. The ISP contains a memory address decoder designed to recognize any memory address less than 1MB (in the 00000000h through 000FFFFFh range). GT1M# is set active whenever the memory address is greater than 000FFFFFh. The state of this signal is used within the EBC's ISA interface unit to determine whether or not to set the SMRDC# or SMWTC# signal active. If the address is below 1MB, SMRDC# or SMWTC# should be set active.

Appendix

Appendix

Glossary

32-bit EISA bus master	EISA-based systems support 32-bit EISA bus master cards. A bus master card typically includes an on-board processor and local memory. It can relieve the burden on the main processor by performing sophisticated memory access functions, such as scatter/gather block data transfers.
82350DT EISA chip set	The Intel 82350DT EISA chip set. The primary chips used by most manufacturers includes the 82358DT EISA Bus Controller, or EBC, the 82357 Integrated Systems Peripheral, or ISP, and the 82352 EISA Bus Buffers, or EBBs
82352 EISA Bus Buffer	Part of the Intel 82350 EISA chip set used for two separate functions: one for the address latching and buffering and one for the data buffering and steering.
82357 ISP	This chip is part of the Intel 82350 chip set and contains a variety of functions including: the DMA controllers, Interrupt controllers, Timers, Arbitration logic, and NMI logic.
8237 DMACs	The Intel DMA controllers used in ISA systems.
AEN	The signal used in ISA systems to disable all I/O address decoders so they do not respond to a DMA address. Also used in EISA systems to independently enable I/O address decoders
AEN logic	Logic responsible for controlling the AEN signal so that DMA cycles, standard access to ISA expansion devices and slot specific I/O addressing occur properly.
address translation	The process of converting one type of address to another. For example: translating the address from an ISA Bus Master (SA0:SA16, LA17:LA23 and BHE#) to a 32-bit address (LA2:LA31 and BE0:BE3) required by 32-bit EISA devices.
arbitration	Efficient bus sharing among the main CPU, multiple EISA bus master cards and DMA channels according to a priority scheme.
arbitration scheme	EISA uses a three-way rotational priority scheme between the Refresh Logic, CPU and Bus Masters (shared), and DMA Channels.

EISA System Architecture

BALE	An ISA bus signal that is a buffered version of ALE. This signal is used by expansion devices to notify them that a valid address is on the ISA bus.
BCLK	An ISA bus signal (bus clock) that provides the timing reference for all bus transactions.
BCPR Services	The legal firm that manages the EISA specification.
bridge	The EISA chip set must allow the addresses and data generated by a bus master to propagate onto all of the system buses so all of the devices in the system can be communicated with. The connection between buses is termed a bridge.
Buffer chaining	A DMA function that permits the implementation of scatter write and gather read operations. A scatter write operation is one in which a contiguous block of data is read from an I/O device and is written to two or more areas of memory, or buffers. A gather read operation reads a stream of data from several blocks of memory, or buffers, and writes it to an I/O device.
Burst bus cycle	A burst transfer is used to transfer blocks of data between the current bus master (or DMA device) and EISA memory. After the initial transfer in a block data transfer, each subsequent EISA Burst bus transfer can be completed in one BCLK period
burst DMA	A DMA bus cycle that supports burst.
Bus Arbitration	A process that determines how bus sharing among the main CPU, multiple EISA bus master cards and DMA channels is handled.
Bus Arbitration Scheme	See arbitration scheme
Bus Arbitration Signals	The signals available on the EISA bus that are used by bus masters to gain ownership of the buses. A pair of signals, MASTER REQUEST and a MASTER ACKNOWLEDGE exist for each bus master.
Bus Cycle Definition	Specifies the type of bus cycle being run. Memory read, memory write, I/O read, I/O write, Interrupt acknowledge, Halt or Shutdown.
bus cycle, EISA std.	Standard EISA bus cycle. A bus cycle based on a default a zero wait-state operation over the EISA bus.

bus master priority	The priority a bus master has in the rotational scheme. The priority changes as bus masters gain control of the buses.
bus timeout	Upon being preempted by removal of its Acknowledge, the current bus master must relinquish control of the buses within a prescribed period of time. Failure to do so results in a bus timeout.
cache controller	A cache memory controller maintains copies of frequently accessed information read from DRAM memory in the cache.
Central Arbitration Control	The logic responsible for managing the bus arbitration process.
command translation	The process of translating between EISA and ISA type commands.
CMD#	CMD# is an EISA signal that is set active by the system board coincidentally with the trailing edge of START#. Only the system board drives the CMD# line. CMD# then remains active until the end of the bus cycle.
configuration file	A file for each expansion card that describes the programmable options available on the card. Used in the EISA automatic configuration process.
Configuration Process	A process that uses information provided by EISA expansion board manufactures and the system manufacturer to configure the system for conflict free operation.
data bus	The group of signal lines used to transfer data between devices.
Data Bus Steering	A process used to ensure data travels over the correct paths between the current bus master and the currently addressed device.
DMA burst bus cycles	DMA bus cycles that supports burst.
DMA cascade channel	The DMA cascade channel connects (cascades) two DMA Controllers together. DMA channel 4 is used as the cascade channel.
DMA clock	The clock used by the DMA Controller to control its data transfer timing. DMA clock also called DCLK is typically one-half the speed of BCLK.

EISA System Architecture

DMA controller	The devices used to perform the DMA transfers in an EISA system. Two modified 8237 DMA controllers are cascaded together to provide support for seven EISA DMA channels.
DMA devices	An I/O device that supports DMA transfers.
DMA Extended Write	A option associated with DMA bus cycle timing that extends the amount of time that the read command line is active.
DMA Page Register	Each DMA channel has an external Page Register used to provide additional address capability. The DMA Controller natively only has the ability to handle 64KB of memory locations.
DMA, Type A bus cycle	DMA bus cycle type that transfers data at a rate of every six BCLK periods.
DMA, Type B bus cycle	DMA bus cycle type that transfers data at a rate of every four BCLK periods.
DMA, Type C bus cycle	See burst bus cycle.
downshift burst	A burst bus cycle performed by a 32-bit EISA bus master when communicating to a 16-bit EISA slave that supports burst.
EBB	See EISA bus buffer
EBC	See EISA bus controller
EISA bus buffer	Two EISA bus buffers (EBBs) are typically used in EISA systems: the Data EBB and the Address EBB. The Data EBB controls the data transceivers when routing data between the host and EISA buses and performs data bus steering when necessary, utilizing latches and data bus transceivers. The Address EBB ensures that the address generated by the current bus master is seen by every host, EISA and ISA slave in the system.
EISA bus controller	Together with the Data and Address EBBs, the EBC provides the bridging, translation and data bus steering functions.
control register	Allows each interrupt request input to the interrupt controller to be programmed to recognize either edge trigger for ISA devices or level triggering for sharable EISA devices.

ELCR	See Edge/Level Control Register.
EX16#	EISA size 16 signal that specifies that a 16-bit EISA device is being addressed.
EX32#	EISA size 32 signal that specifies that a 32-bit EISA device is being addressed.
EXRDY	Used by EISA devices to stretch the default timing beyond zero wait-states if the device's access time exceeds the default ready timing.
HLDA	See Hold Acknowledge
HOLD	See Hold Request
Hold Acknowledge	Hold acknowledge. A microprocessor output that notifies the request device that the microprocessor has given up ownership of the buses.
Hold Request	Hold request. A microprocessor input that is used by bus masters to gain ownership of the buses.
host bus	The bus on which the main CPU and main memory reside.
Peripheral	A chip in the EISA chip set (ISP) that contains a variety of functions including; the interrupt controllers, DMA controllers, arbitration logic, timers, and NMI logic.
interrupt acknowledge	A signal sent to the interrupt controller to indicate that its request is being acknowledged.
interrupt latency	The time that expires between a device requesting service via an interrupt request and when the servicing finally occurs.
interrupts, phantom	An erroneous interrupt triggered at the input of the interrupt controller, usually caused by a noise spike.
interrupts, shareable	The ability of two devices to share a single interrupt request line (IRQ) and operate without conflict.
LA bus	Latchable Address bus. A portion of the ISA bus that connects to 16-bit devices. These address lines are valid earlier that the System Address lines (SA) and provide the ability of 16-bit devices to operate at zero ISA wait-states.

EISA System Architecture

LOCK# signal	Bus Lock. Prevents other bus masters from gaining control of the EISA bus when the current master asserts LOCK# when performing read/modify write operations.
M/IO#	Memory or I/O signal. Used by EISA devices to either specify or determine whether the address currently on the EISA bus is for a memory or I/O device. Also an output from 386 and 486 microprocessors.
MSBURST#	Master Burst signal. Asserted by EISA masters to inform a bursting slave that a burst cycle will be run.
NMI	Non-maskable Interrupt. Used to report serious error conditions to the microprocessor.
Preemption	The ability of bus masters to request and gain ownership of the system buses from the current bus master.
Refresh	The process of keeping dynamic memory from loosing information from the bit cell due to capacitor discharge. All DRAM throughout the system is refreshed approximately every fifteen microseconds.
Refresh logic	The logic that runs refresh bus cycles. The refresh logic is a bus master capable of gaining ownership of the buses on a regular basis.
Ring buffers	A ring buffer reserves a fixed range of memory to be used for a DMA channel. Once the buffer has been filled, data can be stored at the beginning of the buffer again and old information can be over-written if it has already been read by the microprocessor.
rotating priority	A three-way rotational priority scheme between the Refresh Logic, CPU and Bus Masters (shared), and DMA Channels to determine which bus master will be next granted use of the buses.
slave	A term used to refer to target devices with which bus masters communicate in an EISA system.
SLBURST#	Slave burst signal. Used by EISA bursting slaves when addressed to notify the current bus master that they support burst cycles.
slot-specific I/O	The I/O addressing method used by EISA providing independent address space on a slot-by-slot basis to support automatic expansion board configuration.

START#	The EISA signal that goes active at the beginning of address time (T1) and inactive at the end of address time. Asserted by the current bus master.
system timers	The timers that are standard with all EISA systems and are contained in the ISP. These timers include the system timer (0), refresh timer, speaker timer, watchdog timer, and slowdown timer.
Type A DMA bus cycle	See DMA, Type A
Type B DMA bus cycle	See DMA, Type B
Type C DMA bus cycle	See DMA, Type C
W/R#	Write or read. Used by EISA devices to either specify or determine whether the current EISA bus cycle is a write or read operation. Also an output from 386 and 486 microprocessors.

EISA System Architecture

16-bit bus master, 13
16-bit EISA Bus Master and a 16-bit EISA Slave, 151
16-bit EISA Bus Master and a 16-bit ISA Slave, 149
16-bit EISA Bus Master and a 32-bit EISA Slave, 153
16-bit EISA Bus Master and an 8-bit ISA Slave, 147
16-bit ISA Bus Master and a 16-bit EISA Slave, 155
16-bit ISA Bus Master and a 16-bit ISA Slave, 155
16-bit ISA Bus Master and a 32-bit EISA Slave, 156
16-bit ISA Bus Master and an 8-bit ISA Slave, 154
16-bit ISA or EISA bus master, 13
16-bit ISA slave device, 46

32-bit EISA bus master, 13
32-bit EISA Bus Master and a 16-bit EISA Slave, 141
32-bit EISA Bus Master and a 16-bit ISA Slave, 137
32-bit EISA Bus Master and a 32-bit EISA Slave, 144
32-bit EISA Bus Master and an 32-bit Host Slave, 146
32-bit EISA Bus Master and an 8-bit ISA Slave, 132
32-bit Host CPU and a 16-bit EISA Slave, 159
32-bit Host CPU and a 16-bit ISA Slave, 158
32-bit Host CPU and a 32-bit EISA Slave, 161
32-bit Host CPU and a 32-bit Host Slave, 157
32-bit Host CPU and an 8-bit ISA Slave, 157

8-Bit ISA slave, 45
82350DT EISA chip set, 127
82352 EISA Bus Buffer (EBB), 130
82357 Integrated System Peripheral (ISP), 177
82357 Integrated Systems Peripheral, or ISP, 125
8237 DMACs, 59

Address Buffer Control, 161
address bus, 36
AEN, 42
AEN logic, 87
arbitration, 18
arbitration scheme, 7

backward compatibility, 5
BALE#, 42
BCLK, 20

1

BCPR Services, 9
bridge, 118
Burst bus cycle, 79
burst DMA, 6
burst mode (Type C, 39
Bus Arbitration, 7
Bus Arbitration Scheme, 17
Bus Arbitration Signals, 38
bus arbitration, example, 22
Bus Cycle Definition signals, 40
Bus Cycle Timing Signals, 41
bus cycle types, 80x86, 64
bus cycle, EISA burst, 70
bus cycle, EISA compressed, 69
Bus Cycle, ISA DMA, 60
bus cycle, standard EISA, 65
bus master priority, 18
Bus Master, DMA, 165
bus master, downshift burst, 75
Bus Master, EISA, 164
Bus Master, host CPU, 164
Bus Master, ISA, 164
Bus Master, refresh, 165
bus masters, 11
bus masters, ISA, 59
bus masters, number of, 21
bus masters, types of, 13,17
bus timeout, 20
bus timeout, bus master card, 20
bus timeout, DMA channel, 20

cache controller, 18
cascade, 59
Central Arbitration Control (CAC), 11,17
CMD#, 41
configuration, 8
configuration file, 95
configuration file example, EISA, 97
Configuration Process, EISA, 93
configuration program, 94
configuration registers, EISA, 92
Configuration sequence, EISA, 95

connector, EISA, 35,43
CPU priority, 18
CPU Selection, 129

Data Buffer Control, 130
data bus, 38
Data Bus Steering, 7
data bus steering, 122
data bus, system (SD bus), 113
DMA 8237 bus cycle, 60
DMA burst bus cycles, 6
DMA Bus Cycles, ISA, 58
DMA cascade channel, 19
DMA channel four, 19
DMA channel, preemption, 82
DMA channels, 16-bit, 59
DMA channels, 8-bit, 59
DMA channels, number of, 59
DMA clock, 59
DMA Compressed Timing, 8237, 62
DMA controller, 10
DMA controller priority, 19
DMA devices, 5
DMA enhancements, 6
DMA Extended Write option, 62
DMA idle state, 60
DMA memory address range, ISA, 59
DMA Memory Address Register, ISA, 59
DMA Page Register, 59
DMA Transfer Count Register, 59
DMA transfer rates, 81
DMA transfer size, 59
DMA transfer speeds, ISA, 62
DMA wait state, 60
DMA, buffer chaining, 82
DMA, EISA Addressing Capability, 82
DMA, EISA overview, 75
DMA, ISA-compatible bus cycle, 76
DMA, ring buffers, 83
DMA, transfer size, 83
DMA, Type A bus cycle, 77
DMA, Type B bus cycle, 78

DMA, Type C bus cycle, 79
DMA, wait states, 60
DMAC priority, 18

EBB, or EISA bus buffer, 127
EBC, 128
EBC, Cache Support, 173
EBC, Clock Generator unit, 174
EBC, EISA Bus Interface Unit, 172
EBC, Host Bus Interface Unit, 166
EBC, I/O Recovery logic, 176
EBC, ISA Bus Interface Unit, 169
EBC, ISP interface unit, 176
EBC, or EISA Bus Controller, 127
EBC, Reset Control unit, 174
EBC, slot-specific I/O support, 174
Edge/Level Control Register, 31
EISA bus master, 7
EISA chip set, introduction to, 118
ELCR, 31
ENABLE bit, 93
EX16#, 42
EX32#, 42
EXRDY, 41

Feature/Benefit Summary, 9

HLDA (Hold Acknowledge), 10,60
HOLD (Hold Request), 10,60
host bus, 112
host CPU, 112

I/O address space, EISA slot-specific, 86
I/O Address Space, ISA, 83
I/O, slot-specific address decode, 87
Integrated System Peripheral (ISP), 177
intelligent bus master, 12
interrupt acknowledge, 29
Interrupt Handling In the ISA Environment, 27
interrupt latency, 34
Interrupt Pending bit, 33
interrupt request, noise spike, 29

interrupts, 8
interrupts, EISA, 30
interrupts, non-shareable, 30
Interrupts, phantom, 29
interrupts, phantom, 34
interrupts, shareable, 31
IOCHKERR bit, 93
IOCHKRST bit, 93
IRQ15, 29
IRQ7, 29
ISA expansion boards, 5
ISA Memory Transfers, 16-bit memory, 58
ISA-compatible DMA bus cycles, 20
ISP, 125
ISP, Central Arbitration Control (CAC), 180
ISP, DMA Controllers, 178
ISP, Interrupt Controllers, 178
ISP, NMI Logic, 177
ISP, or Integrated Systems Peripheral, 177
ISP, Refresh Logic, 181
ISP, system timers, 179

LA bus, 114
LOCK# signal, 41

M/IO#, 40
master, 13
Memory Capacity, 5
MSBURST#, 40

NMI and bus arbitration, 19
NMI interrupts, 19

Pathfinder, 122
Preemption, 20
product ID, 90
product identification, 9

Refresh logic, 10
Refresh, memory, 23
rotating priority arbitration, 18

Si, 8237 DMAC idle state, 60
signal groups, 10,36
slave, 13
Slave Size Signals, 42
Slaves, types of, 14
SLBURST#, 39
slot-specific I/O, 8
SO state, 8237 DMAC, 60
START#, 41
synchronous transfer protocol, 5

Translation, address, 121
Translation, command line, 121
Type A DMA bus cycle, 6
Type B DMA bus cycle, 6
Type C bus cycles, 39
Type C DMA bus cycle, 6

W/R#, 40

X Bus, 113
XA bus, 114

NOTES

Announcing the
PC SYSTEM ARCHITECTURE SERIES
from MindShare Press

"The books have become **some of the most useful in my library**."
—Mike Demas, Application Support Engineer
Intel Corporation

ISA System Architecture, New revised edition

by Tom Shanley and Don Anderson

- The ONLY book that explains ISA step by step from a system point of view
- Used by hardware and software engineers at IBM, Intel, Compaq and Dell
- Used by Intel Technical Support

PC SYSTEM ARCHITECTURE SERIES · VOLUME 1

> "If you design or test ISA hardware, this is the book you need."

"I recommend this book to all test engineers who test Intel-based printed circuit boards and systems. Shanley and Anderson have a knack for answering your questions about how PCs work. **If you design or test ISA hardware, this is the book you need.**"

–John Swindle, Product Specialist, John Fluke Manufacturing Co., Inc.

"The first technical literature that a new engineer or technician in my group studies is this book ... The book is **an invaluable tool and reference** on ISA architecture and time reading it is time well spent. You might just end up wondering how you ever got along without it!"

–Dave Greenberg, Manager, Test Operations, Dell Computer Corporation

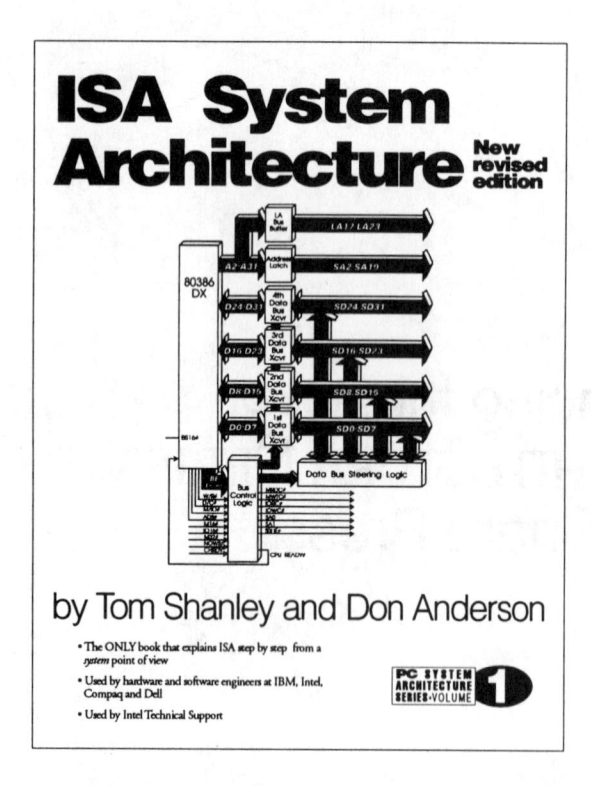

Volume One in the PC System Architecture Series, *ISA System Architecture* explains the architecture of ISA (Industry Standard Architecture) computers.

This includes IBM AT PCs and compatibles. Many concepts also apply to EISA and PS/2 products.

The authors describe all the key parts of an ISA system in detail, with examples and diagrams: bus cycles, addressing, I/O, memory (RAM, ROM and especially cache), decode logic, reset logic, powerup, interrupts, system kernel, DMA, RTC and configuration RAM, timers, microprocessors and more.

This book presents ISA using the "building block" approach. The authors define all concepts and terms as they are introduced. Each new concept builds upon those already described. For those who design or test hardware or software that involves ISA, EISA or PS/2, *ISA System Architecture* will be a valuable, time-saving tool.

Paper (ISBN 1-881609-05-7)   500 pp.   8 1/2 x 11   142 illustrations $39.95

"...to write 486-specific Assembly, you *must* have this book."

"What we have here is a short, crisply-illustrated description of what's inside the 486, written well enough so that software people can make sense of it all. It is by no means a beginner's book, but I followed it clear through, at least in part because *there is no unnecessary information here*. Perhaps the greatest unappreciated skill in writing is knowing what to leave out. Tom Shanley seems to have an intuitive grasp for what matters and what doesn't. ... Knowing the 386 hardware will help a great deal in understanding the book, but **certainly if you're going to attempt to write 486-specific Assembly, you *must* have this book**."

–*Jeff Duntemann,* PC Techniques *magazine*

"*80486 System Architecture* is well-organized, thorough and concise."

–*Peter M. Furgiuele, Paychex Corporation*

Volume Three in the PC System Architecture Series, *80486 System Architecture* explains the hardware architecture of PC products using the Intel 80486 chip, providing a clear, concise explanation of the 80486 processor's relationships to the rest of the system.

An introductory section explains the 80486 microarchitecture and its functional units, including MMU, the Memory Management Unit.

Separate multi-chapter sections cover the 80486 internal cache, the hardware interface, paging, the instruction set, the register set and the 487/487sx and overdrive processors.

This volume is an add-on book to Volume One, *ISA System Architecture*. It explains the 80486 using the "building block" approach. The author defines all concepts and terms as they are introduced. Each new concept builds upon those already described. For those who design or test hardware or software that involves the i486 chip, *80486 System Architecture* will be a valuable, time-saving tool.

Paper (ISBN 1-881609-04-9)   156 pp.   7 x 9   27 illustrations $19.95

PCI System Architecture
by Tom Shanley

- The ONLY book that explains the PCI Local Bus step by step from a *system* point of view
- Used by hardware and software engineers at IBM, Intel, Compaq and Dell
- Used by Intel Technical Support

PC SYSTEM ARCHITECTURE SERIES • VOLUME 4

New edition– Includes Version 2.0

"PCI System Architecture is an excellent resource…"

"One of the major benefits of the PCI specification is that it is defined with many engineering disciplines in mind: architecture, protocol, components, board layout, and software. MindShare's *PCI System Architecture* is an excellent resource for understanding all these aspects and their interrelationships."

    –Todd Koelling, Applications Engineer, Intel Corporation
    Member of the PCI Development Team

Volume Four in the PC System Architecture Series, *PCI System Architecture* is the ONLY book on the high-speed Peripheral Component Interconnect local bus. This bus will be used in IBM-compatible PCs, in Apple Macintoshes, in DEC Alpha computers and in RISC-based computers.

A new edition of *PCI System Architecture* includes changes in PCI due to the recently-released Version 2.0 of the PCI specifications.

An introductory section explains the technical needs that led to the creation of PCI, and compares PCI with ISA, EISA and MicroChannel buses.

Separate multi-chapter sections cover the bus itself (PCI transfer, functional signal groups, commands, read/write transfers, arbitration, premature transaction termination, locking, cache support, 64-bit extension, configuration, error handling, interrupts and expansion slots); the i82420 PCI chip set (features, CDC, DPU, system I/O); and electrical characteristics, including the Speedway.

Paper (ISBN 1-881609-08-1)   370 pp.   7 x 9   70 illustrations $29.95

Pentium™ Processor System Architecture

by Don Anderson and Tom Shanley

- The ONLY book that explains Intel's Pentium™ processor step by step from a *system* point of view
- Used by hardware and software engineers at IBM, Intel, Compaq and Dell
- Used by Intel Technical Support

PC SYSTEM ARCHITECTURE SERIES · VOLUME 5

"... an outstanding job of taking a complex processor—the Intel Pentium—and breaking down all of its aspects..."

"Authors Don Anderson and Tom Shanley have done **an outstanding job of taking a complex processor—the Intel Pentium—and breaking down all of its aspects into well-organized topics** covered in very understandable chapters and subsections within this book. Plenty of examples and well-annotated diagrams are used to illustrate key points and descriptions are kept simple and easy to understand."

–Dave Bursky, *Executive Editor,* Electronic Design Magazine

"This book provides a clear, detailed review of the Pentium microprocessor. It is **more readable and offers more perspective** than Intel's documentation ..."

–Michael Slater, *Publisher and Editorial Director,* Microprocessor Report

"This book is your best guide to Pentium's inner workings and architecture. It takes you inside to see what's going on behind the chip and gives you **the kind of insight you can't find anyplace else.**"

–Keith Weiskamp, *Publisher of* PC Techniques *& author of many computer books*

Volume Five in the PC System Architecture Series, *Pentium™ Processor System Architecture* is the ONLY book on Intel's Pentium™ chip other than Intel's own data books.

This book details Intel's technical strategy behind the Pentium™ processor—not just *how* Intel designed the Pentium™ chip, but *why*. The book points out the differences between 80486 system architecture and new systems based on the new processor, and covers testing and debugging in the Pentium™ processor environment.

It covers the Pentium™ chip's new features, such as using MESI for multi-processing, how the chip interfaces with other hardware components, cache memory use, pipelining and bus cycles.

Paper (ISBN 1-881609-07-3)   332 pp.   7 x 9   74 illustrations $29.95

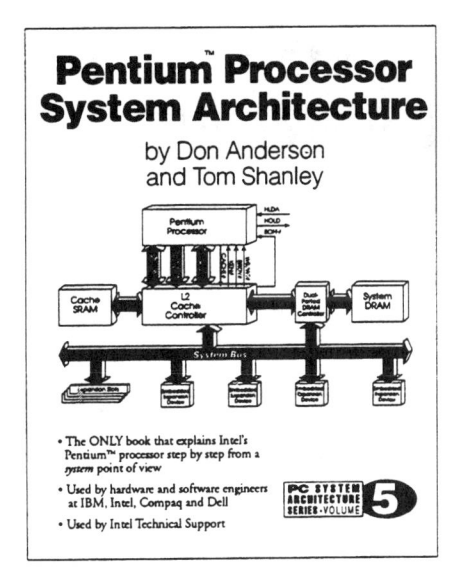

3 Quick Ways to Order the
PC SYSTEM ARCHITECTURE SERIES

1. **PHONE (408) 435-0744**
2. **FAX** this page to (408) 435-1823
3. **MAIL** this form with payment to:

   Order Desk
   **COMPUTER LITERACY
   BOOKSHOPS®**
   2590 North First Street
   San Jose, CA 95131 USA

NAME (Full name, no initials please)

COMPANY/MAIL STOP

STREET ADDRESS (No P.O. boxes)

MORE ADDRESS

CITY   STATE/PROVINCE   ZIP/POSTAL CODE

COUNTRY   **DAY PHONE** (in case we have questions about your order)
REQUIRED FOR 2-DAY RUSH or OVERNIGHT

Method of payment:

❏ Check is enclosed
Charge my:
  ❏ Visa
  ❏ MasterCard
  ❏ American Express
  ❏ Diner's Club/Carte Blanche
  ❏ Discover

Card number _____

Expiration date _____

Signature _____

☐ Please send me information on future MindShare Press books.
☐ I want information on MindShare training classes.

All orders must be prepaid. Prices may change without notice.
If you live in California or Virginia, please add your county's sales tax.
Unless you check a shipping method, we send your order in U.S. via UPS ground.

Quantity		Extended Price
__	**Vol. 1: ISA System Architecture** Order no. AH517867 - $39.95	_____
__	**Vol. 2: EISA System Architecture** Order no. AH517872 - $24.95	_____
__	**Vol. 3: 80486 System Architecture** Order no. AH517888 - $19.95	_____
__	**Vol. 4: PCI System Architecture** Order no. AH544487 - $29.95	_____
__	**Vol. 5: Pentium™ Processor System Architecture** Order no. AH518279 - $29.95	_____

Subtotal _____
CA or VA tax (___%) _____
Shipping _____
TOTAL DUE _____
(U.S. dollars)

SHIP VIA (CHECK ONE)		Continental U.S.	Alaska, Haw., Puerto Rico	Guam, APO/FPO P.O. Box
__ **Regular**	First book	3.75	7.00	7.00
	Each additional	1.75	2.50	2.50
__ **2 day rush**	First book	8.00	13.50	Not available
	Each additional	4.50	5.50	
__ **Overnight**	First book	17.50	20.00	Not available
	Each additional	5.00	6.00	

We ship books in stock no later than the next business day. Your phone no. is required for rush shipment.
We ship anywhere in the world. Please call for shipping charges to other countries.

Phone orders (408) 435-0744 • Fax (408) 435-1823 • E-mail info@clbooks.com